# Solaris™ 9 For Dummies

P9-DTX-582

Cheat Sheet

## CDE Toolbar Options

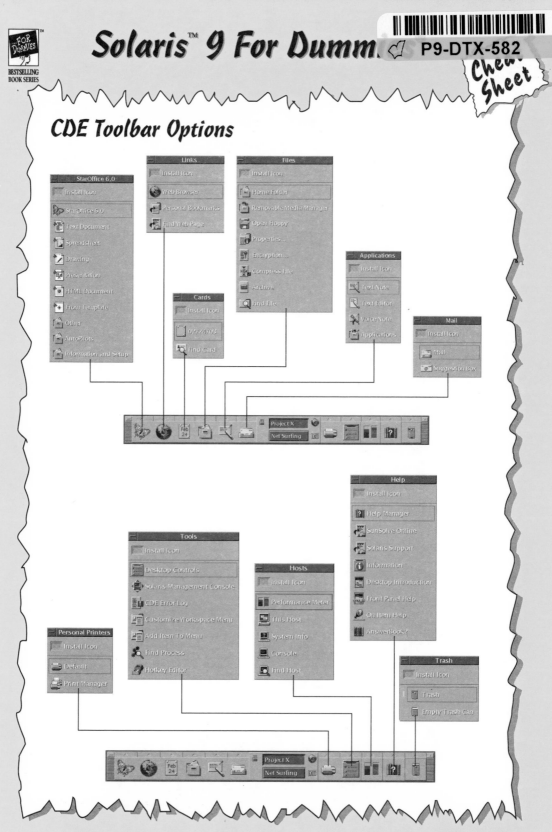

# Solaris™ 9 For Dummies®

Cheat Sheet

## GNOME Applications

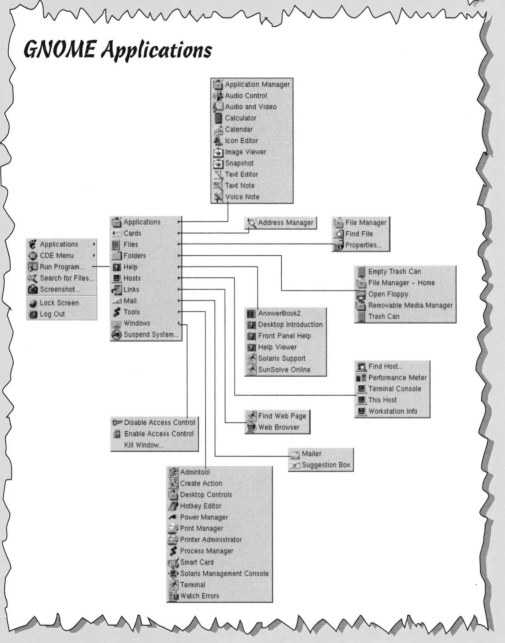

- Applications
  - Application Manager
  - Audio Control
  - Audio and Video
  - Calculator
  - Calendar
  - Icon Editor
  - Image Viewer
  - Snapshot
  - Text Editor
  - Text Note
  - Voice Note
- Cards
  - Address Manager
- Files
  - File Manager
  - Find File
  - Properties...
- Folders
  - Empty Trash Can
  - File Manager – Home
  - Open Floppy
  - Removable Media Manager
  - Trash Can
- Help
  - AnswerBook2
  - Desktop Introduction
  - Front Panel Help
  - Help Viewer
  - Solaris Support
  - SunSolve Online
- Hosts
  - Find Host...
  - Performance Meter
  - Terminal Console
  - This Host
  - Workstation Info
- Links
  - Find Web Page
  - Web Browser
- Mail
  - Mailer
  - Suggestion Box
- Tools
  - Admintool
  - Create Action
  - Desktop Controls
  - Hotkey Editor
  - Power Manager
  - Print Manager
  - Printer Administrator
  - Process Manager
  - Smart Card
  - Solaris Management Console
  - Terminal
  - Watch Errors
- Windows
  - Disable Access Control
  - Enable Access Control
  - Kill Window...
- Suspend System...

- Applications
- CDE Menu
- Run Program...
- Search for Files...
- Screenshot...
- Lock Screen
- Log Out

For Dummies: Bestselling Book Series for Beginners

# Solaris™ 9

## FOR

# DUMMIES®

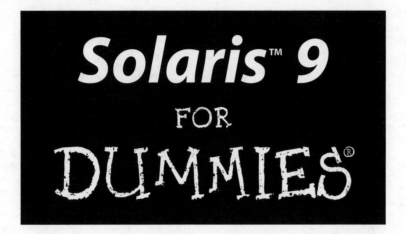

**by Dave Taylor**

WILEY

Wiley Publishing, Inc.

**Solaris™ 9 For Dummies®**

Published by
**Wiley Publishing, Inc.**
909 Third Avenue
New York, NY 10022

www.wiley.com

Copyright© 2003 by Wiley Publishing, Inc., Indianapolis, Indiana

Published by Wiley Publishing, Inc., Indianapolis, Indiana

Published simultaneously in Canada

For general information on our other products and services or to obtain technical support, please contact our Customer Care Department within the U.S. at 800-762-2974, outside the U.S. at 317-572-3993, or fax 317-572-4002.

Wiley also publishes its books in a variety of electronic formats. Some content that appears in print may not be available in electronic books.

Library of Congress Control Number: 2003101892

ISBN: 0-7645-3969-8

Manufactured in the United States of America

10 9 8 7 6 5 4 3 2 1

1O/SS/QU/QT/IN

WILEY    is a trademark of Wiley Publishing, Inc.

# *About the Author*

**Dave Taylor** has been involved with Unix and the Internet since 1980. Former positions include research scientist at HP's Palo Alto R&D Lab, Senior Editor of SunWorld Magazine, intranet columnist for InfoWorld, and founder of two successful Internet startups. He's also written a dozen books on technology, notably Teach Yourself Unix in 24 Hours, Creating Cool HTML 4 Web Pages, and Unix Shell Hacks. He has a bachelor's degree in computer science, a master's degree in educational computing, and an MBA, and currently splits his time between writing, teaching, management consulting work, and outdoor activities. He lives in Colorado with his wife, kids, two dogs, and a cat, just a few miles from the Sun Microsystems Colorado campus.

His e-mail address is taylor@intuitive.com and his Web site is at www.intuitive.com/.

# Dedication

To the pleasure of a productive day, the calm of a loving family, and the security of a world at peace.

# Author's Acknowledgments

I'd like to first acknowledge the gracious help of the folks at Sun Microsystems for their time spent reviewing this book as we've proceeded, their generosity in underwriting my attendance at some Solaris training, and the long-term loan of a Sun Blade100 system to double-check every example and screen image against the latest release on a solid SPARC box. In addition, Tadpole Technology was generous in loaning out a cool SPARCbook 6500 SPARC-based laptop ,and Tenon Software was kind in sending an X Window Server for Mac OS X to allow session interoperability in my network.

There were also a number of people involved in this writing project, notably including the lovely team at Wiley: Terri Varveris, Pat O'Brien, tech reviewer extraordinaire Terry Cummings, and Andy Cummings, a long time friend of mine in the publishing biz. In addition, Dave Miles at Tadpole had some insights into Solaris strategies; Steve Christensen, Webmaster of sunfreeware.com had great ideas about online resources; and Martin Brown and John Meister shared their Solaris expertise. Dee-Ann, as usual, let me vent when needed, and I can't say enough about the great support of my wife, children, dogs, and cat!

## Publisher's Acknowledgments

We're proud of this book; please send us your comments through our online registration form located at www.dummies.com/register/.

Some of the people who helped bring this book to market include the following:

### Acquisitions, Editorial, and Media Development

**Project Editor:** Pat O'Brien

**Acquisitions Editor:** Terri Varveris

**Senior Copy Editor:** Kim Darosett

**Technical Editor:** Terry Collings

**Editorial Manager:** Kevin Kirschner

**Media Development Supervisor:** Richard Graves

**Editorial Assistant:** Amanda Foxworth

**Cartoons:** Rich Tennant, www.the5thwave.com

### Production

**Project Coordinator:** Nancee Reeves

**Layout and Graphics:** Seth Conley, LeAndra Johnson, Stephanie Jumper, Michael Kruzil, Tiffany Muth, Julie Trippetti,

**Proofreaders:** John Tyler Connoley, John Greenough, Angel Perez, TECHBOOKS Production Services

**Indexer:** TECHBOOKS Production Services

### Publishing and Editorial for Technology Dummies

**Richard Swadley,** Vice President and Executive Group Publisher

**Andy Cummings,** Vice President and Publisher

**Mary C. Corder,** Editorial Director

### Publishing for Consumer Dummies

**Diane Graves Steele,** Vice President and Publisher

**Joyce Pepple,** Acquisitions Director

### Composition Services

**Gerry Fahey,** Vice President of Production Services

**Debbie Stailey,** Director of Composition Services

# Contents at a Glance

# Table of Contents

# Foreword

It's my pleasure to introduce you to Solaris, a computer operating environment that has been a important part of my life for more than 20 years. Not that I've paid much attention to it.

The great thing about Solaris, from my perspective, is that it has simply been there for me whenever I need it. To put it plainly, Solaris is pretty darn reliable. And it has always allowed me do several tasks at once — run a spreadsheet, send mail, watch a Webcast, or whatever — with ease.

Even if this book is your first conscious exposure to the Solaris Operating Environment, chances are you've already "used" Solaris. Millions do without ever knowing it. That's because many of the Web sites and Internet applications we use every day run on Solaris. Something like 90 percent of all Internet traffic runs through a Sun server at some point. Eighty-five percent of all NASDAQ trades run on Sun, and every one of the Fortune 100 uses Solaris in some capacity.

We started out in 1983 with Solaris 1.0 and in 2001, we rolled out Solaris 9 with a host of new features and functionality in areas like security, instant messaging, and so on.

Reading this book, you'll learn about the subtleties and strengths of the Solaris environment, including both the command-line and graphical interfaces. Like me, you won't do any programming or advanced system administration, but you will get to know a friendly, reliable co-worker who can help you be more productive.

**Scott McNealy**
Chairman of the Board, President, and CEO

Sun Microsystems, Inc.

# Introduction

*W*elcome to *Solaris 9 For Dummies*! This book covers everything you need to know to be productive with your computer and does it in a fun and engaging manner.

Solaris is the flagship Unix operating system from Sun Microsystems, a company started by a group of graduate students from Stanford and the University of California, Berkeley. In fact, *Sun* comes from the Stanford University Network, where MBA student (and now Sun CEO) Scott McNealy studied.

Unix has a long and interesting history as an operating system, starting with its initial development at AT&T Bell Telephone Laboratories in the early 1960s. The first version of Unix was written so that the BTL folks had a computer that ran *Space War,* a very early computer game. Really!

The first few versions of Sun's Unix OS (initially called SunOS — the Solaris name showed up later) were variants on UC Berkeley's Berkeley Software Distribution (BSD) Unix. Many of the top BSD developers at UCB ended up at Sun, most notably Bill Joy, who shows up time and again in this book.

The Unix community has always been a bit splintered compared to the PC world where Microsoft is a ubiquitous presence. If you were to really explore the history of Unix, with the Posix standardization efforts and shared development efforts of Motif and the Open Software Foundation, you'd find Sun has consistently been at the forefront of both technological development and coolness factor. If you wanted to be a cool Unix type, you'd have a Sun workstation on your desk.

This continues today, and one of the themes in this book is to not only explain the fundamentals of working with the OS, but also reveal some of the coolest features and capabilities. By reading this book, you too will become a smart and productive Solaris user with a higher coolness quotient!

As with all *For Dummies* books, this title has lots of humor, some of which is even funny (I hope!), and great cartoons by Rich Tennant. In addition, to get you into the swing of the Solaris community, I've woven some subtle digs at Microsoft into the book. It's a popular hobby in the Solaris world. Stick with me, and you'll quickly get the hang of it!

# *About This Book*

I like to write books that sound like I'm sitting at a table with you, we're both sipping our cups of tea, and we just happen to have a computer on the table, where I'm demonstrating certain things or letting you explore. As you proceed with this book, I think you'll find it fun, easy to read, and entertaining!

As with any computing topic, the target readers of this book have a wide range of experience and expertise level. This book is geared to neophytes with some basic computing skills (you know what a computer mouse is, for example) up through intermediate users who want to, perhaps, ease the transition from the Sun Common Desktop Environment to the new GNOME graphical world. Any Solaris user can benefit from a brush-up of command shell and terminal skills. They're covered extensively. This book is made up of about 50 percent graphical interface content and 50 percent command line content, so it's like getting *CDE and GNOME For Dummies* and *Working the Solaris Command Line For Dummies* all wrapped up in one neat package!

You will want to have access to a Solaris system on a regular basis. Whether it's SPARC-based or Intel-based won't affect your experience with this book, but everything in this book was run on a SPARC-based Sun Blade100 workstation.

To get an idea of the content, here are some sample sections:

- ✔ Getting Started with GNOME
- ✔ Compressing Big Files
- ✔ Working Effectively with Netscape 7
- ✔ Connecting Securely with SSH
- ✔ Using the vi Text Editor
- ✔ Exploring the Solaris Management Console
- ✔ Configuring Solaris Networking
- ✔ Disabling Unnecessary Internet Services

Although it may seem like this book covers lots of highly advanced technical topics, you'll find that the emphasis is on ensuring you have a productive and secure working environment. Much of the book assumes that you have someone else doing the basic system administration and therefore focuses mostly on the user-level tasks and knowledge needed to avoid any common pitfalls or mistakes. It's fun to use Solaris! It's a sophisticated, powerful, and surprisingly easy-to-use operating system with a ton of great built-in features.

# *How to Use This Book*

This book focuses on the Solaris user experience, interweaving sections on the Sun Common Desktop Environment (CDE), GNOME, and the command line. For each, I use a slightly different approach to detail what you should do at any given point.

When I talk about steps you need to take with a graphical application, you'll find screenshots of pop-up menus, the CDE taskbar, or similar, to ensure that when you're staring at your own computer, you know what you're supposed to do.

Command-line utilities are a little easier: Your input to the command shell is always shown in bold:

```
$ echo "this is a sample command output"
this is a sample command output
```

The first line (other than the $, which is the system prompt) is something you type in. The second line, not in bold, is the output of the command.

Don't try something other than what's shown in the book until you're more confident in your skills. Failure to enter exactly what's shown can sometimes have unfortunate, or at least puzzling, results. For example, there's a world of difference between rm -f x* and rm -f x *. The former removes all files that start with the letter *x,* whereas the latter removes all files in the current directory! Just be careful, okay?

One additional tip: Some command lines are longer than what'll fit in this book — or even on the screen. Rather than have lines wrap willy-nilly, I use the standard Unix trick of ending the partial line with a backslash followed by Enter. Ensure that there's never anything after the backslash on that line. For example, look at the difference between the following two commands:

```
$ cat /usr/local/bin/myapp/data/hidden.data.file | \
> sort | uniq -c | sort -rn | head -5
(output omitted for space)

$ cat /usr/local/bin/myapp/data/hidden.data.file | \
ksh: : command not found
```

Although you can't see this, the second example has a trailing space after the backslash, causing the shell to not only think there's nothing else left to enter (it didn't use the > prompt for more input) but also look for a command called (space character), which isn't found. Hence you get the otherwise puzzling error ksh: : command not found. Just pay attention, and it won't be too much of a problem!

# Solaris Installation: The Missing Topic?

This book diverges from most *For Dummies* computer titles in that it does *not* include any information on Solaris installation and configuration. Unlike the homebrew hacker ethos of the Linux world, Solaris is more straightforward in its installation, and, more importantly, almost all Solaris systems are deployed by a central system administration or information technology group. Solaris users are uniquely shielded from the installation and configuration process.

As a result, I've decided it'd be much more useful to jam as much user level information in this book as humanly possible. Rather than spend 75 pages nattering on about this configuration switch, that disk partitioning scheme, and this other swap space allocation algorithm, you find out how to *use* Solaris.

If you must install and configure your own Solaris system, the Sun installation package makes it a breeze, and the 385-page *Solaris 9 Installation Guide* included with your Solaris 9 distribution does a good job of explaining how to accomplish this task. If you really, really, *really* wish I would have included some information on this topic, please let me know!

Speaking of missing topics, I also don't cover programming, hacking into a Solaris system, or advanced system administration and network configuration topics. You can find plenty of great books on those topics, including *Java 2 For Dummies* and *Exploiting Security Holes For Fun and Profit For Dummies* (just kidding on that one).

# How This Book Is Organized

This book is divided into six parts, arranged to help you proceed logically in your understanding of Solaris. The first few parts primarily focus on what you can do and how to do it, and the later sections are on more advanced topics, ending with a few chapters on important system administration and security topics and the Part of Tens. This book is modular, so you can dig into a specific part, find a topic, and just read that section to find out how to accomplish something or work with a specific application. The index is a terrific resource for jumping directly to a concept, program, or application!

Here's a breakdown of the book:

## Part 1: Getting Acquainted with Solaris

The computer's sitting on your desk, staring at you. Now what? This first part explores how to log in, and how to work with both the Common Desktop Environment and the new GNOME environment. I also delve into the mysteries of the command shell, explore which of the many different shells are best (my choice: Bash), and look at how to redirect input and output, feed the output of one command to another with pipes, and even dabble a tiny bit with shell scripts. This first part ends with an exploration of the different file managers, file permissions, and compression utilities.

## Part 11: The Inevitable Internet Section

Scott McNealy, the CEO of Sun, was the first to coin *The Network Is the Computer*, so it's no surprise that Sun systems have excellent, easy-to-use Internet utilities. The first chapter of this part covers the true killer application of the Internet, e-mail. This part continues by looking at the latest version of Netscape's venerable Navigator browser and then touches on a worthy alternative, Mozilla. I then switch gears and look at how to build Web pages in Solaris, run a Web server, and even analyze Web log files to see who's visiting and what they're viewing. The last chapter considers ftp, telnet, and the superior alternative ssh, the Secure Shell.

## Part 111: Becoming Productive with StarOffice

Until recently, Solaris users faced a dilemma when working with office documents: Either buy a PC or Mac to run Microsoft Office or admit to your colleagues that you couldn't view the presentation, check the figures in the spreadsheet, or proof the latest memo. This all changed when StarOffice showed up on the scene. It has evolved into an excellent alternative, offering complete compatibility with PC and Macintosh office applications.

This succinct part introduces you to the key components of StarOffice, with a particular emphasis on StarOffice Writer, the document processing system. You get a good idea of the power and capabilities of StarOffice so you'll be ready to begin your own exploration.

# Part IV: Editing and Controlling Programs

This part introduces you to the key command-line tools and GUI-based applications for viewing files, analyzing file content, and editing files with vi, CDE Text Editor, or the GNOME Text Editor. I also delve into some of the internals of Solaris to help you understand what processes are running and how to inter-act with them or — if you're feeling particularly aggressive — kill the processes. The last chapter in the section discusses two commands near and dear to every Solaris guru: find and grep. These are definitely worth knowing!

# Part V: Administration and Security Issues

This part addresses something that may be beyond your individual responsibility on your Solaris computer: system administration and security. However, if something goes wrong on your computer, it's your files that'll be lost, corrupted, or stolen. Whether you have a top-notch system administrator or not, it's wise to know something about how to keep your system running optimally, with as many hatches battened down as possible.

The three chapters in this part explore different ways to hook a Solaris system to an existing network, including the popular Dynamic Host Control Protocol (DHCP) and the creaky Point-to-Point Protocol for modem access. You also explore the Solaris Management Console and discover the proper and safe way to stop your computer so you can unplug it.

Never just unplug your computer or flip the power switch to turn it off. *Augh!* That's the worst possible thing you can do to a Solaris system.

Although I don't explore Solaris security in depth, the last chapter in this part offers a good overview of basic security techniques and concepts that can go a long way towards improving the security of your system. It includes information on what Internet services on your computer are potential security holes and how to disable them.

# Part VI: The Part of Tens

This part consists of three incredibly useful lists to ensure you can continue your Solaris journey in safety and comfort — and, of course, keep your hands inside the boat at all times for your own safety!

The three lists are the Ten Best Solaris Web Sites, the Ten Key Security Features in Solaris 9 (just in case you're still running a previous version of

Solaris and need yet another reason to upgrade), and my favorite, the Ten Great Free Add-Ons to Solaris.

# Icons Used in This Book

 This icon tells you that a pointed insight lies ahead that can save you time and trouble as you use Solaris. For example, maybe learning how to type with your toes would help increase your speed in entering commands and moving the mouse at the same time. (And maybe not. . . .)

 The Technical Stuff icon points out places where you may find more data than information. Unless you're really ready to find out more about Solaris — much more — steer clear of these paragraphs the first time you read a given section of the book.

 This icon tells you how to stay out of trouble when living a little close to the edge. Failure to heed its message may have disastrous consequences for you, your drawing, your computer — and maybe even all three.

 Remember when Spock put his hand over McCoy's face and implanted a suggestion in his brain that later saved Spock's life? This icon is like that. Helpful reminders of things you already know but that may not be right at the tip of your brain . . . or whatever.

# Stay in Touch!

With the help of the team at Dummies Press and my friends at Sun Microsystems, I have done the best job I can of covering the most important, interesting, and helpful facets of Solaris, but I don't yet know you and your unique skills, expertise, and interests. I'd love to hear from you, whether you want to share brickbats, kudos, errata reports, or even funny Solaris anecdotes.

Start by checking out my Web site for this book: `www.intuitive.com/solaris/`. Also feel free to contact me via e-mail at `taylor@intuitive.com`.

Thanks and enjoy!

# Part I
# Getting Aquainted with Solaris

The 5th Wave    By Rich Tennant

"We're much better prepared for this upgrade than before. We're giving users additional training, better manuals, and a morphine drip."

# In this part . . .

This part explains how to log in, and work with both the Common Desktop Environment and the new GNOME environment, including a comparison of the two. With that taken care of, we delve into the mysteries of the command shell, explore which of the many different shells are best, and look at how to redirect input and output, feed the output of one command to another with pipes, and even dabble a tiny bit with shell scripts. Finally, this first part ends with an important exploration of the different file managers, file permissions, and compression utilities.

# Chapter 1

# Logging In and Poking Around

*In This Chapter*

▶ Exploring different versions of Solaris

▶ Taking a look at your login account

▶ Using the login panel

▶ Starting a program

▶ Logging out of the system

*T*he best place to start is almost always at the beginning. This book is no different. This first chapter gives you a quick tour of the world of Solaris, describing the evolution of the operating system, how Solaris 9 compares to earlier versions of the operating system, and how Solaris compares to Unix, Linux, Windows, and Mac OS X.

The hands-on part of this chapter focuses on the nuances of the login panel and how to log in to the desktop environment of your choice. Once you're logged in, you'll have a chance to start up a program and practice using the mouse and keyboard, and then log out of the system safely.

## Understanding Solaris Versions

I'm going to travel back in time, just briefly, to the birth of the Unix operating system. It's 1969, at Bell Telephone Laboratories, and Ken Thompson and Dennis Ritchie are interested in taking an old, unused computer and writing a space exploration game called Spacewar. Problem is, the computer doesn't really have any sort of development environment. A few evolutionary steps and Unix was born.

It's no exaggeration to say that Unix has the Internet running through its veins and that the Internet is unquestionably powered by Unix systems —

not just Unix, but Solaris. As Sun CEO Scott McNealy says in his foreword, "Around 90% of all Internet traffic goes through a Solaris system."

As Unix grew, it split into two different operating systems:

- ✔ *System V* (more commonly, *SVR4, System V, Release 4*) was based on the development at Bell Telephone Labs (renamed AT&T Bell Labs, and now a part of Lucent).

- ✔ The *Berkeley Software Distribution (BSD)* flavor came from research and software development efforts at the University of California, Berkeley.

  Unix people refer to all the different versions of Unix, Linux, Solaris, and so on as *flavors* of Unix. Think of ice cream, and you'll smile every time you hear this particular jargon!

Bay Area universities like UC Berkeley are important to the history of Sun Microsystems, too:

- ✔ Sun head scientist Bill Joy was a star at Berkeley.

- ✔ Sun grew from a rival college, Stanford University. In fact, the name SUN comes from *Stanford University Network*.

Andreas Bechtolsheim was a student at Stanford when he saw great potential for computers designed to always have a network connection — a connection to Stanford University Network. Stanford wasn't too interested, so in 1982 Bechtolsheim convinced a couple of fellow Stanford grad students (Scott McNealy and Vinod Khosla) and a friend from UC Berkeley (Bill Joy) to create Sun Microsystems.

The first release of Sun's operating system was called *SunOS.* The last version of SunOS that was called SunOS by the Sun marketing team was SunOS 4.3.1. Since then, the OS has been marketed as *Solaris.*

All versions of Solaris also have the official moniker *SunOS 2.x;* the *x* is the major release number of Solaris. (Yes, Sun went backwards from 4 to 2.) If you want to impress someone who wears the Official Unix Suspenders, call Solaris 9 by its other name, *SunOS 2.9.* (I've heard there's a secret handshake, too.)

# *Solaris 9 Features*

Each release of Solaris adds to the strength and capabilities of the operating system, typically for the key Sun customer running high-speed, high-demand servers or complex multisystem networks. The most important additions to Solaris with the release of Solaris 9 are

✔ Linux compatibility

✔ Significant security enhancements

✔ A new Resource Manager tool

✔ A new directory server

✔ A volume manager and other file system enhancements

✔ An improved multithreaded library

✔ Incremental improvements for installation and configuration

What you don't see on the preceding list are user-level improvements. One of the most exciting changes of Solaris 9 is the gradual transition of the Sun graphical interface from the stale Common Desktop Environment to the exciting new jazzy GNU Object Management Environment, also known as *GNOME*.

# How Linux fits into the puzzle

Linux is a splinter variant, or *flavor,* of Unix created because of frustration with legal restrictions on Unix. Although AT&T freely distributed Unix to the research and commercial community, it kept a tight rein on innovation. Many software developers found the restrictions frustrating, so they started developing operating systems like Unix.

✔ One group of programmers, led by the brilliant and eccentric Richard Stallman, began rewriting a Unix-like operating system from scratch for free distribution. That group was *GNU.* (GNU stands for — I kid you not — *GNU's Not Unix.*) The GNU group developed on expensive minicomputers and mainframes, such as Sun Solaris computers.

✔ Other programmers really wanted a version of Unix running on the low-cost Intel-based IBM PC family of computers. They created systems like Minix. Most importantly, Linus

Torvalds successfully wrote and distributed *Linux,* his own Unix core *kernel* for Intel computers.

Eventually, the GNU group (more commonly known as the Free Software Foundation) and the Linux group got together. Today's Linux, with all the bells and whistles, was created. Over 50 *distributions* of Linux are available today, most notably from well-known distributors like Red Hat and MandrakeSoft.

Linux has evolved to the point where it is important for Sun to ensure strong Linux compatibility (which is one of the major improvements in Solaris 9) while focusing on the Solaris advantages in security, performance, and scalability within the Solaris/SPARC world.

If you want to read more about the history of Sun Microsystems — it's an exciting story — check out www.sun.com/about sun/coinfo/history.html.

This book covers two graphical interfaces:

- ✔ Common Desktop Environment, for those users who are still in the legacy world of CDE
- ✔ GNOME, for users ready to bravely step into the future of Solaris

  By the release of Solaris 10, GNOME will be the primary graphical interface for Solaris. That will be wonderful for all Solaris users, whether guru system administrators or just plain folk trying to be productive and efficient on a Sun SPARC-based computer.

If GNOME isn't an option on your Solaris system, ask your system administrator to install it. It's available for easy download at www.sun.com/gnome/

# *Your Login Account*

The first and perhaps most important step to use a Solaris system is to have an *account* on the system. An account consists of

- ✔ A unique login name
- ✔ A secret password
- ✔ A home directory that you can fill with your files, pictures, and work

Login names are two to eight characters long. Your system administrator should have notified you of your login name. Many organizations use one of these login name formats:

- ✔ First initial, last name (I'd be *dtaylor*)
- ✔ Last name only, unless there's a name conflict (I'd be *taylor* or *dtaylor*)
- ✔ Nicknames, cute words, or whatever else you want (I might be *author* or *heydave*)

The initial password set up with your account probably is a simple word or a random sequence of letters and digits. Both of those are bad passwords, as is your car license, social security number, or any other public information.

The goal of a password is to protect the privacy and security of your account. Anything that makes it easy to break in is bad. Anything that makes it hard is good.

Don't write your password down and don't share it with other people. Ever.

Here are the elements of a good password:

✔ **It's something you can remember.** If you have to write it down, you've just compromised the security of the password.

✔ **It's not a dictionary word or other simple combination of all lower-case letters.** Common password-cracking tools can spin through a dictionary of words and obvious variations (backwards, for example) in an hour or two.

✔ **It's not based on any easily identifiable personal information.** If you pick the name of your daughter, your mother's maiden name, the license of your current vehicle, or even your social security number, a determined hacker can figure it out.

✔ **It's longer, not shorter.** Because passwords can only contain letters, digits, and punctuation, each letter of the password can only have about 80 possible values. If you have a two-letter password, that's only 6,400 possible values. If your password is seven characters long, over 2 billion possible combinations exist!

✔ **It consists of mixed letters, digits, and punctuation, not just letters.** If there are 2 billion possible seven-letter mixed letter/digit/punctuation passwords, how many are there if you just use lowercase letters? Instead of $80^7$, you have a possible password space of only $26^7$, many, many fewer possibilities.

How do you invent a secure, memorable password? Try these strategies:

✔ **Replace a letter with a punctuation character.** Instead of using *sparky* as a password, try *Sp@rky!* instead. It's easy to remember and difficult to guess.

✔ **Take a phrase and create a password from the first letter of each word.** If you're fanatical about all things Tolkien, you might take the phrase *one ring to rule them all* and turn it into *ortrta*. Then add some mixed (upper and lower) case, punctuation, and digits. A great, memorable password would be *OR+trta!* It looks completely random but isn't if you know its derivation.

Don't use the # character in your password. If not properly configured, a Unix login program interprets # as a backspace.

✔ **Take a phrase and replace a word like *for* with a digit.** The Shakespearean phrase "Wherefore art thou, Romeo?" could be shortened a bit and turned into *wh4Rmeo?* with very good results.

Adding punctuation is an easy way to increase security for any password. It's easy to start or end a password with !, ?, +, -, or &.

## *Working with the login panel*

Enough chitchat. Log in!

When you turn on your Solaris system, you are presented with a blank screen that contains the login panel.

The login panel confirms which computer you'll be connecting to once you're logged in.

If you're impatient, you can type in your account name, press Enter, type in your password, press Enter again, and log in, but first take a moment to see what choices are available before you proceed. Patience, patience!

From left to right, the buttons along the bottom are

- ✔ OK (which acts the same as if you'd pressed Enter on your keyboard)
- ✔ Start Over (if you get confused about where you are in the login process, this'll start you back at the beginning, ready for your account name)
- ✔ Options
- ✔ Help

    Click the Help button, and you'll see an informative reminder of the various options available with the login panel, as shown in Figure 1-1.

The Options button of the login panel is where all the power of the screen is hidden. Click it, and you're presented with a range of alternatives:

- ✔ With a local connection, these items are on the Options menu:
    - • Language
    - • Session
    - • Remote Login
    - • Command Line Login
    - • Reset Login Screen

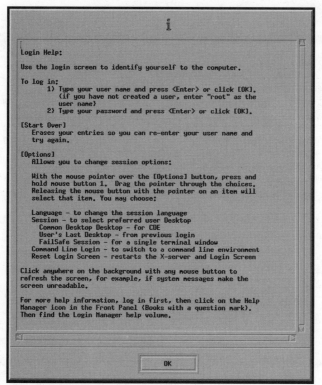

```
                              i

Login Help:

Use the login screen to identify yourself to the computer.

To log in:
        1) Type your user name and press <Enter> or click [OK].
           (if you have not created a user, enter "root" as the
           user name)
        2) Type your password and press <Enter> or click [OK].

[Start Over]
   Erases your entries so you can re-enter your user name and
   try again.

[Options]
   Allows you to change session options:

   With the mouse pointer over the [Options] button, press and
   hold mouse button 1. Drag the pointer through the choices.
   Releasing the mouse button with the pointer on an item will
   select that item. You may choose:

   Language - to change the session language
   Session - to select preferred user Desktop
      Common Desktop Desktop - for CDE
      User's Last Desktop - from previous login
      FailSafe Session - for a single terminal window
   Command Line Login - to switch to a command line environment
   Reset Login Screen - restarts the X-server and Login Screen

Click anywhere on the background with any mouse button to
refresh the screen, for example, if system messages make the
screen unreadable.

For more help information, log in first, then click on the Help
Manager icon in the Front Panel (Books with a question mark).
Then find the Login Manager help volume.


                              OK
```

**Figure 1-1:**
Help
available in
the login
panel.

✔ If you're connected to a Solaris computer through the network, your login is like Figure 1-2. (The remote login says "remote host aurora" to tip you off: "aurora" is the name of the other system to which we're connecting.) The Options menu on a remote login consists of these items:

- Language

- Session

- Connect to Local Host

Unlike Windows and other graphical environments, Solaris supports multiple environments in a remarkably simple fashion. You can easily log in to a session with GNOME running, give it a test drive, log out, change the Options⇨ Session setting to the Common Desktop Environment (CDE), and log in again. Poof — a completely different style of interacting with the environment.

**Figure 1-2:**
The remote
login panel
for Solaris 9.

All of these options are configurable, so your choices may be different from a user in a different organization. On my system, for example, I have the following list of available languages:

✔ POSIX

✔ Canada

✔ U.S.A.

✔ U.S.A. (Euro)

✔ Mexico — Spanish

✔ Canada — French

Your list may be different, depending on what languages are installed and how your system is configured.

It's usually best not to change the default language.

The most interesting of the options for logging in is changing the session, the window manager, and the user environment. On a minimal Solaris 9 installation, you'll have only CDE and Failsafe as choices, but on a full version you should have these choices:

✔ Common Desktop Environment (CDE)

✔ GNOME 2.0 Desktop

✔ User's Last Desktop

✔ Failsafe Session

By default, Solaris 9 logs you in to the session you most recently used on a previous login.

✔ If you're a CDE nut, you can log in without checking the Session value.

✔ If you're interested in other desktop management environments, choosing Options⇨Session⇨GNOME lets you try GNOME, and choosing Options⇨ Session⇨Common Desktop Environment puts you back in the older legacy CDE environment.

Chapter 2 addresses the differences between GNOME and CDE at length, with lots of screen shots. You might want to preview that chapter before doing too much experimentation.

Some installations are configured with even more sessions available, including the K Desktop Environment, Motif, or even earlier versions of GNOME (the latest is 2.0). If so, try them out when you have a few minutes to spare.

If you'd rather work in the raw, unadulterated Unix command line, skipping windows, graphics, mice, and all that fancy jazz, you can choose Command Line Login to shut down the windows environment temporarily. (This is only an option on a local connection. If your configuration doesn't have your display directly wired to the Sun computer, this won't be a choice.)

The command line is a different sort of world. If you're curious about the many, many commands you can use at the command line, how they work, and how you can use them for maximum efficiency on a Solaris computer, please see Chapter 3.

## *Just log in already!*

To log in to the Solaris system, follow these steps:

1. **Enter your account name in the text box on the screen and then either click the OK button or press Enter on your keyboard.**

   Your account name (sometimes called *login name*) is case sensitive, so make sure that you enter it exactly as given. Account name *Taylor* is not the same as account name *taylor* in Solaris.

   After you've successfully entered your account name, the login screen changes to say "Welcome *name*," and it reminds you what type of session you have scheduled to start up, as shown in Figure 1-3.

2. **Type in your password.**

   Your password *isn't* echoed on the screen. This can be confusing when you first start using a Solaris system, especially if your password is a sequence of random letters, digits, and punctuation. It's for your own good. (Can't you just hear your mother saying that?) You're already following good security by not writing down your password, so having it in clear text on your computer screen where a passerby can see it is also a bad idea.

**Figure 1-3:**
Continuing
the login
process.

If you enter the password incorrectly, the login panel informs you in a pretty non-threatening way, giving you another chance to log in.

The password is case sensitive! If you're having trouble logging in, make sure that you don't accidentally have the Caps Lock selected: It changes the key sequence you're sending.

If you can't log in, call your system administrator for assistance.

Once you are successfully logged in, your screen will flash, the login window will vanish, and you'll see the splash screen and other parts of the window manager you've selected appear as the system starts all the programs needed.

## *Launching a Program*

After you've logged in, a splash screen momentarily indicates what version of CDE you've installed (probably Version 1.5).

The results of the login depend on the windowing system you choose.

✔ If you start CDE, the startup screen shows the version of CDE, then quite promptly switches to the default CDE view.

Although not glamorous or full of snazzy three-dimensional graphics, CDE is quite functional and has a helpful control panel along the bottom of the screen, making it easy to see what's happening on your computer (including the current time and system load). It's also easy to launch applications.

✔ If you start GNOME, the startup screen shows the launch of Metacity (as shown in Figure 1-4).

GNOME starts lots of helper applications and has a transitional startup screen called Metacity. On a Solaris system, it looks like Figure 1-4. Watch the gradual progression of icons on your own screen as each component of GNOME starts.

After all the components are running, GNOME takes over your window, looking much more like Windows or the Macintosh than CDE does, as shown in Figure 1-5.

## Launching an application in CDE

If you're running the Common Desktop Environment, you can launch applications by either of the following methods:

✔ Finding them on one of the panels that emerge when you click on the top edge above the icons on the control panel

✔ Typing the command into a terminal window at the command line

For the purposes of this first foray into CDE, click the globe in the lower-left part of the control panel. It shows the current time, and it is the shortcut for launching the Web browser. If your CDE configuration launches the browser automatically, you're ahead of the game and have saved an entire mouse click.

After the browser starts up, it has a screen full of information about the plug-ins and other configuration details.

After a few seconds, that vanishes, and your home page appears (probably www.sun.com/).

Congratulations! You've successfully logged in and launched a program within the Common Desktop Environment.

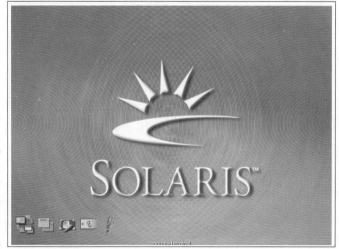

**Figure 1-4:**
Metacity
helps
GNOME
start.

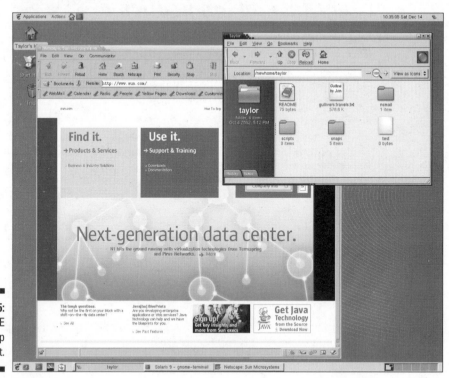

**Figure 1-5:**
The GNOME
desktop
environment.

## Launching an application in GNOME

If you've opted for the world of GNOME, be assured that there aren't little people running around looking for geodes. It's in a graphical environment that should feel familiar if you're used to Windows or Macintosh computers.

The little foot icon in the bottom-left corner of the screen is the GNOME equivalent of the Start button in Windows. Click it, and a menu of choices pops up.

As an example, choose Applications⇨Games⇨Gnometris to launch the GNOME version of the computer game Tetris.

TIP

Spend a few minutes playing Gnometris. It's easy and also demonstrates that moving from Windows or the Mac to the more powerful world of Solaris doesn't have to be all serious!

# Logging Out

Whether you're enjoying the simple legacy world of the Common Desktop Environment or the more colorful modern graphical interface of GNOME, the final task at the end of a workday is to log out of the system. You accomplish this in different ways on different systems:

- ✔ **CDE:** Look for the small EXIT sign in the middle of the control panel. Click it, and you're asked if you really want to log out, as shown in Figure 1-6.
- ✔ **GNOME:** Log out by clicking the small computer screen with the little moon icon on the lower left, just next to the GNOME footprint logo. You're asked if you want to log out., as shown in Figure 1-7.

**Figure 1-6:**
Sure you
want to log
out of CDE?

Logout Confirmation

Exiting the desktop session...

Application updates you have not saved may be lost.

Your current session will be saved and returned to
upon your next login. For more detail, select Help.

Continue Logout?

OK          Cancel          Help

**Figure 1-7:**
Ready
to quit
GNOME?

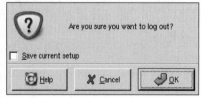

Whether you're using CDE or GNOME, click "yes" or "okay." Everything shuts down, the screen goes blank, and the login panel shows up again. The computer is waiting for you or someone else to log in.

Done! Not too bad, was it?

# Chapter 2

# Graphical Window Managers

After logging in to your Solaris system, the next step is to personalize it to meet your needs, wants, and interests. Think of it as putting the *personal* into *personal workstation*.

The path you take depends on which desktop environment you've chosen. This chapter explores the Common Desktop Environment, with an emphasis on its powerful Control Panel, but focuses more on GNOME; it's the future of the Solaris environment. Either way, if you prefer a certain color scheme, larger type, sound, or other changes, this chapter shows you how to make those changes.

As with all subsequent chapters, log in to your Solaris system before you proceed with this material.

## Digging Around in CDE

The most notable feature in the Common Desktop Environment is the large, visually interesting Control Panel along the bottom of the screen, as shown in Figure 2-1. It's primarily a launch pad for applications. Almost every icon or graphic that you click causes something to happen on your computer.

**Figure 2-1:**
The CDE
Control
Panel.

From left to right, these are the icons on the Control Panel:

- ✔ The butterfly represents the StarOffice components.

- ✔ The globe is a clock and launches the Netscape Web browser.

- ✔ The calendar page enables you to access a CDE calendar.

- ✔ The file cabinet offers a file and directory browser.

- ✔ The note with a pushpin and a pencil enables you to access the text editor.

- ✔ The inbox is a shortcut to the e-mail client program.

- ✔ The small lock icon lets you lock your system if you leave it for any amount of time.

  To unlock it, enter your account password.

- ✔ The four buttons labeled One, Two, Three, and Four represent four different *workspaces*, essentially four virtual computer monitors.

  This is a helpful feature because you don't have any window overlap or worries about the size of your monitor. For example, you can have the

  - Open files of a project in one workspace

  - Your mail program in a second workspace

  - A game running in a third workspace

  - A fourth workspace available for other tasks

- ✔ To the right of the workspace buttons is a small icon of planet Earth. Unlike the large Earth icon that launches Netscape Navigator, this smaller icon opens a Go dialog box where you can type such information as

  - Web site address

  - Remote hostname

  - e-mail address

- ✔ The small EXIT sign is the fast way to log out of the Common Desktop Environment when you're done for the day.

- ✔ The printer enables you to access the Solaris print management system.

✔ Next is a preferences area (a section I examine in closer detail later in this chapter).

✔ The CPU disk icon enables you to access a CPU and disk usage monitor.

✔ The question mark icon enables you to access the online Sun document library.

✔ The wastebasket, where you drag files that you don't want to keep and where you can also manage your trash, pulling out files that you changed your mind about deleting.

Above each icon is a small button with a triangle pointing upwards. Clicking this button opens a *pop-up menu* of choices in that category.

## The world of pop-ups

If you click the small rectangular button above the butterfly icon, a menu of options slides up, as shown in Figure 2-2. Instead of pointing upwards (which is a visual clue that there's a menu underneath the button), the triangle now points downward, indicating that clicking the same spot will close the menu and change the triangle back to its initial state.

The Sun mouse has three buttons. In this book, unless stated otherwise, always use the left mouse button to click things. The other two buttons are primarily for copying and pasting.

**Figure 2-2:**
The
StarOffice
menu.

The menu stays open until you click the small triangle at the bottom. This is a nice feature but can take some time getting used to if you've spent time using Windows or Mac systems.

Figure 2-2 shows the StarOffice menu. StarOffice, included with the full Solaris 9 distribution, is a suite of terrific applications that give you the functionality of Microsoft Office. StarOffice is covered in Part III of this book.

From this menu, you can launch

- ✔ StarOffice central control area (the default item that's highlighted in Figure 2-2)
- ✔ Text document
- ✔ Spreadsheet
- ✔ Drawing palette
- ✔ Presentations
- ✔ HTML (Web) document
- ✔ Templates
- ✔ File and configuration options for StarOffice

On the top left of this menu's title bar is a small box that has what looks like a dash or hyphen within. This is the *window menu button.* Click it to see a set of options, as shown in Figure 2-3.

**Figure 2-3:**
The CDE window menu.

A variation of this window control menu shows up in almost all windows in the CDE environment, though the options vary based on the application running in the window. For the Control Panel pop-up menu, the choices are

- ✔ **Restore:** Restores the menu to full size. This option is grayed out in Figure 2-3 because the menu is already restored — full size.

✔ **Move:** Enables you to move the menu to your favorite spot on the screen. Drag the menu to the desired location and then click the mouse to stick it there.

✔ **Lower:** Doesn't do anything in this context.

Some applications support using Lower as a way to minimize the window to a desktop icon (skip forward to Figure 2-5 to see desktop icon examples), but StarOffice does not let you minimize the floating menu, so Lower won't do anything here.

✔ **Close:** Closes the pop-up menu. The StarOffice menu slides neatly back into the Control Panel, leaving things as they were in Figure 2-1.

If you click the window menu button in the top-left corner of the main Control Panel (refer to Figure 2-1), you see similar choices, as shown in Figure 2-4:

✔ Restore (again, grayed out)

✔ Move

✔ Minimize

✔ Lower

✔ Refresh

✔ Log Out — enables you to quickly log out of the CDE environment

**Figure 2-4:**
The Control
Panel menu.

The most interesting option is Minimize. Poof! The Control Panel disappears, and a small 1-x-1-inch icon appears in the top-left corner of the screen, as shown on the right in Figure 2-5. The name *One* is the name of the current workspace.

**Figure 2-5:**
The Control
Panel,
minimized,
with
Netscape
adjacent.

This concept of minimizing, or *iconifying,* applications to get them out of the way is a powerful aspect of the Unix environment because the application is still running when minimized. You can minimize your Web browser (as shown on the left in Figure 2-5), e-mail program, StarOffice applications, and anything that you can run within CDE.

Clicking a minimized application opens another window menu (see Figure 2-6). This time Restore is *not* grayed out.

✔ Choose this option to change the icon to a full window again.

✔ You can also restore iconified applications by double-clicking the icon.

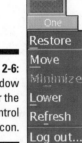

**Figure 2-6:**
The window menu for the Control Panel icon.

For iconified applications, it's helpful to see the expanded menu of options for a regular program as compared to a special CDE application like the Control Panel. Because Netscape Navigator is already iconified, that's a good place to start.

Click the icon, and it changes, as shown in Figure 2-7.

**Figure 2-7:**
The window menu for the Netscape icon.

The Netscape icon name expands to show the name of the Web site that's currently loaded (Sun Microsystems, in this example).

## *Wandering through workspaces*

The window menu options added for a regular application are

- ✔ Occupy Workspace
- ✔ Occupy All Workspaces
- ✔ Unoccupy Workspace (grayed out)

A *workspace* is a virtual computer screen available for use. The buttons One, Two, Three, and Four represent the four workspaces.

To see how workspaces work, follow these steps to move the Netscape application from Workspace One to Workspace Two:

1. **Restore the Netscape window, as shown in Figure 2-8.**

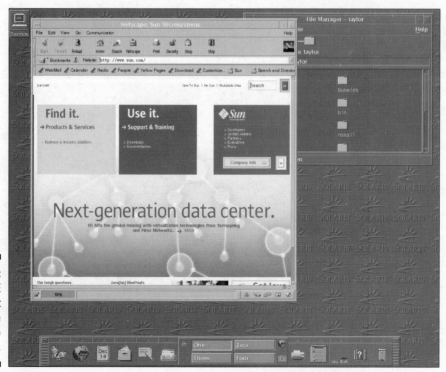

**Figure 2-8:** The CDE environment Netscape restored to full size.

2. **Click Two in the Control Panel to confirm that it's a big, empty workspace with no iconified applications, as shown in Figure 2-9.**

   It has a different background, so it's not identical to Workspace One.

3. **Click One in the Control Panel to return to Workspace One.**

4. **Click the window menu button in the top-left corner of the window to reveal the window menu.**

   The options in the window menu are identical to Figure 2-7. In this case, Restore is grayed out, and Minimize isn't.

5. **Choose Occupy Workspace.**

   You see the dialog box shown in Figure 2-10.

6. **Select Two and click OK.**

   The application vanishes! Where did it go? To workspace Two, of course. Click Two in the Control Panel, and you'll find the wandering application safe and sound.

**Figure 2-9:**
Workspace
Two with no
applications.

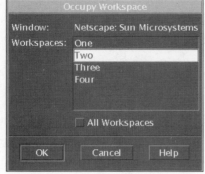

**Figure 2-10:**
Occupy
which
work-
spaces?

Here are a few additional points to remember about workspaces:

✔ If you want an application to live in all workspaces, select the All Workspaces check box in the Occupy Workspace dialog box.

✔ If you want an application in all but one workspace, use these steps:

  1. Select All Workspaces in the Occupy Workspace dialog box.

  2. Jump to the workspace you want to exclude.

  3. Choose Unoccupy Workspace from the window menu.

✔ To rename a workspace, use these steps:

  1. Double-click the workspace name, which changes the color of the icon and adds a cursor.

  2. Use the mouse to select the text

  3. Type a new name over the existing text.

Change all four workspace names, and you might have something similar to Figure 2-11. (In Figure 2-11, the fourth workspace has been selected, but no new name has been entered.)

**Figure 2-11:**
Customized
workspace
names.

CDE remembers all of these customizations when you log out and log in again. That's what the message, "Your current session will be saved and returned to upon your next login," means when you log out of a CDE session.

## Working with CDE windows

Clicking the top-left box on a CDE window produces a menu of options. Two of these options are Minimize and Restore.

Click the Text Editor icon (the piece of paper with the pushpin and the pencil). A small edit window pops up, as shown in Figure 2-12.

**Figure 2-12:**
An empty
Text Editor
window.

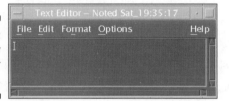

On the top right, you see two boxes, one with a dot, and one with a large box:

- ✔ The dot box is the Minimize button. Click it to minimize the application.

- ✔ The box with the large square in it is the *zoom box;* click it to maximize the application window, similar to the Microsoft Windows zoom feature.

More functionality is hidden in the window frame:

- ✔ **To move the window:** Click the title bar (where it says *Text Editor*), and while holding down the mouse button, move the mouse. This is a simple shortcut for moving windows in the Common Desktop Environment.

- ✔ **To restore the window to full size:** Double-click the title bar. Double-click it again, and you're back to the original small application window.

- ✔ **To resize the window:** Click carefully on one of the narrow edges of the window and then move the mouse while holding the mouse button down. This is a shortcut for resizing the window in that dimension. Click a corner, and you can drag in two directions at the same time. You can make a window any size and dimensions you want.

Most of this behavior is identical in Microsoft Windows. Try some of these shortcuts next time you're near a Windows 98, NT, or XP system.

The menu choices within the application window are controlled by the application. File, Edit, Format, Options, and Help are all part of the Text Editor application. The Text Editor is explored in Chapters 11 and 12.

# Back to the Control Panel

This section takes a quick peek at a few other interesting menus that pop up from the top edge of the Control Panel.

### File Manager

One notable menu is the Applications menu. To open this menu, click the triangle button just above the Text Editor icon. The choices shown in that menu are

- ✔ Text Note
- ✔ Text Editor
- ✔ Voice Note
- ✔ Applications

Click Applications to run the CDE File Manager, as shown in Figure 2-13.

The folder opened by default is the applications and tools folder, causing File Manager to label itself Application Manager instead. Underneath, it's the CDE File Manager.

**Figure 2-13:**
The CDE File Manager displaying applications and tools.

Though not as glamorous as Windows and nowhere near as sexy as the pulsing three-dimensional look of Apple's Mac OS X Aqua interface (let alone the GNOME file manager, Nautilus), this is the basic file manager for the Common Desktop Environment. Click a folder to open it. Click an application to launch it. The name of the window is the name of the currently displayed folder.

For example, click the Desktop_Apps icon in the top-left corner of the window. The result is shown in Figure 2-14. You have 32 applications available to launch, and a .. (go up) shortcut that takes you to the original Applications level.

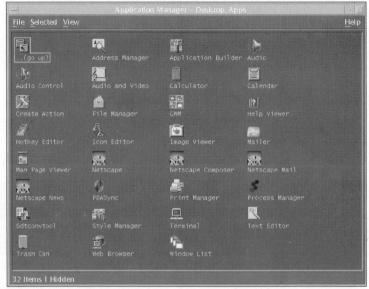

**Figure 2-14:** A bunch of useful desktop applications.

The Control Panel is another way to access many of these applications. When you click the globe clock, for example, you launch the Web Browser application shown in Figure 2-14. Click the bookshelf with the question mark icon, and you get the help viewer from this group.

To close the CDE File Manager, click the top-left box and choose Close from the menu.

### Style Manager

A more interesting area to explore is the CDE Style Manager. In the Control Panel, click just above the Preferences icon (next to the printer) to open the Tools menu, and then choose Desktop Controls.

The resulting file manager window shows a variety of customization tools, as shown in Figure 2-15.

The most useful choices here are

- Backdrop Style Manager, which makes it a breeze to change the wallpaper in any or all of the workspaces.
- Color Style Manager for picking different themes.

**Figure 2-15:**
CDE
custom-
ization
nirvana!

✔ Power Manager to customize when your system

- Sleeps

- Spins down the hard disk

- Shuts off the display on inactivity

✔ Screen Style Manager to customize screen saver modules, as shown in Figure 2-16.

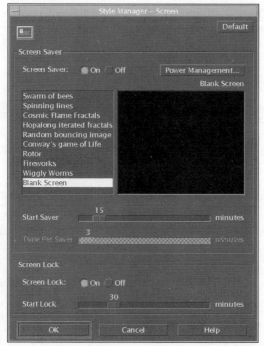

**Figure 2-16:**
Easily
customized
screen
saver
settings.

In the Screen Style Manager, you

- Select screen saver graphics

- Enable or disable having to enter a password when returning from screen saver mode

- Access the Power Management features directly

The Common Desktop Environment Style Manager is automatically launched when you select any of the customization tools, as shown in Figure 2-17. From here, it's easy to figure out how to customize your CDE environment for your preferences and needs.

**Figure 2-17:**
The CDE
Style
Manager.

Go into the Color Style Manager and check out Mustard. It's one of my favorite color schemes for CDE. Then go to Backdrop and check out Southwest. They're a good combination of color and style.

If you want to change the number of workspaces in CDE, click Workspace Manager Controls in the file manager window. You can choose from 1 to 50 workspaces. Select too many, and the Control Panel gets a bit wacky, as shown in Figure 2-18!

**Figure 2-18:**
Maybe this
is too many
workspaces
after all.

There's much more to customizing and using the Common Desktop Environment than can be reasonably covered in this book, but the fundamental question is *why?* Sun Microsystems makes it clear that the future direction of Solaris is with GNOME, covered in the next section. Although CDE will be included for *legacy* support ("footdraggers who hate change"), CDE will be less important as time passes.

If CDE is your preferred windowing environment for Solaris 9, be prepared for a big change. In fact, now's a great time to get started! Ask your system administrator to install GNOME if it's not already part of your operating system install. (System administrators can start by reading the latest information and downloading the newest programs at `www.sun.com/gnome/`). Then use it. Switch over. All CDE applications are still accessible within the GNOME environment, and all the GNOME applications are there, too.

# Getting Started with GNOME

By contrast with the CDE world, GNOME has a tendency to spread out and use all the nooks and crannies of your desktop.

Figure 2-19 shows GNOME, with a taskbar along the bottom and a menu bar along the top of the window.

**Figure 2-19:** The world of GNOME.

# Menu bar

Without changing the default settings, the main controls for GNOME are along the top menu bar. The important details of the top menu bar are shown in Figure 2-20 and described from left to right in the following list:

**Figure 2-20:**
The GNOME menu bar.

✔ The *foot* icon is the GNOME equivalent of the Apple icon on the Macintosh. It's the shortcut to the Applications menu, which enables you to access all applications and functionality within GNOME.

✔ Adjacent to the Applications menu is the Actions menu, shown in Figure 2-21. It enables you to

 • Run programs from a command line

 • Search for files

 • Take a screenshot

 • Lock your screen

 • Log out of GNOME

**Figure 2-21:**
The GNOME Actions menu.

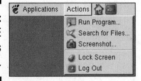

✔ The small house icon opens the Nautilus file manager at your home directory.

✔ The tiny computer screen launches a terminal window for working at the command line (as discussed in Chapter 3).

✔ The right side of the menu bar includes the following:

 • The date and time.

 • A small speaker icon for quick access to the audio controls within GNOME.

- An icon showing the current application in the foreground.

  Known in the world of the X Window System as the application
  with *focus*, it receives the information when you press keys on the
  keyboard, and its window frame is usually a different color from
  the others on the screen. Clicking the currently running application icon shows all running applications, even those in different
  workspaces. Figure 2-22 shows that three applications are running
  in this workspace, and one in another.

**Figure 2-22:**
The GNOME
running
applications
menu.

 Two different Netscapes are running in Figure 2-22, and the title of each Web
site being viewed is shown. This information is helpful when things are going
on simultaneously!

## Taskbar

The taskbar at the bottom of the screen is useful even in the default configuration. The taskbar shows which applications are running offering

- An easy way to jump between applications
- Access to the Workspace Switcher

Figure 2-19 shows three applications running and a panel of small boxes on
the bottom right.

A closer look at the bottom-right corner of the taskbar is shown in Figure 2-23.
The small panel with six boxes is the GNOME version of workspaces; by
default, there are six. Because five are as-yet unpopulated in Figure 2-23,
they're blank. (In the Common Desktop Environment, the default configuration has four workspaces, initially labeled One, Two, Three, and Four.)

**Figure 2-23:**
The right
edge of the
taskbar.

To move to a workspace, click it. All your open applications vanish and move to a new, clean desktop. You can start applications in each workspace and move them between workspaces, but not quite as flexibly in GNOME as within CDE:

- ✔ A GNOME application can either run in either one workspace or all workspaces.
- ✔ CDE applications can be excluded from some workspaces and included in others.

## Customizing your taskbar

GNOME is easy to customize. Right-click just about anything, and you can change it to your heart's content.

Start by right-clicking the Workspace Switcher on the bottom right of the taskbar. To change your Workspace Switcher preferences, choose Preferences. The Workspace Switcher Preferences dialog box appears, as shown in Figure 2-24.

**Figure 2-24:**
Changing
preferences
in the
Workspace
Switcher.

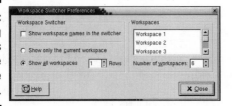

- ✔ To change the number of workspaces, enter the desired number in the Number of Workspaces box.
- ✔ To change the name of a workspace, follow these steps:

    1. Click the name in the Workspaces list on the right

    2. Type the new name.

    3. Click the Show Workspace Names in the Switcher check box.

Click Close to close the preferences dialog box. Figure 2-25 shows a new, improved Workspace Switcher.

**Figure 2-25:**
The new
Workspace
Switcher
view.

Continuing to customize the taskbar, click the small vertical separator bar on the far left of the taskbar. With your mouse button held down, move this bar about two inches to the right so there's a blank space to the left. Right-click that blank space to see the menu of choices shown in Figure 2-26.

**Figure 2-26:**
Customizing
your
GNOME
taskbar.

It's easy to pick a few useful functions and add them to the left corner of the GNOME taskbar. You have to re-launch the menu after each choice — that's just a right-click. For example, choose GNOME Menu, Log Out Button, and Lock Button. The result is three small icons on the bottom-left corner, as shown in Figure 2-27.

**Figure 2-27:**
New
GNOME
taskbar
functions,
all in a row.

To change the order of icons, right-click an icon and choose Move from the menu that pops up.

I prefer to have the GNOME menu on the left, then the logout icon, and then the lock icon. I also add a few shortcuts for commonly used programs: Netscape and the terminal application. To add Netscape, for example, right-click on a blank spot and choose Add to Panel➪Launcher from Menu➪Internet➪Netscape Web Browser.

You can also add or delete panels (menubars), because the same underlying program controls the taskbar and the top menu. If you'd rather live in a more Windows-like world, zap the top panel by right-clicking the menu and choosing Delete This Panel; then customize the bottom to meet your preferences.

I like to add a weather monitor to either the taskbar or the menu bar. Just Right-click a blank area and then choose Add to Panel➪Accessories➪Weather Report.

By default, the weather is for Pittsburgh, Pennsylvania. If you're not planning a picnic in the Steel City, though, you can change the location with these steps:

1. **Right-click the little weather graphic and choose Preferences from that menu.**

   The Weather Preferences dialog box opens, as shown in Figure 2-28.

**Figure 2-28:**
Customizing
the weather
report.

2. **Pick the appropriate city from the list (it's organized by state) and then click the General tab.**

   This ensures that the default configuration is good — it usually is fine.

3. **Click Close and right-click the weather forecast and choose Refresh from the options.**

Now it's your local weather forecast, updated every 30 minutes. Neat, eh? And people say Solaris is dull!

## The GNOME menu

Click the foot icon at either the top or bottom of your screen — depending on how you configured things — and you'll see a number of choices on the Applications menu, including

- Applications
- CDE Menu
- Run Program
- Search for Files
- Screenshot
- Lock Screen
- Log Out

Of these, the CDE Menu is most worth mentioning because it offers access to *all CDE applications within the GNOME environment.*

A neat trick!

This is one big reason why it's easy for Common Desktop Environment users to transition to GNOME. When running GNOME on Solaris, you have access to all the great GNOME applications and still have easy legacy access to CDE applications, too, all of which work fine. Figure 2-29 shows GNOME running a typical CDE application, Text Editor, and also shows the CDE Menu⇨ Applications list.

Not only do CDE applications run happily in GNOME, they look better and more modern. Figure 2-29 shows the CDE Calculator in GNOME, which looks nicer than in CDE.

## The desktop menu

A hidden gem in GNOME is the menu that pops up on the main desktop area when you right-click. The menu is shown in Figure 2-30. The following list describes some of the options available from this menu:

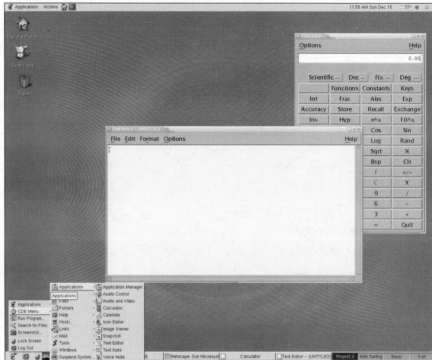

**Figure 2-29:**
CDE
applications
within
GNOME.

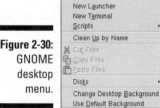

**Figure 2-30:**
GNOME
desktop
menu.

> ✔ **New Window:** Opens a Nautilus file manager window with your home
> directory shown.
>
> Nautilus is explored in depth, including day-to-day Nautilus tasks, in
> Chapter 4.
>
> ✔ **New Folder:** Creates an unnamed folder, logically enough. You can
> rename the folder by right-clicking the folder and choosing Rename.

✔ **New Launcher:** Enables you to tie a desktop icon to the invocation of a specific program. Getting it to work properly is beyond the scope of this book, so we'll leave it alone.

✔ **Clean Up by Name:** A quick way to reorganize your desktop icons if they've sprawled out of control. It's analogous to the same function in Windows.

✔ **Disks:** This submenu offers quick access to the floppy and CD-ROM disks.

Selecting a disk opens up Nautilus with the contents of the appropriate device displayed. GNOME tries to show removable media on the desktop automatically upon being inserted, but it doesn't always work. This is a fast and easy alternative.

✔ **Change Desktop Background and Use Default Background:** GNOME includes several desktop backgrounds. It's easy to change to a different background picture or even a color or gradient.

    1. **Choose Change Desktop Background to access Background Preferences.**

    2. **Click the miniature version of the current desktop on the top left to access a browser.**

    3. **Move to either images or tiling_patterns to see your choices.**

       Figure 2-31 shows one of the images in the standard distribution previewed. Nice!

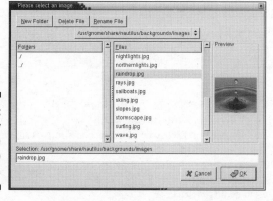

**Figure 2-31:** One of many possible desktop images.

One advantage that CDE has over GNOME is that you can have different desktop images for each workspace. In GNOME, workspaces share the background desktop image, which is one of the few disappointments for CDE users transitioning into the brave new world of GNOME.

# Customizing GNOME

You can poke around and tweak the visual characteristics of GNOME many ways to meet your preferences, from weather forecasts to named workspaces, from duplicate GNOME menus to shortcuts for your favorite applications. However, you can change a lot more under the proverbial hood of the program.

Although you can reach each preference from the GNOME menu, stepping through all the possible areas is awkward. A smarter way to accomplish this is to click the Start Here map and compass icon on the desktop. This launches a Nautilus file manager window, as shown in Figure 2-32.

**Figure 2-32:** Start Here offers easy access to lots of customization.

Because this section focuses on GNOME, double-click Desktop Preferences. You see the list of customizable elements shown in Figure 2-33. The icons that list a certain number of items beneath the icon name (such as Advanced, which lists *5 items*) denote that those items are folders and that there are, for example, five different items within the Advanced folder.

Ahhh. So many choices, so little time!

Start customizing by picking a different background:

**Figure 2-33:**
GNOME
desktop
preferences.

✔ Double-click the Background icon, and you'll see the same Background Preferences window you encounter from the desktop menu, as shown in Figure 2-34.

✔ To change the image, click the Select Picture box on the top left and navigate to your preferred image.

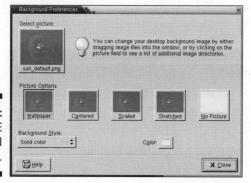

**Figure 2-34:**
GNOME
background
preferences.

Crazy pictures can seem fun, but simple, calm low-color background graphics and solid colors offer the least invasive desktop for productive work. The best choice is a *gradient* that gently transitions from one color to another; it's more attractive than a solid color background. Pick a gradient by following these steps:

**1. Click the white No Picture box.**

Your desktop becomes, um, as pure as the driven snow.

2. **To change the background color, click the small Color button.**

It opens a color chooser window, as shown in Figure 2-35.

3. **To select a new color, click different spots on the color wheel or within the color triangle, and then click OK to proceed.**

You can go wild and have dark blue transitioning to bright pink, but a nice low-key background can be a gradient from one dark color to another, perhaps dark blue to dark purple.

Gradients can be oriented *horizontally* or *vertically*.

4. **Click the Background Style pop-up menu, and you can choose from**

> **Solid Color**
>
> **Horizontal Gradient**
>
> **Vertical Gradient.**

5. **When everything is to your liking, click Close to make your change permanent and return to the Desktop Preferences area.**

## *Of fonts and mice*

Two of the great improvements of modern graphical computing are

- ✔ The ability to use a pointing device, like a mouse, for rapid and precise cursor motion
- ✔ The ability to change typefaces to improve the clarity and legibility of information displayed on-screen

### *Choosing Typefaces*

You can change the default typefaces used in applications and on the desktop, but you have less control in GNOME than in Windows or Macintosh systems. Figure 2-36 shows the default font choices out of a relatively small list accessible from the Font Preferences window.

**Figure 2-36:** GNOME Font Preferences.

Unless you have a strong desire to tweak things, I suggest leaving the application and desktop fonts to their default values of sans 10 and sans 12, respectively.

*Sans* means a *sans-serif typeface.* (*Serifs* are tiny feet on the bottom of letters.) Sans-serif type is more readable on a computer screen. The text you're reading now in the book is in a *serif typeface* (like a newspaper) because it makes letters this size easier to read when they're printed on paper.

### Running with Mouse Preferences

The mouse preferences are more interesting. Double-click Mouse in the Desktop Preferences window to see the many ways you can customize the mouse. Figure 2-37 shows both the Buttons and Motion tabs.

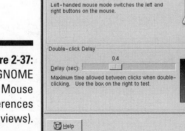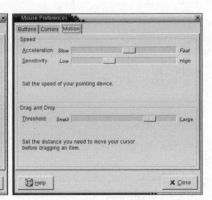

**Figure 2-37:** GNOME Mouse Preferences (two views).

  ✔ **Buttons tab:** If you're left-handed, you'll be delighted by the first option on the Buttons tab: Left-Handed Mouse. Choosing this option flips the behavior of the left and right mouse buttons. The mouse will work better with your left hand and ensure that no one else can use your system without getting hopelessly befuddled!

- ✔ **Cursors tab:** This tab enables you to change cursors, but I don't recommend doing so.

- ✔ **Motion tab:** This tab enables you to customize the behavior of your mouse. If you have a large screen, increasing the mouse acceleration is often helpful and can save lots of dragging on-screen. Think of it as the add/delete cat function (cat chases mouse, mouse goes faster, get it?).

When you're done fine-tuning the behavior of your mouse, click Close to have your changes take effect.

## The rest of the preferences

Once you get up to speed with GNOME, one of the most enjoyable tasks is to customize various facets of your workspace and desktop.

Many additional preferences can make your workspace reflect your personality.

### Tweaking Menus and Toolbars

Menus & Toolbars enables you to change the Nautilus window, among others, to look less like a Web browser (this visual similarity isn't a coincidence, by the way).

If you're working on a small screen, switching the toolbars to text-only can save a lot of screen space in GNOME-controlled windows.

### Listening for Sound Preferences

If you like audio feedback and aren't in an office environment where people will be annoyed by it, the Sound Preferences offer the ability to make GNOME just as fun as a standard Windows configuration. You can get audio feedback for such events as

- ✔ Startup
- ✔ Shutdown
- ✔ Error messages
- ✔ Warnings

Make sure that you enable the sound server startup.

The Sound Events tab enables you to identify and fine-tune audio feedback played for different events. Some Web sites have even more free sound sets to download for the GNOME Sound Manager.

GUI Central, at `www.guicentral.com/`, is a great source for background images, sound sets, screen savers, and lots of other Solaris system goodies.

### Ensuring thematic consistency with Theme Preferences

The Theme Preferences window, shown in Figure 2-38, enables you to quickly change colors and typefaces. What's nice is that the changes occur instantly. You can easily click each theme in the list to see how it looks.

**Figure 2-38:**
Theme
Preferences.

If you really want to change the appearance of your GNOME Desktop, hop onto the Internet. Freshmeat.net is a great place to download new themes to make your GNOME experience fun. This developer site also has lots of technical content if you're dying to know exactly what makes the wheels turn. Start at `themes.freshmeat.net/browse/930/` to see the themes organized in categories. (Atomic is a great theme, particularly if you like green!)

By default GNOME makes a window your system's *focus* (the window that receives keyboard events and mouse clicks) when you *click* in the window. If you prefer to have the focus change as soon as the mouse *points* at a window, choose the Window Focus preference in the Desktop Preferences list.

# Chapter 3

# Interacting with the Shell

*O*ne of the most striking differences between the powerful Solaris operating system and Microsoft Windows is that Solaris has a crude but tremendously powerful environment lurking underneath the pretty graphical face. The Unix that's the foundation of the Solaris operating system offers hundreds of commands and thousands of options that can be combined in millions of ways. Windows has, well, the DOS prompt.

For many Solaris users, the command line world is the interface of choice for using the system. (I'm typing this chapter in the vi editor from a command line, within a terminal program.) Although not as visually attractive or user friendly as CDE or, especially, GNOME, the Solaris command line is a powerful friend to have, whether you use it daily or once in a blue moon.

This chapter explores the basic idea of the command line and demonstrates how to be most productive when faced with a % or $ prompt rather than a window full of buttons, tabs, and icons.

## Surviving the Command Line

To get to the command line, you need to launch a terminal program. You can easily accomplish this in either CDE or GNOME:

✔ If you're a Common Desktop Environment user, click the small rectangular region above the CPU and Disk performance graph to open the Hosts menu, as shown in Figure 3-1. Choose This Host from the menu to open a terminal window, as shown in Figure 3-2. Now you can type in Unix commands to your heart's content.

✔ The path to finding a terminal in GNOME is trickier because it's buried deep in the menu path. Click the GNOME menu (the foot), and then choose Applications➪System Tools➪Terminal, as shown in Figure 3-3. In a few seconds, a terminal window pops up on the GNOME desktop, as shown in Figure 3-4.

**Figure 3-1:**
The Hosts
menu
in CDE.

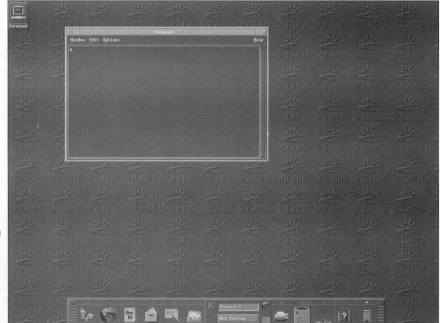

**Figure 3-2:**
Terminal
window
ready to
go in CDE.

**Figure 3-3:**
Finding the
terminal in
GNOME.

**Figure 3-4:**
GNOME
terminal
ready
for duty!

Think of the terminal as the *wrapper*. The program that runs within the
terminal — the program that you interact with — is a *command shell*. Over a
dozen different shells exist in the Unix community. Solaris 9 ships with four
major choices:

✔ The ancient, primitive Bourne shell (sh)

✔ The Sun-favorite Korn shell (ksh)

✔ The powerful TENEX-inspired C shell (tcsh)

✔ The Bourne Again shell (bash)

All shells follow the same concept. They're empty vessels waiting for you to type in an instruction and give them something to do. Leave them alone for a weekend, and they'll sit quietly, waiting for you to return and start typing. When you type in a command, the shell invokes the specified program, feeds it whatever input you enter, and sends its output to the terminal window.

For example, type **ls**, and the shell invokes the ls (list files) command, which shows you what files are in the current directory. It looks like this:

```
$ ls
03.txt            Library    Perl:JS Complete     Uni Phoenix
Email Explained   Merrick    Shell Script Hacks
```

The convention in this book is to show user input (what you type) in bold. When faced with a $ prompt from the shell, type the letter *l*, and the letter *s*, and then press Enter on your keyboard. The results won't be the same as shown here because you have different files and folders in your home directory.

After the shell finishes running a command, it prompts with another $ and awaits the next instruction. (Of course, some shells use a different prompt: csh uses % as its main prompt, for example.)

## Leaving the shell

One of the most important commands to know is exit. It ends the terminal program and lets you go back to the GUI world quickly and efficiently. Of course, you can also simply switch the focus on your screen to another application by moving the mouse and clicking in that window. Or you can minimize the terminal window by clicking the Minimize button on the title bar
or choosing Minimize from the window menu. It's okay to leave a terminal running, even if you're not currently using it.

## Poking around the system

The Solaris file system is organized as a file tree, where your home directory is located in /export/home, along with all other users on your system. You can move up or down the file system tree at the command line. You can also jump directly to other spots in the file system.

These are the commands to move around:

- ✔ pwd reveals your present working directory.

- ✔ cd changes the directory. Give cd a specific spot in the file system, and it takes you there directly. Omit a specific spot, and it takes you back to your home directory, wherever you are.

The commands work like this:

```
$ pwd
/export/home/taylor
$ cd /tmp
$ pwd
/tmp
$ cd
$ pwd
/export/home/taylor
```

The cd command on line three didn't return any feedback to indicate that it had successfully moved to the specified directory (/tmp). As is typical with Unix commands, only an error generates output. When things work properly, there is no output.

This lack of confirmation is one reason why the Solaris operating system intimidates many users. There's really no reason to be anxious. In fact, a basic understanding of how to work with the shell can help you become a power Solaris user!

When moving around, it's useful to see what's in a given location. That's the job of the ls command. Without any arguments, it displays the contents of the current directory. Specify a directory, and it shows you what's inside, without taking you there:

```
$ ls
03.txt              Library     Perl:JS Complete    Solaris for Dummies
Email Explained     Merrick     Shell Script Hacks  Uni Phoenix
$ pwd
/export/home/taylor
$ ls /tmp
com.symantec.NAV_AP_LAUNCH.log          vi.zCGsqY
$ pwd
/export/home/taylor
```

The ls command can output its results in a variety of ways. You can change the behavior of the program with command *options,* single-letter arguments preceded by a single dash. For example, to see the files listed with their sizes, use the -s flag to the ls command:

```
$ ls -s
total 8
8 03.txt              0 Merrick            0 Solaris for Dummies
0 Email Explained     0 Perl:JS Complete   0 Uni Phoenix
0 Library             0 Shell Script Hacks
```

The -l flag has a different result, requesting the long output format for the listing:

```
$ ls -l
total 8
-rw-r--r--   1 taylor   staff   1321 Dec 16 15:06 03.txt
drwxrwxrwx   9 taylor   staff    306 Oct 20 12:12 Email Explained
drwxr-xr-x  27 taylor   staff    918 Dec  4 12:57 Library
drwxrwxrwx  21 taylor   staff    714 Oct 21 21:17 Merrick
drwxrwxrwx  17 taylor   staff    578 Dec 15 22:39 Perl:JS Complete
drwxrwxrwx  11 taylor   staff    374 Dec 15 23:27 Shell Script Hacks
drwxrwxrwx  13 taylor   staff    442 Dec 15 23:28 Solaris for Dummies
drwxrwxrwx  26 taylor   staff    884 Oct 24 11:37 Uni Phoenix
```

This shows more of what's going on with the contents of the home directory:

✔ The first column of the output (for example, "-rw-r—r—" for the file "03.txt") indicates the permissions of the file or directory.

• If the first letter is a *d,* it's a directory or folder.

• - denotes a regular file or program.

✔ The third column shows the owner of the file or directory.

✔ The fifth column is either

• Size of the file

• Size of the folder's directory

The size column of ls doesn't show the summary size of the directory's contents. That's generated by the du command.

✔ The sixth column shows the date the file or directory was last modified.

✔ The seventh column shows the name of the file.

To change to a specific directory, use the cd command and specify the directory by name. If the name has spaces in it, wrap the name in quotes, as shown here:

```
$ cd "Solaris for Dummies"
$ pwd
/export/home/taylor/Solaris for Dummies
$ ls
539698-00.doc        539698-02.doc        Sync with TheBox
539698-01-Snaps      Older Material       Table of Contents.doc
539698-01.doc        SFD14 Snaps
539698-02-Snaps      SFD14.doc
```

A useful flag for the ls command is -F, which appends a / after each directory name so you can easily differentiate between files and directories in an ls output:

```
$ cd
$ ls -F
03.txt              Merrick/            Solaris for Dummies/
Email Explained/    Perl:JS Complete/   Uni Phoenix/
Library/            Shell Script Hacks/
```

Now you can see that the home directory contains only one file — this chapter.

Many more command flags for ls are covered in depth in Chapter 4, if you're curious, but these three flags — -s, -l, and -F — are enough to explain how flags work in Solaris.

## Working with flags

Command flags should always appear *after* the command name and *before* any filenames or directories you specify. Compare these examples:

✔ This form is valid:

```
ls -s /tmp
```

✔ This form is not valid and will generate an error message:

```
ls /tmp -s
```

Where logical, you can also specify multiple flags at the same time as separate arguments or all bunched together. The order in which you specify the command flags counts only in rare situations. The following lines are functionally identical:

```
ls -lF
ls -l -F
ls -F -l
```

Solaris is case sensitive. For example, ls and LS are not the same command.

Be careful not to have the Caps Lock key down, which'll change your input and cause the Solaris system to get quite confused. Uppercase commands almost never work at the shell.

Flags and filenames are also case sensitive, as with the ls command:

✔ A lowercase s shows the size of files.

✔ An uppercase F denotes directories with a trailing slash.

Some commands are oddballs that take full-word flags, not single-letter abbreviations. The `find` command is the most commonly used of these commands. It's common to see a command like this:

```
find . -name "*.c" -print
```

This is different from the typical Solaris flag usage. The `find` command and its many usage options is covered more extensively in Chapter 14, giving you an opportunity to truly master this powerful and helpful Solaris tool.

## Wildcards

However, the asterisk (*) in the `find` command is one of a set of shell wildcards. Knowing how to work with shell wildcards can save you lots of typing.

There are two basic wildcard characters:

- ✔ matches *zero or more* characters.
- ✔ matches *exactly one* character.

You can use more than one wildcard in a pattern.

For example, an easy way to produce a long listing of all C source files is

```
ls *.c
```

If you want to limit that to files that start with the letter *A,* the correct pattern is

```
ls A*.c
```

To match a certain *number of letters* in the filename, ? comes into play. To show all files that have exactly four letters in their names, you can use:

```
ls ????
```

The `echo` command is helpful for understanding how to work with shell wildcards because it expands as appropriate and lists the results:

```
$ echo *.c
cat.c dog.c long_filename_test.c
$ echo ???.c
cat.c dog.c
$ echo c*t*c
cat.c
```

The last echo example (echo c*t*c) works because it requests all files that start with the letter *c,* have zero or more other characters, followed by a letter *t,* followed by zero or more characters, and ending with a *c.*

# Online documentation

For the graphical world, many documents are available to help you find out more about Solaris, CDE, GNOME, and the like. The command line is not as well documented. If you spend any time in the shell, the one super-important command to know is man.

The Solaris documentation is divided into individual manual pages for each command, all easily accessible with the man command. To find out more about the echo command, for example, type this:

```
man echo
```

At the end of each page, press the spacebar to continue to the next page of information, or type **q** to quit and go back to the shell prompt.

Because it's impossible to always know which command is which, the man command also has a -k flag for keyword searching. For example, use this to discover which commands work with floppy disks:

```
$ man -k floppy
eject        eject (1)       - eject media such as CD-ROM and
                               floppy from drive
fd           fd (7d)         - drivers for floppy disks and
                               floppy disk controllers
fdc          fd (7d)         - drivers for floppy disks and
                               floppy disk controllers
fdformat     fdformat (1)    - format floppy diskette or PCMCIA
                               memory card
fdio         fdio (7i)       - floppy disk control operations
rmmount      rmmount (1m)    - removable media mounter for
                               CD-ROM, floppy, Jaz drive, and
                               others
volcheck     volcheck (1)    - checks for media in a drive and
                               by default checks all floppy
                               media
vold         vold (1m)       - Volume Management daemon to
                               manage CD-ROM and floppy,
                               ZIP/JAZ, and DVD-ROM devices
volmissing   volmissing (1)  - notify user that volume
                               requested is not in the CD-ROM
                               or floppy drive
```

These results are a bit cryptic. They show the matching name, the matching manual page entry name, and the one-line description of that command. In the first example, the command `eject` is described as `eject media such as CD-ROM and floppy from drive`.

The number in parentheses is the *section* of the online man page system where the specific command was found. Here's the lowdown on the different sections:

- ✔ Section 1 is user commands.
- ✔ Sections 2 and 3 are for software developers.
- ✔ Section 4 is file formats.
- ✔ Section 5 is publicly accessible data files.
- ✔ Sections 7 and 8 are for system administrators.

A good place to start is by typing `man intro` at the command line.

# Managing File Redirection

It's useful to explore exactly how input for a command comes from the keyboard, and output goes to the screen, because this mechanism underlies much of the power of the Unix command line.

Any command that's run in the shell has two assigned I/O channels: *standard input* and *standard output.* (They're called *stdin* and *stdout* by the cognoscenti.) They start out as the *keyboard* and the *display screen (e.g., your monitor),* respectively, but you can change them depending on how you invoke the command.

For example, you can save the output of a command to a file rather than display it on-screen. To do so, redirect stdout with the special > character, followed by a new filename. The following command causes the output of the `pwd` command to be saved to a new file with the name `my-present-directory`:

```
$ pwd > my-present-directory
```

You can verify this with a quick invocation of `ls`. The new file is included in the output.

```
$ ls -sF
total 32
24 03.txt                 0 Merrick/              0 Solaris for Dummies/
 0 Email Explained/        0 Perl:JS Complete/     0 Uni Phoenix/
 0 Library/                0 Shell Script Hacks/   8 my-present-directory
```

The > symbol causes the contents of the output file to be replaced, which isn't always the desired result. To append the results to the output file, not replace it, use >> instead of >. The following command appends the results of the ls -l command to the existing output file from the pwd command:

```
$ ls -l >> my-present-directory
```

You can also change standard input with a similar redirection symbol, pointing the other way: <. Again, follow it with the name of the file you want to replace stdin. Using the helpful wc (word count) command, here's how you can have it analyze the my-present-directory file:

```
$ wc < my-present-directory
      11      91     600
```

The preceding output is a bit cryptic (typical Unix!). It shows the number of lines, words, and characters in the specified file.

File redirection creates several challenges:

✔ What happens when you redirect the output to a file that already exists?

Depending on the settings of your shell, redirecting output to an existing file can cause an error to be output instead, as demonstrated here:

```
$ ls > my-present-directory
my-present-directory: File exists.
```

Rather than stomp on what might be a useful file, the shell protects you from your own zeal with this warning message.

✔ What happens when you want to append output to a file that doesn't exist?

An append can also generate an error instead of successfully finishing, as demonstrated here:

```
$ ls >> doesnt-exist
doesnt-exist: No such file or directory.
```

Don't disable this feature. Be safe. Ensure that you don't want to keep the file in question, and then explicitly remove the file with the rm command if it's safe to delete. If you absolutely want to turn this behavior off, ask your system administrator to help you disable the noclobber setting in your shell configuration file.

The rm command is *dangerous*. Unlike Windows and Macintosh systems, there's no *unrm* or *undelete* capability. If you remove something with rm in the shell, it's gone, gone, gone. Note that this doesn't apply to the GUI environment: in both CDE and GNOME, if you drag a file to the trashcan, you can still retrieve it until you manually empty the trash.

# Building Command Pipes

Unquestionably, the most powerful capability of the Solaris command line is being able to easily build command *pipes*. By using a pipe (invoked by inserting the '|' symbol between two different commands), you can feed the output of one program as the input to another. This is a tremendous addition to the shell functionality, and well worth a detailed examination.

As a simple example, you can easily figure out how many files are in a large directory by building a command pipe to do the job: couple the output of ls to the input of the wc word count program:

```
$ ls /usr/bin | wc -l
575
```

As you can see, the | character is the magic incantation that enables Solaris to hook input and output together. In the preceding example, a listing of the files in /usr/bin is fed to the word count command, and the -l flag to wc requests that only *the number of lines* are output, rather than lines, words, and characters.

In less than a second, all 575 files in the /usr/bin directory are counted (something you wouldn't want to do by hand).

Here are a few key commands to use with pipes:

- ✔ grep lets you screen only those lines that match a specified pattern.
- ✔ sort lets you sort things alphabetically.
- ✔ tr lets you translate one set of characters for another on the input stream.
- ✔ sed lets you substitute patterns in the pipeline data.

## Finding matches with grep

grep is an oddly named command. You can think of it as *match* or *find* if you want. (But there's already a find in Solaris, so that might just be confusing.)

The basic use of grep is to produce only those lines in its input that match the specified pattern. Typical grep usage is either grep *pattern* inputfile or, as seen in this instance, grep *pattern* to search the input stream for matches. To see which files in /usr/bin contain the letters *sh,* you could use this command:

```
$ ls /usr/bin | grep sh
bash
csh
glib-genmarshal
hash
jsh
ksh
pfcsh
pfksh
pfsh
remsh
rksh
rsh
sh
showrev
ssh
ssh-add
ssh-agent
ssh-keygen
tcsh
zsh
```

The preceding result can also be generated with `ls /usr/bin/*sh*`.

Here's a slightly different example. It counts how many commands in `/usr/bin` do *not* have the letter *a* as part of their name.

There's no special wildcard pattern for the shell that does an exclusionary pattern. It's a perfect task for `grep` and the `-v` flag, which requests a "not" match. The `grep -v` pattern only shows lines that do *not* have the specified pattern, like this:

```
$ ls /usr/bin | grep -v a | wc -l
376
```

The preceding example is a *three-command pipe.* The *output* of `ls` is the *input* of `grep`, and the *output* of `grep` is the *input* of `wc`.

For the next few examples, look at the text to *Gulliver's Travels,* conveniently saved as `gullivers.travels.txt`.

You can also download a copy of this story in text form from the *Solaris For Dummies* Web site: `www.intuitive.com/dummies/`.

How many lines are in this file?

```
$ wc -l < gullivers.travels.txt
10064
```

That's a long story! But of those 10,064 lines, how many have the word *Gulliver* in them? It's another job for `grep`:

```
$ grep -i gulliver < gullivers.travels.txt | wc -l
9
```

Amazingly few, eh? The `-i` flag to `grep` results in it ignoring the case in matches. *Gulliver* and *gulliver* both match the specified pattern. Without the `-i` flag, there are no matches to gulliver as a pattern.

Here are the nine matches:

```
$ grep -i gulliver < gullivers.travels.txt
Gulliver's Travels into Several Remote Nations of the World
The author of these Travels, Mr. Lemuel Gulliver, is my
ancient and mother's side. About three years ago, Mr.
Gulliver growing weary that country, several tombs and
monuments of the Gullivers. Gulliver had spoken it.
that Mr. Gulliver may be a little dissatisfied. But I was
resolved
A LETTER FROM CAPTAIN GULLIVER TO HIS COUSIN SYMPSON
though earlier in the work, Redriff is said to have been

Gulliver's
```

One of the preceding matches is all uppercase, but the `-i` flag to `grep` caught it anyway.

The following pipe is trickier: Screen out the occurrences of *Gulliver's* from the list of lines that contain the case-insensitive pattern 'gulliver':

```
$ grep -i gulliver < gullivers.travels.txt | grep -v "Gulliver's"

The author of these Travels, Mr. Lemuel Gulliver, is my
ancient and mother's side. About three years ago, Mr.
Gulliver growing weary
Although Mr. Gulliver was born in Nottinghamshire, where his
Father that county, several tombs and monuments of the
Gullivers.
Gulliver had spoken it.
that Mr. Gulliver may be a little dissatisfied. But I was
resolved
A LETTER FROM CAPTAIN GULLIVER TO HIS COUSIN SYMPSON.
```

The same command can appear more than once in a pipeline, as in the preceding example.

# Changing text in the pipeline

Gulliver has always struck me as a funny name. I've wondered how it might read as Miguel or Chin instead. With Solaris, you can test this with the sed stream editor:

```
$ grep -i gulliver < gullivers.travels.txt | sed 's/Gulliver/Miguel/'

Miguel's Travels into Several Remote Nations of the World
The author of these Travels, Mr. Lemuel Miguel, is my ancient
and mother's side. About three years ago, Mr. Miguel growing
weary
Although Mr. Miguel was born in Nottinghamshire, where his
Father that county, several tombs and monuments of the
Miguels.
Miguel had spoken it.
that Mr. Miguel may be a little dissatisfied. But I was
resolved
A LETTER FROM CAPTAIN GULLIVER TO HIS COUSIN SYMPSON.
though earlier in the work, Redriff is said to have been
Miguel's
```

Definitely has a different vibe, doesn't it? The all-capitalized GULLIVER didn't change because sed was only looking to substitute Miguel for Gulliver.

Instead of Miguel, what if in a perverse moment you decide you want to change all occurrences of the letter *l* to an *m?* That's easy to do, too:

```
$ grep -i gulliver < gullivers.travels.txt | tr 'l' 'm'
Gummiver's Travems into Severam Remote Nations of the Wormd
The author of these Travems, Mr. Lemuem Gummiver, is my
ancient and mother's side. About three years ago, Mr.
Gummiver growing weary
Amthough Mr. Gummiver was born in Nottinghamshire, where his
father
that county, severam tombs and monuments of the Gummivers.
Gummiver had spoken it.
that Mr. Gummiver may be a mittme dissatisfied. But I was
resomved
A LETTER FROM CAPTAIN GULLIVER TO HIS COUSIN SYMPSON.
though earmier in the work, Redriff is said to have been
Gummiver's
```

Not quite the spirit of Swift's original, but *Gummiver* has some potential.

In the preceding example, every occurrence of *l* was replaced by an *m. Travels* became *Travems, World* became *Wormd,* and *little* became *mittme.*

## But what's the point?

Few people will monkey around with a novel like *Gulliver's Travels* on their Solaris box, so why bother with all this stuff?

Because the capabilities demonstrated in this example are quite powerful. If you have a series of documents that reference a member of your team, and the documents need to be identified promptly, it's much faster to use grep across a directory of matching files than to laboriously step through each possible file in StarOffice, searching for the specified pattern. In addition to removing vowels, tr can also easily translate uppercase into lowercase, for example (tr '[A-Z]' '[a-z]'). sed can make it a breeze to correct the reference number in a set of documents in a few seconds, rather than a few hours.

The tr command can also *remove* specified letters from the input stream so you can also quickly produce the shorthand version, *Gllvr's Trvls*:

```
$ grep -i gulliver < gullivers.travels.txt | tr -d 'aeiou'
Gllvr's Trvls nt Svrl Rmt Ntns f th Wrld
Th thr f ths Trvls, Mr. Lml Gllvr, s my ncnt nd
mthr's sd. Abt thr yrs g, Mr. Gllvr grwng wry
Althgh Mr. Gllvr ws brn n Nttnghmshr, whr hs fthr
tht cnty, svrl tmbs nd mnmnts f th Gllvrs.
Gllvr hd spkn t.
tht Mr. Gllvr my b lttl dsstsfd. Bt I ws rslvd
A LETTER FROM CAPTAIN GULLIVER TO HIS COUSIN SYMPSON.
thgh rlr n th wrk, Rdrff s sd t hv bn Gllvr's\
```

Uppercase letters weren't specified to tr, so they weren't affected by the translation.

## *More useful piped commands*

Many pipes in Solaris have a very helpful part: wc. The wc command has three possible flags: -w for words, -l for lines, and -c for characters. wc -l only outputs lines, but wc -w can force just the number of words to be shown:

```
$ wc -w < gullivers.travels.txt
104290
```

The final command to consider in a pipe is sort, which can sort alphabetically or numerically, ascending or descending.

### Sorting Output

You've already seen that the -s flag to ls produces an indication of each file's size. Now sort that output and see what happens:

```
$ ls -sF | sort
   0 539698-01-Snaps/
   0 539698-02-Snaps/
   0 539698-03-Snaps/
   0 Older Material/
   0 SFD14 Snaps/
  72 539698-00.doc
  72 Sync with TheBox
  80 Table of Contents.doc
 112 539698-01.doc
 120 539698-03.doc
 136 539698-02.doc
 280 SFD14.doc
1136 gullivers.travels.txt
```

The directories are not useful information with their size indicated as zero. You can screen them out with a grep command using a pattern of /$. (The $ is a special character that matches the end of the line, so this pattern only matches lines where the / is the last character in the line):

```
$ ls -s | grep -v '/$' | sort
  72 539698-00.doc
  72 Sync with TheBox
  80 Table of Contents.doc
 112 539698-01.doc
 120 539698-03.doc
 136 539698-02.doc
 280 SFD14.doc
1136 gullivers.travels.txt
```

This is sorted numerically, but you can reverse its order. You do this with the -r flag:

```
$ ls -s | grep -v '/$' | sort -r
1136 gullivers.travels.txt
 280 SFD14.doc
 136 539698-02.doc
 120 539698-03.doc
 112 539698-01.doc
  80 Table of Contents.doc
  72 Sync with TheBox
  72 539698-00.doc
```

### Calculating disk usage

The du command shows disk usage for a given directory and any subdirectories, enabling you to see the size of directories. It is a perfect candidate for a numeric sort, as shown here:

```
$ du -s *
26000     BWA Traffic Logs
56        CTEK Advisor.doc
1752      Email Explained
656       MWJ_20021216.pdf
48872     Merrick
14928     Perl:JS Complete
8952      PhotoSIG
5336      Shell Script Hacks
98320     Solaris for Dummies
12600     Uni Phoenix
```

Which is the largest of these directories? A quick call to sort makes it obvious:

```
$ du -s * | sort
12600     Uni Phoenix
128       Amtrak Reservations Service.doc
14928     Perl:JS Complete
1752      Email Explained
26000     BWA Traffic Logs
48872     Merrick
5336      Shell Script Hacks
56        CTEK Advisor.doc
656       MWJ_20021216.pdf
8952      PhotoSIG
98320     Solaris for Dummies
```

Does that look right to you? It shouldn't. By default, sort considers the dictionary order of entries. A line beginning with 1 comes before a line beginning with 2, odd though that looks. The earlier sort of the ls -s output worked because the numbers were prefaced by spaces so that they were right-aligned. By lucky coincidence, it sorted as if they were numbers, but sort was considering the lines only as dictionary-sorted strings.

To force sort to consider lines as numeric values, use the -n flag. Combined with the -r flag to reverse the order of the sort, the output is now a listing of files and folders, from largest to smallest:

```
$ du -s * | sort -rn
98320     Solaris for Dummies
48872     Merrick
26000     BWA Traffic Logs
14928     Perl:JS Complete
12600     Uni Phoenix
8952      PhotoSIG
```

```
5336    Shell Script Hacks
1752    Email Explained
656     MWJ_20021216.pdf
56      CTEK Advisor.doc
```

This is just the tip of the iceberg with pipes. If you want to find out more, check out the man pages for uniq, tee, grep, sort, tr, and sed.

# Korn versus Bash: Which Is Best?

A lot of power is available at the Solaris command line. And a number of shells offer different interactive features. The grandfather of all shells is the Bourne Shell, written by Steven Bourne at Bell Telephone Labs eons ago. It's good for simple scripts, but it's not a user-friendly shell, lacking useful features such as aliases, history, filename completion, and sophisticated control structures.

From the seed of the Bourne Shell, over a dozen different shells, varying in interactive features and programmability, have emerged. These are the most popular:

  ✔ Bourne Again (/bin/bash)

    In the Linux world, the Bourne Again Shell (bash) is the most popular choice.

  ✔ Korn (/bin/ksh)

    In the Solaris world, the Korn Shell (ksh) is the most popular choice.

---

## Shells left on the beach

When you have a couple of winners, you have some also-rans. Whether their time has passed or has not come to pass, these shells are seldom used as login shell by Solaris users:

  ✔ Bourne (/bin/sh)

    The grandfather of all shells. It's good for simple scripts, but not a very friendly user shell, lacking useful features like aliases, history, filename completion, and sophisticated control structures.

  ✔ C (/bin/csh)

    This is a graft of the C programming language atop the Bourne Shell. Its descendant Korn supersedes it and is a better choice.

  ✔ Z (/bin/zsh)

    This is an attempt to merge the best of the other shells into a coherent whole, but it's much less popular than the Korn and Bourne Again Shells in the Solaris community.

## Which shell are you using?

To find out which shell you're using is surprisingly easy. Using the ps processor status command, type the special shortcut $$ that uniquely identifies your own shell in the operating system. The resulting information is the shell you're running:

**$ ps -p $$**

PID TTY  TIME CMD

3891 pts/6  0:00 bash

In this instance, the bash shell is responsible for interpreting commands entered in the terminal.

If you have a Linux system at home and a Solaris system at work, bash might be a better shell choice shell; bash is the default with Linux systems, and it's available on Solaris 9. Korn Shell and the Bourne Again Shell both are fine choices in the Solaris environment. The difference really comes into play if you're working in a *multi-vendor* environment. Whatever shell you choose, it's easier to use the same shell all the time.

I use bash on all of my Unix and Unix-like systems, including Linux, Solaris, and Mac OS X. This book uses bash for examples; none of them are different for Korn Shell users.

One note: Solaris doesn't let you change your own login shell; if you'd like to switch to using Bash instead of the Korn Shell, you'll need to ask your system administrator to make the change. If you're your own system administrator, you can edit your account entry in the /etc/passwd file, changing /bin/ksh to /bin/bash, or use the Solaris Management Console. See Chapter 16 for details.

Both the Korn Shell and the Bourne Again Shell have inherited such C Shell features as job control, aliases, functions, and a command history. To this, the Korn Shell and the Bourne Again Shell add:

✔ Command-line editing

    This is critical to a useful and useable shell and saves vast amounts of retyping commands to fine-tune your interaction.

✔ Integrated programming features including the incorporation of test, echo, and getopt capabilities within the shell

✔ Additional programmatic control structures

✔ More sophisticated regular expressions

✔ Lots of environment variables to allow environment customization

- ✔ Security features
- ✔ Text manipulation facilities
- ✔ Additional built-in commands

Many of these features are important only if you're developing scripts to run in the shell environment itself — shell scripts — which is addressed briefly at the end of this chapter.

## Korn Shell features

The Korn Shell has these features that are missing from the Bourne Again Shell:

- ✔ Floating point arithmetic.
- ✔ A more sophisticated pattern-matching language.
- ✔ Support for the += variable assignment operator.
- ✔ The `-a` flag to `getopts` is available.

Other differences are not significant for day-to-day use of the shell.

## Bourne Again Shell features

A few features in the Bourne Again Shell aren't included in Korn Shell, but they're not important for casual shell usage:

- ✔ The prompt string `PS1` can have dynamically expanded values like date, current directory, hostname, and so on.
- ✔ The `EMACS` command history editing environment can be customized.
- ✔ You can remap keystrokes in `vi` command history editing mode.

## Creating Aliases

A helpful way to refine your shell experience is to redefine commands to include your favorite flags. You can even create new commands that have more mnemonic names than the famously obscure Unix counterparts.

Fortunately, this is easy in the shell. The basic syntax is

```
alias command="the specific Unix commands to run"
```

If you want the -F flag to always be specified when you run the ls command, you can easily achieve this with:

```
alias ls="ls -F"
```

Watch how this changes things:

```
$ ls
Dummies                         myspellscript
Mail                            nsmail
bin                             scripts
components                      snaps
errors                          test
gullivers.travels.txt           vnc-3.3.6-sparc_2.5
$ alias ls="ls -F"
$ ls
Dummies/                        myspellscript*
Mail/                           nsmail/
bin/                            scripts/
components/                     snaps/
errors                          test
gullivers.travels.txt           vnc-3.3.6-sparc_2.5/
```

To find out what aliases you have defined, type **alias** without any qualifiers. In both shells, the format for specifying an alias is identical.

✔ In the Bourne Again Shell, you'll likely have just one defined alias, ls:

```
$ alias
alias ls='ls -F'
```

✔ In the Korn Shell, about a half-dozen are already defined:

```
$ alias
autoload='typeset -fu'
command='command '
functions='typeset -f'
history='fc -l'
integer='typeset -i'
local=typeset
ls='ls -F'
nohup='nohup '
r='fc -e -'
stop='kill -STOP'
suspend='kill -STOP $$'
```

An alias like the redefined ls command only hangs around until you log out or close the terminal window. To make it permanent, add it to your system. The exact command depends on your shell:

✔ If you're using the Bourne Again Shell, enter this command:

```
echo 'alias ls="ls -F" ' >> ~/.bashrc
```

✔ If you're using the Korn Shell, enter this command:

```
echo 'alias ls="ls -F"' >> ~/.profile
```

Use the >> not > to *append* the alias to the end of the file. Don't *replace* the contents of your login file with the alias!

After you've added the alias to your file, launch a new terminal window and type **alias** to confirm that the new, improved ls is available for use.

# Advancing with Shell Scripts

Just as a commonly typed command can be turned into an alias to save time, a sequence of commands can be dropped into a file and then saved as a shell script for later use. Similar to Windows batch files, the different shells' scripting environments are one area where the difference between ksh and bash can sometimes matter.

The concept is straightforward. Say that every time you log in to your system you want to check whether your friend Joan is logged in. To see everyone who's logged in, you'd use the who command. Because you're only interested in one user, Joan, this is a job for who and grep together, like this:

```
who | grep joan
```

Now I'll make this a bit trickier. If it's not a weekday between 9 a.m. and 5 p.m., you don't want to check because you know that if she is logged in after hours, it's because she forgot to shut off her computer.

To determine the time, use the date command, with a special argument that indicates that you're only interested in the hour or the day of the week. You specify the hour and day by using a special % notational format. You determine the hour of the day with date +%H and the day of the week date +%a as shown:

```
$ date +%H
19
$ date +%a
Tue
```

You can use variables to assign a mnemonic name to values within scripts. Create an hour and dayname variable like this:

```
hour="`date +%H`"
dayname="`date +%a`"
```

These variables can be used in conditional tests to see whether they're a value you want:

```
if [ $dayname != "Sat" -a $dayname != "Sun" ] ; then
   if [ $hour -ge 9 -a $hour -le 17 ] ; then
     it's a weekday between 9 and 5
   fi
fi
```

Read this as "if dayname isn't Sat and dayname isn't Sun, then . . ." and "if hour is greater than or equal to 9 and hour is less than or equal to 17, then . . ." All that's left is to add the who command within the conditionals, and you have a fully functional script that shows only if Joan is logged in if it's a weekday between 9 a.m. and 5 p.m. Here's the entire script:

```
hour="`date +%H`"
dayname="`date +%a`"

if [ $dayname != "Sat" -a $dayname != "Sun" ] ; then
   if [ $hour -ge 9 -a $hour -le 17 ] ; then
     who | grep joan
   fi
fi
```

This script isn't something you'd want to type into the command line every time you want to check if Joan's online. It's also too complex for an alias. Instead, it's a text file created with Text Editor, gedit, or even vi or emacs (learn how to use both the command line-based text editor vi and the CDE and GNOME text editors in Chapter 12 ) and saved to either your home directory or a subdirectory called bin in your home directory, with a mnemonic name, perhaps *joan* or something similar.

To test if Joan's online, you'd just type this to find out:

```
$ sh joan
```

Alternatively, mark the file as executable (with chmod +x joan) then you can type in the script name directly on the command line:$ **joan**.

## The tip of the iceberg

Shell scripts are a remarkably complex topic. If you need more information, the Sun documentation suite is a good resource (start with the AnswerBook material already included with the Solaris operating system).

Learning how to write shell scripts is fun and can help you customize your environment. It can also make you more productive and efficient when you delve into the world of the terminal program and the shell.

The next step in shell script mastery is to learn more about functions, command flow, and variables, all of which are well explained in *Mastering Unix Shell Scripting,* by Randal K. Michael (Wiley). For more sophisticated example scripts and a chance to learn by example rather than explanation, my advanced *Shell Script Hacks* (O'Reilly & Associates) is a very good choice.

# Chapter 4

# Managing Files and Directories

• • • • • • • • • • • • • • • • • • • • • • • • • • • • • • • • • • • • • • • • • • • • • • • • • • • • •

## In This Chapter

▶ Managing your files and directories with File Manager and Nautilus

▶ Listings files at the Command Line with ls

▶ Understanding and changing File and Directory permissions

▶ Creating directories and Subdirectories

▶ Moving and copying files

▶ Compressing large files

*Y*ears ago, computer people talked about the "paperless office." Although it's proven to be a bit of a myth (doesn't your office still have lots of paper laying around?), many documents have migrated online. In fact, a modern Solaris desktop has analogs for quite a few different physical document management systems, including file folders (directories), two-sided printing to shrink documents (compression), and security mechanisms for documents (file and directory permissions).

This chapter focuses on the key applications for managing your files and directories — File Manager in the Common Desktop Environment and Nautilus in GNOME — and shows keyboard equivalents for the shell command line. As always, the goal is to choose the environment that will enable you to be efficient and productive.

## Using File Manager and Nautilus

If you've spent any time on a Windows or Macintosh system, you have worked with a file management system. The idea of clicking a directory and having its contents shown as a set of clickable icons is an expected part of interacting with a graphical desktop environment.

Whether you're a CDE or GNOME aficionado, the graphical file manager is one of the best-designed applications in Solaris. Many users more often use the file manager than any other application because it offers an easy way to explore the file system, rename files, move them from one directory to another, make new directories, change file permissions, and much more.

# The CDE File Manager

The CDE File Manager usually runs automatically after you're logged in to the CDE desktop. If it isn't running, launch it by clicking the Home Folder icon (the file cabinet) on the Control Panel. The icon is shown in Figure 4-1.

**Figure 4-1:**
The Home
Folder icon
from the
CDE Control
Panel.

## Exploring the File Manager window

The File Manager automatically displays your home directory, as shown in Figure 4-2.

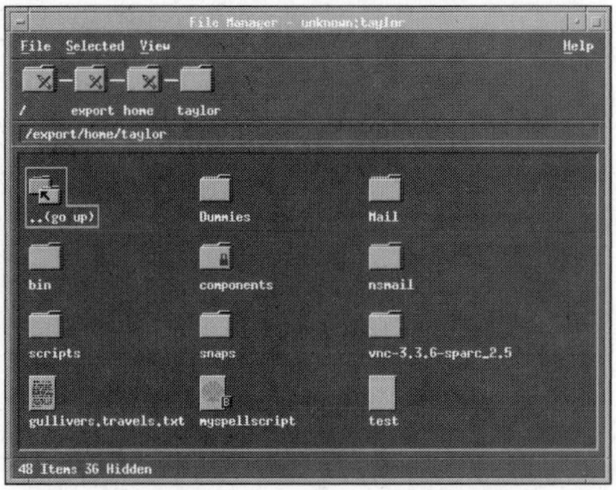

**Figure 4-2:**
The default
view of the
CDE File
Manager
home
directory.

### The top

Here's a tour of the top of the File Manager window:

- Three menus are available within File Manager:
  - File
  - Selected
  - View

✔ The icons below the menus show you the path of the current directory. The parent directories in Figure 4-2 are /, export, and home.

✔ A text box shows the directory path. In Figure 4-2, this path is /export/home/taylor.

To change directories quickly, click in the current directory display box, type in a new directory, and then press Enter. You're whisked away to that directory without any fuss.

### The main panel

The main panel of the window is the most interesting part. The view in Figure 4-2 shows 12 items; eight are directories. The first entry, .. (go up), is a special entry because clicking it enables you to move up to the parent directory. Double-clicking a directory such as Dummies moves you into that directory, with the contents of that directory replacing the current set of icons.

The components directory icon in Figure 4-2 has a *padlock*. That means it's a *read-only directory*. It's probably owned by CDE or another application.

Three files are shown in Figure 4-2:

✔ gullivers.travels.txt is a plain text file. It has tiny writing on its icon to denote its content type.

✔ myspellscript is a shell script. A small seashell is superimposed on the icon. The tiny box indicates what shell is required for the script. In this case, it's a *B* because the script is written for the Bourne Shell.

✔ test is an unknown format to File Manager, so it shows a generic plain grey icon. The only thing you can conclude is that it's not a directory.

### The bottom

The bottom of the File Manager window indicates how many items are in the directory and how many of those items are hidden. In Figure 4-2, 48 items are in the directory (the home directory), and 36 are hidden.

Any file or directory name that starts with a period is a hidden item, so there are 36 entries with names like .gnome and .bash_login. To see these *dot* files (as they're colloquially called), modify the Show Hidden Objects setting on the View menu. By default, hidden files, are, well, hidden. Most of the time you can safely ignore them.

## Changing view and configuration settings

To access view and configuration settings, choose View⇨View Options to open the Set View Options dialog box, shown in Figure 4-3. Here's a rundown of some options in this dialog box:

✔ **Headers:** These are your options:

- **Iconic Path:** Select this option to show the current path as a series of icons at the top of the File Manager.

- **Text Path:** Select this option to show the current path in a text box.

- **Message Line:** Select this option to display how many entries are in the current directory and how many are hidden.

✔ **Representation:** The default view is large informative icons that enable you to quickly identify the content type. You can choose a name-only, small icon, or full informational listing view format. Regardless of what view you choose, you can change how icons are organized.

✔ **Order:** You'll almost always stick with Alphabetically as the sort order. You also have the option to sort by date (to see which files are newest) or by size (to see which are largest).

**Figure 4-3:**
View
options in
the CDE File
Manager.

## *Examining file properties and permissions*

The Selected menu in File Manager is *contextually sensitive* (its contents depend on what icon you've selected). Figure 4-4 shows the options with the gullivers.travels.txt file selected.

This menu is the heart of the File Manager. You can move or copy files, rename them, drop them into a workspace (that is, have them show up on the desktop of the selected workspace), delete them, print them, or change their properties.

Choosing the Properties option on the menu opens the File Properties dialog box. This dialog box has two main views: Information and Permissions.

### *Information view*

The Information view, shown in Figure 4-5, reveals such useful information about the file as

✔ Who owns it

✔ Which group owns it

This is the group ownership of the file, not the group that your account has been assigned, that is, in addition to an owner, each file and directory in the file system is assigned to a group, and this is showing us that datum. Usually all your files will be owned by the group you've been assigned, but files and directories beyond your own home directory have different owner and group values as part of Solaris system security.

✔ The size of the file

✔ When it was last accessed

✔ When it was modified

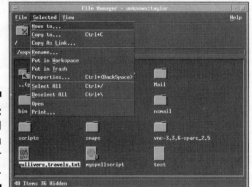

**Figure 4-4:**
Selected
menu
options for
a text file.

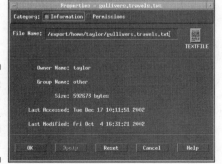

**Figure 4-5:**
File
properties,
Information
view.

## Permissions view

The Permissions view is also important because it controls whether others can read and even alter or delete your files and directories, as shown in Figure 4-6.

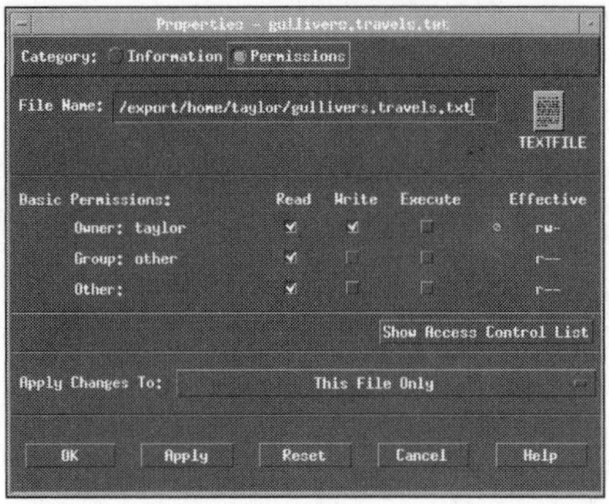

**Figure 4-6:**
File
properties,
Permissions
view.

Solaris has a three-level permissions model for files and directories, with the owner of the file, the group that the file is a part of, and the rest of the accounts on the system (also known as *other*). Files can have any combination of read, write, or execute permission for each of the three possible groups (owner, group, and other), for a combination of 27 different permissions. Usually, you'll stick to a few typical combinations, one of which is shown in Figure 4-6:

✔ Read and write permission for the owner

✔ Read-only permission for other members of the group and everyone else on the system

Execute permission is reserved for things that can be executed (run) by the system, such as shell scripts and executable programs. You probably won't need to worry about execute permission for files. You'll learn more about file permissions and how to ensure that your private files are private and public files are public later in this chapter.

In the Permissions view, you can apply changes to either the *current file* or *multiple files or directories.* This is a quick shortcut to changing lots of file permissions at once, but be sure to make these changes carefully. The choices for the Apply Changes To option are

✔ This File Only

✔ All Files in the Parent Directory

✔ All Files in the Parent Directory and its Subdirectories

# *Working with GNOME's Nautilus*

The CDE File Manager is a capable program, but one of the gems of GNOME is its equivalent program, the Nautilus file manager. To launch Nautilus, double-click your home icon on the GNOME desktop. The Nautilus window is shown in Figure 4-7.

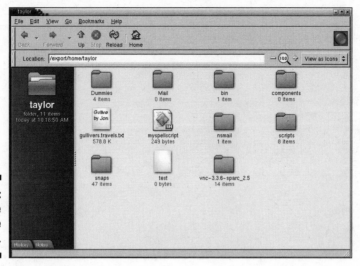

**Figure 4-7:**
Nautilus, the
GNOME file
manager.

Nautilus is more like the Windows and Macintosh file management displays, which isn't a big surprise because the programmers who created Nautilus were from the Apple user interface team.

As you can see in Figure 4-7, each folder icon lists the number of items in that folder, and each text icon has the first few words of the file's text and lists the file's size. Like File Manager, different types of files have different icons. The interface is similar to a Web browser, with Back, Forward, Up, Stop, Reload, and Home buttons along the top, as well as a zoom feature with zoom in (+) and zoom out (–) shortcuts on either side of the magnifying glass.

Adjacent to the zoom feature is a menu of view options. Your options are View as Icons (the default), View as List, and View As. The View As option enables you to customize views and change which icons are associated with which file types.

To fine-tune the current view, choose from a variety of options on the View menu, as shown in Figure 4-8.

Choose the Arrange Items options to customize how items are arranged in the directory. Here are some of your choices:

- **By Name, By Size, or By Modification Date:** These options are identical to those of the CDE File Manager.

- **By Emblems:** Emblems are unique to GNOME. They let you associate files and directories with a graphical symbol.

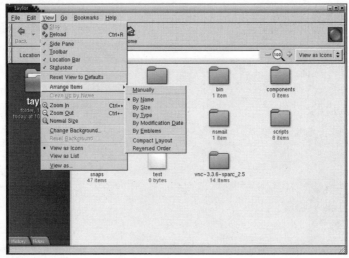

**Figure 4-8:**
View menu
options,
Nautilus.

To further explain GNOME Emblems, go directly to the Properties window for
the `gullivers.travels.txt` file. To change the properties of an individual
icon, you can either

✔ Select the icon and then choose Properties from the File menu.

✔ Right-click the icon and choose Properties from the pop-up menu that
appears.

Either way, you end up with the Properties dialog box shown in Figure 4-9.
The Properties dialog box has three views:

✔ The **Basic** view is shown in Figure 4-9. You can see the filename (which
is editable), type, size, current location, and modification and access
times. You can also set a custom icon if you're feeling creative or eager
to spice up the Nautilus display of your home directory.

✔ The **Emblems** view is shown in Figure 4-10. Emblems enable you to organize and categorize files just as a doctor might use colored dots on file
folders to denote certain characteristics about a patient. Some of the
emblems are just for fun (like the Oh No unhappy face), and others are
quite useful.

To see how this feature works, designate the `gullivers.travels.txt`
file as Cool: Click the check box adjacent to the Cool icon (the one
with the sunglasses) and then click Close. Figure 4-12 shows the new
Nautilus view of the directory with the nifty sunglasses displayed on
the `gullivers.travels.txt` file icon.

✔ The **Permissions** view, which is similar to the CDE File Manager, is shown in Figure 4-11. The only important change is that if you're a member of more than one group, Nautilus makes it easy for you to change the group associated with the specified file. To change settings across all files in the same directory, you must select all the files before launching the Properties dialog box.

Whether you opt for Nautilus and GNOME or File Manager and CDE, both applications make it a breeze to move around the file system and manage files and directories.

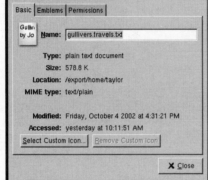

**Figure 4-9:**
File
properties
in Nautilus,
Basic view.

**Figure 4-10:**
File
properties
in Nautilus,
Emblems
view.

**Figure 4-11:**
File
properties
in Nautilus,
Permissions
view.

**Figure 4-12:**
Emblems
add visual
pizzazz to
Nautilus.

# Listing Files with ls

By contrast with the attractive and easy-to-use graphical file managers, the shell requires you to type in every request.

To get to the shell, you need a running terminal program:

- ✔ In CDE, select This Host from the Hosts menu (just above the performance meter).
- ✔ In GNOME, right-click on the desktop background and then choose New Terminal.

Many of the file managers' functions are accomplished on the command line with the combination of ls for listing files and directories, cd for changing directories, and pwd to show the current directory:

```
$ pwd
/export/home/taylor
$ ls
Dummies/              gullivers.travels.txt    snaps/
Mail/                 myspellscript*           test
bin/                  nsmail/                  vnc-3.3.6-sparc_2.5/
components/           scripts/
```

This output arranged the files and directories in alphabetical order, with the
contents sorted down the columns. To sort by date, use the -t option:

```
$ ls -t
snaps/                vnc-3.3.6-sparc_2.5/     nsmail/
Mail/                 myspellscript*           scripts/
Dummies/              bin/                     test
components/           gullivers.travels.txt
```

This output shows that the snaps directory was most recently accessed, and
test was least recently accessed. The ls command can't sort by size, but you
can accomplish the same net result with a command like

```
ls -s | sort -rn
```

To find out more about a specific file, the -l flag offers more information.
Specify a directory, and the ls output will show you the information about
every file in that directory, like this:

```
$ ls -l gullivers.travels.txt
-rw-r--r--   1 taylor    other       592673 Oct  4 16:31 gullivers.travels.txt
```

In an abbreviated form, the file permissions are read and write for the owner
and read-only for the group and everyone else. (I address file permissions
fully in this chapter.) The file is owned by taylor, is assigned to group
other, is 592,673 bytes in size, and was last modified on 4 October at 16:31
(4:31 p.m.).

It might be more convenient to have this output across multiple lines in a
more readable format, but what would happen if you wanted to see permissions for a bunch of files at once? It would take oodles of space. The -l
output to ls offers the same information succinctly, like this:

```
$ ls -l scripts
total 22
-rw-r--r--   1 taylor    other         1269 Oct  4 16:31 DIR.sh
-rw-r--r--   1 taylor    other          240 Oct  4 16:31 available.sh
-rw-r--r--   1 taylor    other          190 Oct  4 16:31 changepositional.sh
-rw-r--r--   1 taylor    other          130 Oct  4 16:31 junk.sh
-rw-r--r--   1 taylor    other          344 Oct  4 16:31 lotsofparams.sh
-rw-r--r--   1 taylor    other          256 Oct  4 16:31 myquota.sh
-rwxr-xr-x   1 taylor    other         1109 Oct  4 16:31 normdate.sh*
-rw-r--r--   1 taylor    other         1851 Oct  4 16:31 validate.sh
```

To see all the otherwise hidden dot files, the -a flag makes them all suddenly visible, as in this new listing of the home directory:

```
$ ls -a
./                      .gnome2/                .sversionrc*
../                     .gnome2_private/        .themes/
.ICEauthority           .java/                  .user60.rdb
.TTauthority            .login                  .xftcache
.Trash/                 .mc/                    .xscreensaver
.Xauthority             .metacity/              Dummies/
.bash_history           .mozilla/               Mail/
.bash_login             .nautilus/              bin/
.cshrc                  .ncftp/                 components/
.dt/                    .netscape/              gullivers.travels.txt
.dtprofile*             .netscape6/             myspellscript*
.esd_auth               .profile                nsmail/
.gconf/                 .sh_history             scripts/
.gconfd/                .smc.properties         snaps/
.gnome/                 .solregis/              test
.gnome-desktop/         .ssh/                   vnc-3.3.6-sparc_2.5/
```

By default, ls wants to show you what's inside each directory specified on the command line, as shown when I used the command ls -l scripts. Want to see the scripts directory entry itself? Here's where the -d flag to ls is a valuable addition. It forces ls to show you directories, not their contents. In the following example, the first command output (without the -d option) shows the contents of the directory; the second command (with the -d option) shows the directory entry, not its contents:

```
$ ls -l .
total 1206
drwxr-xr-x   2 taylor    other         512 Dec 10 20:05 Dummies/
drwx------   2 taylor    other         512 Dec 14 16:23 Mail/
drwxr-xr-x   2 taylor    other         512 Oct  4 17:58 bin/
drw-r--r--   2 taylor    other         512 Dec 10 19:16 components/
-rw-r--r--   1 taylor    other      592673 Oct  4 16:31 gullivers.travels.txt
-rwxr-xr-x   1 taylor    other         249 Oct  4 21:22 myspellscript*
drwx------   2 taylor    other         512 Oct  4 16:31 nsmail/
drwxr-xr-x   2 taylor    other         512 Oct  4 16:31 scripts/
drwxr-xr-x   3 taylor    other        2560 Dec 18 11:47 snaps/
-rw-r--r--   1 taylor    other           0 Oct  4 16:31 test
drwxr-xr-x   3 taylor    16000         512 Nov 26 09:41 vnc-3.3.6-sparc_2.5/
$ ls -ld .
drwxr-xr-x  29 taylor    other        1024 Dec 18 11:53 ./
```

The combination of ls and cd enable you to move around in the file system. Without any arguments, cd takes you directly to your home directory, a fail-safe if things get too confusing.

---

# Using `file` to ascertain file type

The `file` command tries its best to tell you what kind of file you're asking about:

```
$ file gullivers.travels.txt
    test scripts/available.sh
gullivers.travels.txt:  English
    text
test:                   empty file
scripts/available.sh:   exe-
    cutable shell script
```

---

# Using and Changing Permissions

File and directory permissions are critical for being a successful Solaris user.

## Interpreting file permissions

File permissions are straightforward. The Solaris world has three classes of users:

✔ Owner

✔ Group

✔ Everyone else

Figure 4-13 illustrates the overlapping relationships between the user classes.

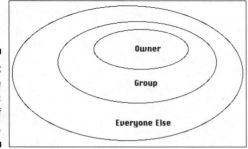

**Figure 4-13:** The concentric circles of access.

Owner

Group

Everyone Else

The owner of the file is the center of everything, then the group, and, finally, on the outside, the rest of the people who use and access the computer. You're the owner of all files you create, but you may not be the owner of everything in your home directory. You probably won't be either the owner or in the group that owns system commands.

To better understand the nuances of file and directory permissions, dissect the permissions string shown at the beginning of each line of `ls -l` output. Start with the `gullivers.travels.txt` file, and then consider the `..` directory. It's the directory that's the parent of your home directory.

The `..` (go up) icon in File Manager represents the `..` directory.

First, a simple file:

```
$ ls -l gullivers.travels.txt
-rw-r--r--  1 taylor    other      592673 Oct  4 16:31 gullivers.travels.txt
```

The file is owned by `taylor`, is a part of group `other`, and has the permissions string `-rw-r—r—`. Figure 4-14 shows how to interpret this permissions string properly.

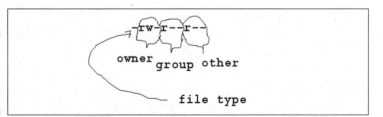

**Figure 4-14:** Deciphering permission strings.

Permission strings are always composed of a single letter that indicates whether it's a file (`-`) or a directory (`d`), followed by three letters that indicate read, write, or execute permission for each of the three classes of owner, group, and other. With `gullivers.travels.txt`, the permission string denotes a regular file (the first character is `-`), with read and write permission for the owner (`r` and `w`, but not `x` in the next three characters), followed by read-only permission (no `w` for write, no `x` for execute) for group and other.

Here's another example:

```
$ ls -ld ..
drwxr-xr-x  9 root    root       512 Dec 12 13:09 ../
```

This directory is owned by `root` and is also part of the group `root`. The permissions string is interpreted as a directory (the first character is d) with read, write, and execute permission for the owner, but only read and execute permission for group and other.

File permissions allow different operations. Some make sense, and others are a bit weird:

- **Read** allows such operations as printing the file and using `grep` to search the file for patterns.

- **Write** lets you change the file.

- **Execute** lets your shell run the file as if it were a program. This is only for shell scripts or other software programs.

The preceding example shows that the owner (`taylor`) has read and write access to the `gullivers.travels.txt` file. He can scan through it and change it, as wanted. Members of the group `other`, and others on the system, can only read the file.

Permissions can change. If this were a private message, perhaps a memo to the boss, it might have either of these permissions:

`-rw------` grants read and write permission to the owner, but no access to anyone else.

`-rw-r---` grants read access to other members of the group, but no access to the rest of the local Solaris user community.

## Understanding directory permissions

Directory permissions are trickier than file permissions. Unix differentiates between permission to see

- The *list* of directory entries (names of files and subdirectories)
- The *content* of the directory entries (the data in the files)

To see (list) the directory entries, you need read permission on the directory. That permission doesn't mean you can access the file's contents, but you can see that the file exists. Here's a quick cheat:

✔ **Read** allows you to view the contents of the *directory record* but not the contents of the directory itself.

It's an incredibly subtle difference. You can *find* the names of files in the directory, but you can't *list* them or *access* them in any manner. Almost always, directories either have *both* read and execute permission, or *neither.*

✔ **Write** allows you to

- Delete entries from the directory

- Modify files through editing or appending data

- Delete files

If read and execute permissions are denied, you'll need to already know the name of the file to accomplish these tasks. You'll never encounter a directory with write-only permission.

✔ **Execute** allows you to view the contents of the directory *if you already know its name.*

If you don't and you can't read the directory contents (read permission) then you can't list the contents of the directory to find out what's inside. Almost always, directories either have *both* read and execute permission, or *neither.*

To demonstrate the nuances of different directory permissions, use the chmod (change permission mode) command, which is explained in detail in the next section:

```
$ ls -ld scripts
drw-r--r--   2 taylor  other  512 Oct  4 16:31 scripts/
$ ls scripts
scripts/available.sh: Permission denied
scripts/myquota.sh: Permission denied
scripts/lotsofparams.sh: Permission denied
scripts/junk.sh: Permission denied
scripts/changepositional.sh: Permission denied
scripts/DIR.sh: Permission denied
scripts/validate.sh: Permission denied
scripts/normdate.sh: Permission denied
```

Read-only permission on the directory enables you to see information about the directory itself, but doesn't give you permission to see any information about each entry. You can, puzzlingly, see an error for each filename and therefore extrapolate the filenames therein. Does this mean you can list those files, though? No:

```
$ ls -l scripts/available.sh
scripts/available.sh: Permission denied
```

Now change permissions to have execute but not read permission. The results are just as peculiar:

```
$ chmod a-r scripts
$ chmod a+x scripts
$ ls -ld scripts
d-wx--x--x 2 taylor   other      512 Oct 4  16:31 scripts/
$ ls -l scripts
scripts: Permission denied
$ ls -l scripts/available.sh
-rw-r--r-- 1 taylor   other      240 Oct 4  16:31 scripts/available.sh
```

With read-only permission, you can view the individual contents of a directory, but you cannot view the directory contents itself.

If this makes about as much sense as a fish on a bicycle, the good news is that you really don't have to worry about this too much. By convention, Unix people either set *both* read and execute, or *neither*.

A couple of common permission strings are really useful:

✔ To create a directory where you can make whatever changes, deletions, and additions you want, but keep it from prying eyes, a good permission string would be `rwx------`.

✔ Want to let other people in your group see the directory but not change its contents? Use `rwxr-x---` to accomplish the job.

## Changing permissions with chmod

The `chmod` command *changes* permissions. These are the most important and most common permission modes.

You can use this command a couple of ways, the easiest of which is a *mnemonic equation* (yes, it really is the easiest!). You must assemble the string from all three of these sets of options:

✔ *One* of these *user* specifications:

u (user)

g (group)

o (other; everyone who isn't the owner and isn't in the group that owns the file or directory)

a (all, a shorthand way to specify user + group + other)

✔ *One* of these *modifier* options:

+ (add)

- (remove)

= (make exactly)

✔ *One or more* of these *permissions:*

r (read)

w (write)

x (execute)

✔ To add write permission for the user, use u+w.

✔ To remove write permission from group and other, use either of the following pairs of equations, separated by a comma:

```
go-w
g-w,o-w
```

✔ To turn off all permissions, specify 0

Here are a few examples:

✔ In the following example, chmod 0 turns off all permissions for anyone, making this a very secure directory: Even the owner can't see what's inside.

```
$ ls -ld scripts
drwxr-xr-x  2 taylor    other        512 Oct  4 16:31 scripts/
$ chmod 0 scripts
$ ls -ld scripts
d---------  2 taylor    other        512 Oct  4 16:31 scripts/
```

✔ In one somewhat complex call to chmod, the following example adds read, write, and execute permission for the user, and read and execute permissions to group.

```
$ chmod u+rwx,g+rx scripts
$ ls -ld scripts
drwxr-x---  2 taylor    other        512 Oct  4 16:31 scripts/
```

✔ This example gives everyone else read and write permission:

```
$ chmod o+rw scripts
$ ls -ld scripts
drwxr-xrw-  2 taylor    other        512 Oct  4 16:31 scripts/
```

✔ When everyone on the system has been granted different permission to access this directory, you can alter the permission to have the file mode a bit more normal with this example:

```
$ chmod a-w scripts
$ ls -ld scripts
dr-xr-xr--   2 taylor    other          512 Oct  4 16:31 scripts/
$ chmod u+w,o+x scripts
$ ls -ld scripts
drwxr-xr-x  2 taylor    other          512 Oct  4 16:31 scripts/
```

You can change the permission on lots of files at the same time with a *shell wildcard*. For example, chmod go-rw * takes away read or write capabilities to group or everyone else for each file and directory matched by the * wildcard.

# Making Directories

To make new directories, use the mkdir command. If you have write permission in your current directory and the requested directory name doesn't yet exist, you can create a new directory with the command:

```
$ mkdir newdir
$ ls -ld newdir
drwxr-xr-x  2 taylor    other          512 Dec 18 17:43 newdir/
```

By default, the permissions of newly created directories give you read, write, and execute permission and everyone else read and execute permission. As expected, the new directory is owned by taylor, the person who created it.

You can change the default permissions of newly created files and directories by altering your umask setting. See the man page for more information.

What if you don't have write permission in the current directory? The mkdir command fails, of course:

```
$ mkdir /mydir
mkdir: Failed to make directory "/mydir"; Permission denied
$ ls -ld /
drwxr-xr-x  44 root     root          1536 Dec 14 15:26 //
```

To confirm your user ID (which is the same as your account name) and primary group membership, use the id command. To get a list of all groups you're in, use the groups command:

```
$ id
uid=100(taylor) gid=1(other)
$ groups
other
```

In the preceding example, the / directory has write permission for its owner, root, but only read and execute permission for everyone else, hence the error.

Try to make a directory that already exists, and you'll see a slightly different error:

```
$ mkdir newdir
mkdir: Failed to make directory "newdir"; File exists
```

To remove a directory, use rmdir. (For your protection, rmdir only removes empty directories. )

# Moving and Copying Files

The two commands explored in this section allow you to gain control over which files live where.

Absolute control of file copying is surprisingly difficult to accomplish on a GUI-based interface. Sometimes, dragging an icon to a new directory moves the file; other times, it copies the file.

On the command line, you have more precise control: to move files, use mv, and to copy files, use cp.

## Copying files with cp

Using the command line, you can copy files just as easily as you can in the File Manager or Nautilus:

```
cp gullivers.travels.txt newdir
```

This creates a copy of the gullivers.travels.txt file in the directory newdir, with the same name:

```
$ ls -l gullivers.travels.txt newdir
-rw-r--r--   1 taylor    other      592673 Oct  4 16:31 gullivers.travels.txt

newdir:
total 1184
-rw-r--r--   1 taylor    other      592673 Dec 18 18:06 gullivers.travels.txt
```

These are two distinct copies of the file, though they are identical. If `newdir` didn't exist, however, the `cp` command would have created a copy of the `gullivers.travels.txt` file called `newdir`, which would doubtless be confusing.

To copy a file to a new area of the file system, use a directory path along with a filename:

```
cp gullivers.travels.txt /tmp/swift.txt
```

This copies the file into the `/tmp` directory and renames it `swift.txt` at the same time.

Where the shell shines is when you want to copy a group of files. To copy everything from the current directory into `newdir`, use:

```
cp * newdir
```

To copy just those files that have the `.txt` filename suffix, use

```
cp *.txt newdir
```

## Moving files to new directories with mv

The `mv` command works similarly, the only difference being that a copy of the file isn't left upon completion, of course. What might not be obvious is that the `mv` command is also the Unix rename function. To rename `gullivers.travels.txt` in the current directory, for example, the following command does the trick:

```
mv gullivers.travels.txt swift.txt
```

With both commands, you can ensure a slightly safer operation by adding a -i flag, which blocks the command from overwriting an existing file:

```
$ cp -i test gullivers.travels.txt
cp: overwrite gullivers.travels.txt (yes/no)? no
```

If you like that capability, create two aliases that make it an automatic part of your future interaction with the shell:

```
alias mv="mv -i"
alias cp="cp -i"
```

You can find out more about aliases in Chapter 3.

To remove a file, use `rm`.

Solaris doesn't have any sort of undelete or unrm function. After the file or directory is deleted, it's gone.

# Compressing Big Files

Running out of disk space is a constant concern for Solaris users. As with any computer operating system, Solaris likes to take lots of space to run efficiently and maintain a historical archive of activity. (Unix folk call these archives *logs* or *log files.*)

As a result, many Solaris installations have system administrators who pay very close attention to individual disk usage and might even have set up a quota for your personal disk space. Type the following to see if you have a quota set up:

```
$ quota -v
Disk quotas for taylor (uid 100):
Filesystem    usage  quota  limit    timeleft  files  quota  limit    timeleft
```

In the preceding example, there's no quota, which you can determine by the lack of data after the column headers. (Yes, Unix isn't always friendly!)

Whether or not you have a disk space quota, if you have large data files or graphics that you don't need for a while, it's good manners to compress these large files so there's more free disk space for other files.

You can compress files in Solaris 9 three ways:

- ✔ `compress`
- ✔ `gzip`
- ✔ `bzip2`

They all do the same basic task. Give them a big file, and they shrink it down to a smaller file. Which one works best? The difference is more historical: `bzip2` tends to do the best job of compression and it's also the newest of the three.

In general, `bzip2` is best. Sometimes `gzip` or `compress` shrink a file further.

All three of these compression tools are *zero loss compression systems*. Whatever you compress, the restored original will be identical to the file you started with, whether it's a JPEG graphic, a StarOffice `.doc` file, or a humble `.txt` file.

The following example compresses the `gullivers.travels.txt` file with each tool and shows the size of the compressed file:

```
$ ls -l gullivers.travels.txt
-rw-r--r--  1 taylor   other      592673 Oct  4 16:31 gullivers.travels.txt
$ compress -v gullivers.travels.txt
gullivers.travels.txt: Compression: 59.32% -- replaced with
               gullivers.travels.txt.Z
$ ls -l gullivers.travels.txt.Z
-rw-r--r--  1 taylor   other      241071 Oct  4 16:31 gullivers.travels.txt.Z
```

The example shows which compression tool saves the most disk space. The `compress` utility saved almost 60% of the disk space, shrinking down the 592,673 byte file to only 241,071 bytes. The newly compressed file has a `.Z` suffix added, which indicates that it's been compressed with `compress`.

Follow these rules to name and recognize compressed files:

Z is a `compress` file

.gz is a `gzip` file

.bz2 is a `bzip2` file

To restore a file that's been shrunk with `compress`, use the `uncompress` command:

```
$ uncompress gullivers.travels.txt.Z
```

Compressing a file with `gzip` is accomplished in a manner identical to the `compress` command:

```
$ gzip -v gullivers.travels.txt
gullivers.travels.txt:   62.3% -- replaced with gullivers.travels.txt.gz
$ ls -l gullivers.travels.txt.gz
-rw-r--r--  1 taylor   other      223139 Oct  4 16:31 gullivers.travels.txt.gz
```

Not bad, it's even a little smaller. This time the newly compressed file has a `.gz` suffix, indicating that it has been compressed with `gzip`. To uncompress a `gzip` file, use `gunzip`. Then compress it one more time, with the more powerful `bzip2` program:

```
$ gunzip gullivers.travels.txt.gz
$ bzip2 -v gullivers.travels.txt
  gullivers.travels.txt:  3.589:1,  2.229 bits/byte, 72.14% saved, 592673 in,
            165126 out.
$ ls -l gullivers.travels.txt.bz2
-rw-r--r--   1 taylor    other       165126 Oct  4 16:31 gullivers.travels.txt.bz2
```

This compression tool has done the best job, shrinking the file considerably more than the two alternatives. This time, the filename suffix is .bz2, and the tool to uncompress it is bunzip2:

```
$ bunzip2 gullivers.travels.txt.bz2
```

With any luck, the file ends up the same size:

```
$ ls -l gullivers.travels.txt
-rw-r--r--   1 taylor    other       592673 Oct  4 16:31 gullivers.travels.txt
```

# Part II
# The Inevitable Internet Section

The 5th Wave                    By Rich Tennant

WHAT DO YOU MEAN
THERE'S A UNIX
OPERATING SYSTEM
IN THE LOBBY?

# In this part . . .

With a Sun computer, The Network really is The Computer. It's no surprise at all that Sun systems have excellent and quite easy-to-use Internet utilities. Starting with a chapter on the true killer application of the Internet, email, this part continues by looking at the latest version of Netscape's venerable Navigator browser and then touches on a worthy alternative, Mozilla. We then switch gears and look at how to build Web pages in Solaris, run a Web server, and even analyze Web log files to see who is visiting and what they're viewing. The last chapter considers ftp, telnet and the superior alternative to both, ssh, the secure shell.

# Chapter 5

# Doin' That E-Mail Thing

***E***-mail enables users to instantaneously communicate with family and friends throughout the world. E-mail is the so-called *killer app* of the Internet.

From its humble beginnings in the 1970s in the Unix community, e-mail has become the main reason many folks are connected to the Internet. Because Sun has always believed the network *is* the computer, it's no surprise that Solaris includes a number of different e-mail applications.

You may also want to check out some wonderful graphical and command-line-based mail programs that aren't included in the standard Solaris 9 distribution. If you're interested, ask your system administrator to download these free alternative applications that are ready to go on Solaris 9.

Regardless of which mail program you choose, sending and receiving e-mail is a "killer skill" for anyone using the computer. This chapter offers an introduction to working with e-mail from all three major environments: the command line, the Common Desktop Environment, and GNOME.

## Getting to Know Mailer

Within the Common Desktop Environment, Mailer is the only mail program. Easily accessible from the Control Panel (click the inbox icon), it's likely that the program will launch the first time without any inbox or configuration, as shown in Figure 5-1.

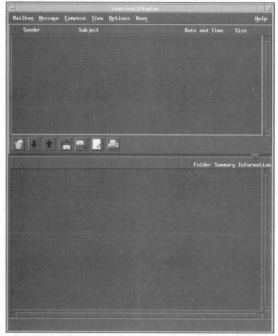

Figure 5-1:
Mailer
with no
messages.

# Configuring the program

To configure the program, choose Mailbox⇨New Mailbox. This opens the dialog box shown in Figure 5-2.

You can set up a local mailbox, as discussed in this section, but Mailer will probably automatically recognize a local mailbox without any additional effort.

## An IMAP connection

Many Solaris users have their mail centrally stored on an IMAP server.

To configure an IMAP connection, click the IMAP Server button near the top of the configuration dialog box. This opens the IMAP configuration dialog box, shown in Figure 5-3.

**Figure 5-2:**
The Mailer
configuration
dialog box.

**Figure 5-3:**
The IMAP
configura-
tion dialog
box.

✔ **Password:** If you're concerned about security, you don't have to enter your password in this dialog box. Mailer will prompt you for a password each time it checks your incoming mailbox.

✔ **Retrieve Attachments:** You have the option to retrieve attachments automatically, or leave these potentially large additions on the server until you determine whether they're worth downloading.

On most systems, your connection to the mail server is sufficiently speedy that there's rarely any visible slowdown for retrieving all attachments. You can configure this option either way without a problem.

E-mail within Solaris is less susceptible to viruses than Windows programs — a reason to cheer, and a reason to be less paranoid about the possible dangers lurking in e-mail attachments.

### *Using a local mailbox instead*

If you don't have an IMAP account, you can specify your mailbox with these steps:

1. Click Local in the configuration dialog box.

2. Search for the specific mailbox in question, as shown in Figure 5-4.

**Figure 5-4:**
Finding a
local
mailbox.

# *Viewing the mailbox*

After the mailbox is identified, the program

✔ Opens the mailbox

✔ Scans through all the messages

✔ Presents an attractive and easy to navigate view of all the messages, as shown in Figure 5-5.

In this default mailbox view, here's what you see:

✔ The top pane is a table of contents of all messages.

✔ The middle area shows

• A summary of the mailbox

• A set of control elements

The mailbox in Figure 5-5 contains 575 messages and message 568 is currently shown.

From left to right, the Mailer toolbar contains these controls:

- Delete

- Move down the list to the next message

- Move up the list to the previous message

- Reply

- Forward

- Compose a new e-mail message

- Print message

✔ The bottom pane of the window is the specific message in question, formatted in an attractive manner.

In the top pane, each message lists

✔ Sender

✔ Subject

✔ Date and time sent

✔ Size

Mailer offers other sophisticated display options:

**Figure 5-5:**
Viewing a
mailbox in
Mailer.

✔ An optional status indicator of a diamond or *N* indicates new messages.

✔ By default, the message list pane sorts the messages by date sent, oldest to newest.

✔ The message view window shows almost all headers in an e-mail message, screening out a few by default. If you want to hide more of the headers (such as X-UIDL and MIME-Version), search for message view preferences in the Help system (see the top-right corner of the Mailer menu bar).

✔ Mailer doesn't understand how to display messages using fancy formatting (typically HTML). If you receive lots of newsletters from Web sites, some messages may be unreadable in Mailer. Mailer recognizes and activates all Web site addresses it encounters in messages: In Figure 5-5, the URL for the Frontier Airlines Web site is in a different color. Click that, and the site opens in the Web browser.

✔ If the message has an attachment, the bottom pane shows the attachment in icon form, indicating the file's

   • Name

   • Type

✔ Right-click on the attachment to see a variety of options for the file processes:

   • Saving

   • Opening

   • Editing

In Figure 5-5, Mailer recognizes an HTML format attachment and displays it.

## *Changing the sorting order*

You can organize your message display in several ways:

✔ The default setting of sorting messages from oldest to newest is usually a good choice.

✔ If you want to sort the messages by sender, subject, and so on, click the View menu, as shown in Figure 5-6.

 If your mailbox contains a ton of messages, it may be useful to sort the messages by sender and then select all of those messages and save them in a new mailbox for that sender:

1. Right-click the set of selected messages.

2. Choose the option to save to a new mailbox.

**Figure 5-6:**
Mailbox
sorting
options for
Mailer.

# Sending mail

Sending mail and responding to messages from others are the two most common Mailer tasks.

## Responding to a message

To respond to a message, follow these steps:

1. **Select the original message.**

   For example, I selected a Frontier Airlines message. I want to reply to thank the airline for its lovely holiday wishes.

2. **Click the reply icon (the one with the letter and the blue arrow pointing to the person) or choose Compose⇨Reply.**

   A message window opens, as shown in Figure 5-7.

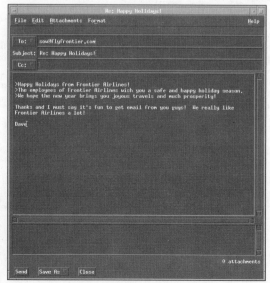

**Figure 5-7:**
Responding
to an e-mail
message.

3. **By default, the Reply button includes the text: If you don't want to include the original text with your reply, choose Reply from the Compose menu.**

   The original message text is included at the top of the new message. The original text is prefaced by a > on each line, by convention.

   As a matter of good form and netiquette, I deleted the extraneous material in my response, as shown in Figure 5-7, before typing in a response.

4. **Fill in the appropriate fields as desired.**

   The compose window has five input areas:

   - To
   - Subject
   - Cc
   - The message body
   - An attachment area for dragging and dropping attachment files or pictures

     When you reply to an existing message, the To and Subject fields are automatically filled in. Both the message body and attachment windows have useful pop-up menus; just right-click in the appropriate space. This is also an easy way to add attachments.

5. **When the message is ready to send, click the Send button, and away it goes.**

### Creating a new message

Creating a new e-mail message is just about as simple as replying to one:

1. **Click the Compose icon on the toolbar. (It's the icon that looks like a blank piece of paper with a pencil laying on top.)**

   A blank New Message window opens.

2. **Type in an address, subject, message, and so on.**

   Figure 5-8 shows an example message.

3. **When you've finished composing the message, click Send.**

Mailer is a good, simple e-mail program that lets you manage a simple flow of incoming and outgoing e-mail. However, its inability to render HTML messages and lack of sophisticated filtering and other modern amenities make it feel dated compared to many of the other choices available.

**Figure 5-8:**
Composing
a new
message in
Mailer.

# Using Netscape Messenger

The alternative mail application for GNOME users (and CDE users, if desired) is a part of Netscape Navigator, as included with Solaris 9.

## Configuring an e-mail account

Follow these steps to configure an e-mail account:

1. **Launch Netscape 7.**

2. **Click the Window menu.**

    This menu offers a variety of options, as shown in Figure 5-9.

    If you don't have Netscape 7 on your Solaris system, it's an extremely worthwhile download. Go to `www.sun.com/netscape` to get started.

Figure 5-9:
The many
faces of
Netscape 7.

Window   Help
Navigator                                    Ctrl+1
Mail & Newsgroups                            Ctrl+2
Instant Messenger                            Ctrl+3
Composer                                     Ctrl+4
Address Book                                 Ctrl+5
• 1 Netscape

**Figure 5-9:**
The many
faces of
Netscape 7.

### 3. Choose Mail & Newsgroups.

A window opens, indicating that you haven't configured the e-mail preferences yet, as shown in Figure 5-10.

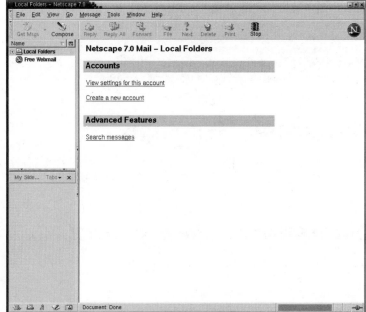

**Figure 5-10:**
No e-mail
accounts
have been
added to
Netscape.

### 4. Choose Create a New Account.

A window asks what type of account you want to create.

### 5. Select the default value, Email Account. Click Next to proceed.

### 6. In a manner similar to Windows task wizards, Netscape prompts you, window by window, for the information needed to create the new e-mail account. Follow the prompts.

Figure 5-11 shows the first window, asking for your

- Name

- E-mail address.

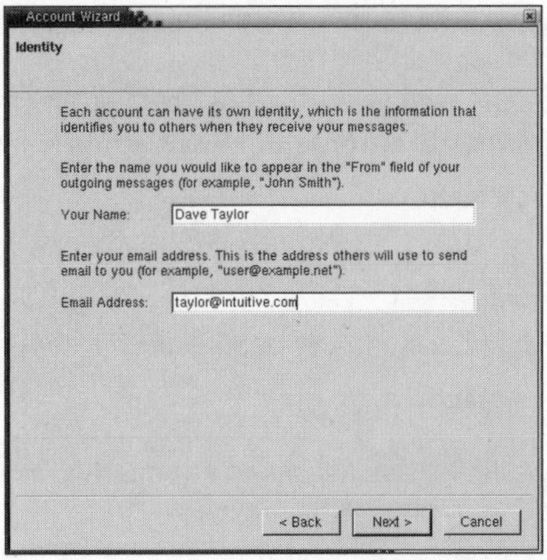

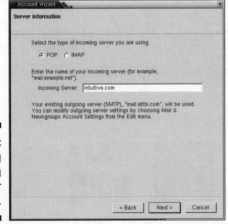

**Figure 5-11:**
Personal
identity
settings in
Netscape.

7. **Once you've entered the appropriate information, click Next again to configure your**

   • **POP or IMAP server**

   • **Outbound mail server information**

   In Figure 5-12, the wizard recognized that I configured my outbound mail server when I first set up the Web browser. It shows me that the outbound mail server is set to `mail.attbi.com` instead of prompting me to specify a new server.

**Figure 5-12:**
Specifying
incoming
mail server
settings.

8. **To configure an incoming mail server, enter the server name as supplied by your ISP or system administrator.**

9. **Specify the type of server you'll be accessing (POP or IMAP) and click Next to somewhat redundantly enter your e-mail account name.**

10. **Label this account, if you want.**

    Netscape 7 supports multiple e-mail accounts, but you'll probably leave the default user@host value shown.

    After you deal with the label, a summary of all values is shown.

11. **Click Finish to set up the account.**

I also set up an account that allows easy access to an America Online mailbox. Figure 5-13 shows how the mailbox is displayed.

## Examining the Netscape window

Netscape 7 has an attractive display, as shown in Figure 5-13. The main window consists of four main areas by default:

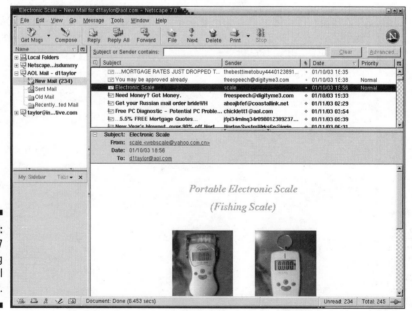

**Figure 5-13:** Netscape 7 displaying new e-mail in the Inbox.

✔ A list of folders and accounts in the upper-left pane

✔ A sidebar in the lower-left pane

   You can remove the sidebar by clicking the X button.

✔ A list of messages in the current folder or mailbox in the upper-right pane

✔ The current message in the lower-right pane

Netscape can render complex HTML e-mail messages, as shown in the message at the bottom of Figure 5-13. This display of portable fishing scales, while perhaps a bit lame, is more attractive than the primitive display of the Frontier Airlines message in the CDE Mailer program (see "Working with incoming mail," later in this chapter).

These are some of the folders in the upper-left pane:

✔ **Sent Mail:** By default, a copy of all messages you send are saved in the Sent Mail folder.

✔ **Old Mail:** Messages you've read but haven't filed or otherwise disposed of can later be found in the Old Mail folder.

✔ **Recently Deleted Mail folder:** This folder stores messages that you have marked for deletion. You can retrieve them if you change your mind.

Similar to Mailer, the main Netscape 7 toolbar offers quick access to the main functions of the mail program, as shown in Figure 5-14. Most of these buttons should be familiar if you've sent e-mail and used a Web browser. Netscape checks for new mail every ten minutes by default. (You can change that setting in your Preferences.) You can force a quick check by clicking the Get Msgs button.

**Figure 5-14:**
The
Netscape
toolbar.

## *Menu options and sorting*

The available menus in Netscape are

- ✓ File
- ✓ Edit
- ✓ View
- ✓ Go
- ✓ Message
- ✓ Tools
- ✓ Window
- ✓ Help

Sorting is one of the many options available on the View menu, as shown in Figure 5-15. If you thought Mailer had a lot of mailbox sorting options, you'll be even more impressed with Netscape, which has 22 ways to organize your view. As with Mailer, the default sorting order in Netscape is likely to keep you happy for years of e-mail activity.

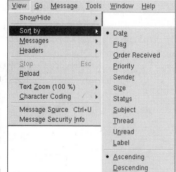

**Figure 5-15:**
Sorting
options and
the View
menu.

- ✓ The Message menu, shown in Figure 5-16, offers options for creating a message.

The most interesting and unusual option on this menu is Edit Message as New, which lets you edit messages you've received. This sounds kind of wacky, but I find it quite useful to improve subject lines on messages before I save them to an archive folder: "Skylight Bid from Outlook Renovation, without painting" is a much better subject than "Re: Remodeling" when you're later digging around the folder.

✔ You can access your Address Book by using the Tools menu (refer to Figure 5-9). The Address Book is a handy feature that enables you to manage a list of everyone with whom you send and receive e-mail.

**Figure 5-16:** The Message menu.

## Sending and responding to e-mail

To respond to an e-mail message, click the Reply button on the navigation bar, or choose Message⇨Reply (refer to Figure 5-16). Figure 5-17 shows the beginning of my response to the note about the fishing scale.

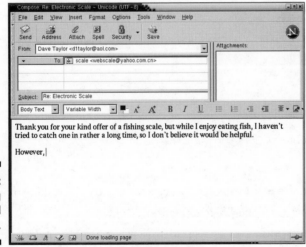

**Figure 5-17:** Responding to an e-mail message.

A remarkable number of options are available to customize your e-mail message:

✔ The most important thing to notice about the composition window is that, by default, messages are composed and sent in HTML format. If your recipient is using Mailer, well, there's a mismatch. For many user communities, HTML-friendly e-mail programs are quite common, and the most popular Windows and Mac e-mail applications all support rich, colorful HTML.

✔ An important capability in Navigator is the spell checker. Click the Spell button on the navigation bar, and the program helps you avoid looking foolish with spelling hiccups. It can't help with grammar and word choice, but it is a terrific addition to the mail program.

✔ In the panel with the To address, the To button is actually a pull-down menu. You can specify that an address should actually be a Cc or Bcc address instead.

Choose the Options menu, and you'll see a number of useful message options, as shown in Figure 5-18. You can

✔ Encrypt and digitally sign messages

✔ Request a return receipt

✔ Assign various priorities

If you're sending attachments, you can specify how the attachments should be packaged to ensure that they arrive at their destination in a useable format. You can safely leave the default configuration unless you're getting complaints from colleagues, in which case I recommend working with your system administrator to determine the ideal settings.

**Figure 5-18:**
Message
Options
menu.

The Format submenu lets you choose

✔ HTML-only messages (the default)

✔ Text-only messages (no different typefaces, no colors, and so on)

✔ A hybrid of both plain text and fancy HTML.

Recipients are shown one or the other based on the sophistication of their mail program.

The hybrid option might sound ideal, but remember this means that two copies of every message are sent to each recipient:

• A fancy HTML version

• A plain text version

If your messages are a half-dozen lines, that's no big deal. But if you regularly send friends or colleagues 10 to 20-page messages, they might get testy about the waste of bandwidth and disk space.

To write a new message, you just follow a simple process:

1. Create the new document with one of these steps:
   - Click the Compose icon on the toolbar
   - Choose Message⇨New Message

2. Add the information to the document:
   - Address
   - Subject
   - Message text.

Figure 5-19 shows an example message.

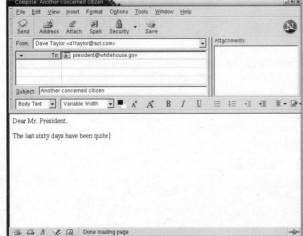

**Figure 5-19:**
A new
message,
partially
composed.

The Netscape mail program is very sophisticated and has many options:

✔ If you opt to use this e-mail program, I suggest using the Help menu to explore the program's capabilities.

✔ You may also want to go through the different panels of the Preferences area to customize the program to your liking.

# Command-Line Communication

I stick with Berkeley mail, `mailx`, because it is included with Solaris 9 and has long been a part of the Sun operating system. It's not sexy but offers a surprisingly efficient mechanism for working with electronic mail.

Without additional software, `mailx` cannot interact with POP or IMAP mailboxes. If you're using Solaris to process mail that comes via an ISP or is sequestered on a central mail server until you grab it, you need to move up to a graphical mail application.

Freeware POP and IMAP applications, most notably `fetchmail`, are available for Solaris, but you need to have your system administrator install them from the Internet. To find out more about `fetchmail`, go to `www.tuxedo.org/~esr/fetchmail/`.

## Sending mail with mailx

Whether or not you can receive your e-mail at the command line, it's likely you can send a quick message using `mailx`.

By default, Solaris 9 is configured properly to send out messages if your system is on the Internet.

To send a message, follow these steps:

1. Type mailx followed by the e-mail address of the intended recipient or recipients.

   It'll then prompt for a subject

2. Enter as much text as you'd like, ending with a Ctrl-D:

   ```
   $ mailx taylor@intuitive.com
   Subject: Thanks for all the fish!

   Just wanted to send a quick note saying "thanks" for ...
   ```

   This is part of a sample message.

   - The `mailx` program lets you type in as much material as you'd like.
   - You can cut and paste other text from other messages.

3. When you're done entering the message, press Ctrl+D (press the Control key down and, while it's depressed, press D) on its own line to complete the message:

   ```
   ... all the fish.

   Dave
   EOT
   $
   ```

The `EOT` (end of text) is output when you press Ctrl+D. That's it. The message is now on its way to the recipient somewhere on the Internet.

The `mailx` program offers some additional message capabilities, and you can generate a list of them with the sequence ~? on its own line. These are the most useful of the escape commands:

```
~?
-------------------- ~ ESCAPES ---------------------------
~b users           Add users to Bcc list
~c users           Add users to Cc list
~e                 Edit the message buffer
~f messages        Read in messages, do not right-shift
~h                 Prompt for Subject and To, Cc and Bcc lists
~m messages        Read in messages, right-shifted by a tab
~p                 Print the message buffer
~q,~Q              Quit, save letter in $HOME/dead.letter
~r,~< file         Read a file into the message buffer
~r,~< !command     Read output from command into message
~R                 Mark message for return receipt
~s subject         Set subject
~t users           Add users to To list
~v                 Invoke (vi) display editor on message
~w file            Write message onto file (no header)
~x                 Quit, do not save letter
~!command          Run a shell command
~|,~^ command      Pipe the message through the command
~?                 print this help message
-------------------------------------------------------
```

To include the file `gullivers.travels.txt` at the end of a message, for example, type `~r gullivers.travels.txt` on its own line. The commands ~e and ~v are useful for editing the message. (One uses your default editor, and the other uses the `vi` editor, as discussed in Chapter 12.)

## *Working with incoming mail*

If your system is configured so that your e-mail lives in a local mailbox, you can read and respond to your e-mail from the command line and never have to take your hands off the keyboard.

To check your e-mail, use the `mailx` command but don't specify any arguments:

```
$ mailx
mailx version 5.0 Sat Apr  6 14:57:29 PST 2002  Type ? for help.
"/var/mail/taylor": 14 messages
>O  1 Midwifery Today    Thu Dec 12 02:19 1038/41234 E-News 4:38 - Obstetric I
 O  2 Robbie Dunlap      Thu Dec 12 11:08   28/1210  <no subject>
 O  3 Lori Kats          Thu Dec 12 12:16   72/4086  Donna Eden Suggests:  Ask
```

```
O  4 james@emissaryofli Fri Dec 13 02:20    41/3427  GREAT EXPERIMENT III
O  5 Figureskater      Fri Dec 13 10:25   107/3967  Re: S-Mart Order
O  6 Lester, Emily     Sat Dec 14 12:12    81/3511  RE: Hello!
O  7 Colette Donahue   Sun Dec 15 10:00    73/2806  RE: chicken pox
O  8 Roy R. Dunlap     Sun Dec 15 15:11   241/9813  Fwd: Fw: Re: one dollar
O  9 news@909shot.com  Mon Dec 16 11:49   122/5160  [NVIC] 5 in 1 vaccine liv
O 10 Don Taylor        Mon Dec 16 16:46   201/6620  (no subject)
O 11 FrontierAirlines@f Tue Dec 17 04:38    80/4614  Happy Holidays!
O 12 A Feehan          Tue Dec 17 11:22 1113/82036 Hi
O 13 james@emissaryofli Tue Dec 17 15:04    42/4034  Washington Mobilizes For
O 14 Melissa Cohen Insu Tue Dec 17 15:56    51/1725  Re: cancellation of home
?
```

In the preceding example, 14 messages are in the mailbox
/var/mail/taylor; they're listed from oldest to newest. The fields from left
to right are

✔ The message status (0 is old)

✔ A unique message number

✔ The sender

✔ The date and time the message was sent

✔ The size in lines/characters

✔ The subject

For example, the first message is from *Midwifery Today*. It was sent Thursday,
December 12th at 2:19, and is 1,038 lines (41,234 characters) long. The subject of the message is E-News 4:38 - Obstetric I.

To read a message, type its index number at the ? prompt. For example, to
read the message from Frontier Airlines (#11), type 11 at the prompt and then
press Enter:

```
? 11
Message 11:From FrontierAirlines@flyfrontier.com Tue Dec 17
04:38:04 2002
X-UIDL: b-;!!77K!!V\7"!\#k"!
X-Sender: FrontierAirlines@flyfrontier.com
Date: Tue, 17 Dec 2002 01:00:08 -0700
X-Sybari-Trust: b53a39e6f6624f78c4b24ea600000109
From: <FrontierAirlines@flyfrontier.com>
To: "taylor@intuitive.com" <taylor@intuitive.com>
Subject: Happy Holidays!
MIME-Version: 1.0
--MWZAlternativeMessage  Content-Type:text/plain
```

```
Happy Holidays from Frontier Airlines!
The employees of Frontier Airlines wish you a safe and happy
holiday season. We hope the new year brings you joyous
travels and much prosperity!

Cancun and Mazatlan Sale Fares!!
For all the exciting sale details and to make reservations,
Visit <http://www.frontierairlines.com>.
Spirit of the Web
Due to the high volume of air travelers expected over the
weekend, Spirit of the Web fares will not be offered this
week. Thank you for your continued support and look for a
Spirit of the Web update.
?
```

It's certainly not the most attractive e-mail message, but `mailx` does offer a crude, functional interface. To respond to the message, type `reply` at the ? prompt, or to ensure you're responding to the correct message, you can also type `reply 11`:

```
? reply
To: sow@flyfrontier.com
Subject: Re: Happy Holidays!

Thanks for your lovely note. Happy Holidays to you too!

Best,

DT
EOT
?
```

Again, the `EOT` is displayed when you press Ctrl+D to denote the end of message input. With a reply, the program automatically grabs the recipient's address and subject from the original message.

You can do more with `mailx`, and additional, more sophisticated e-mail programs are available for hard-core shell users, but you'll probably use a graphical mail program.

To find out more about `mailx`, check the extensive man page. To learn about Elm, Pine, Mutt, and other alternative e-mail programs, check out `www.sun freeware.com/`.

# Chapter 6

# Exploring the World Wide Web

*W*hether you're looking for a wedding dress, a spouse, or a hubcap for your Yugo, you can find it on the Web.

Working with the Web in the Solaris environment is slightly different from on a PC or Macintosh system; the browsers and the windowing system are different. Worse, many Web sites are designed for Windows-specific browsers — particularly Microsoft Internet Explorer, which isn't available on Solaris — and don't always work as intended in other environments.

For most Solaris users, encountering a Web site that doesn't work is cause for some grumbling, sending an occasional e-mail message to the site's Webmaster, and exploring other places online.

This chapter covers Netscape 7 (the Web browser shipped with Solaris 9). I introduce you to some interesting Web sites along the way — I can't resist — but primarily focus on the tools themselves.

This chapter doesn't differentiate between the Common Desktop Environment and GNOME because Netscape works fine in both environments. The only differences are button layout and window colors. Outside of those superficial elements, the browsers are identical in either environment, with the same dialog boxes, menus, and configuration oddities.

## Starting Netscape 7

Netscape first released the Version 4.7 browser in September 1999. Subsequent to that release, the Internet standards groups agreed on a different core architecture for Web browsers. Netscape has since released Version 6 and Version 7 browsers for most platforms. I focus on the newer and more sophisticated Netscape 7.

TIP

If you don't have Netscape 7, ask your system administrator to download it from www.sun.com/netscape/. Netscape 4.78 is the version that might be on your Solaris 9 distribution; this version is nearly an orphan.

The process for starting Netscape 7 depends on your interface:

✔ If you're running CDE, launch Netscape 7 by clicking the clock icon (the picture of planet Earth), as shown in Figure 6-1.

**Figure 6-1:**
The Earth
icon
launches
Netscape 7
in CDE.

✔ In the GNOME environment, you have a couple of options:

• Click the foot icon to pop up the GNOME menu and then choose Applications⇨Internet—Netscape Web Browser, as shown in Figure 6-2.

• If you personalized GNOME as described in Chapter 2, you can click the small N on the control panel.

**Figure 6-2:**
Launching
Netscape 7
from the
GNOME
menu.

The Web browser loads the Sun Microsystems home page as the default home for the browser. It looks like Figure 6-3.

**Figure 6-3:**
The Sun
home page.

# Changing Preferences

You can customize Netscape 7 a million different ways.

To get to the Preferences area, choose Edit⇨Preferences. You see the Preferences dialog box, shown in Figure 6-4, by default.

The small boxes on the left side of the category indicate *subcategories* under that category.

- ✔ Click the tiny *plus signs* to see hidden subcategories.
- ✔ Click the tiny *minus signs* to hide subcategories.

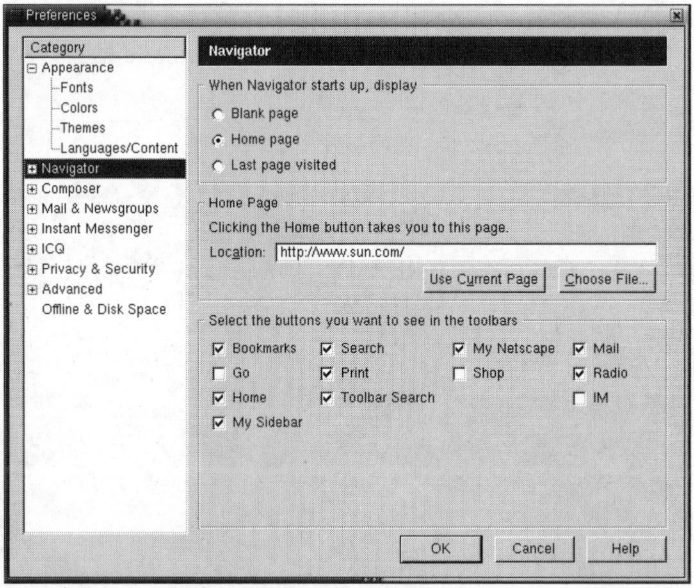

**Figure 6-4:**
Netscape 7
Preferences,
default
view.

Here's the lowdown on the Preferences categories:

- ✔ Appearance lets you change how pages are displayed in the browser, including such subcategories as

    - Fonts

    - Colors

    - Themes

    - Languages/Content

- ✔ Navigator lets you change such subcategories as

    - History

    - Languages

    - Helper Applications

    - Smart Browsing

    - Internet Search

    - Tabbed Browsing

    - Downloads

- ✔ Composer is a simple Web page development environment.

✔ Mail & Newsgroups lets you fine-tune the presentation of the Netscape mail program and the Netnews program, including these subcategories:

   • Message Display

   • Composition

   • Send Format

   • Addressing

   • Labels

   • Return Receipts

Chapter 5 explains Netscape e-mail.

✔ Instant Messenger customizes these AOL settings:

   • Privacy

   • Buddy Icons

   • Notification

   • Away

   • Styles

   • Connection

✔ ICQ customizes these message settings:

   • Privacy & Authorization

   • Notification & Sounds

   • Away

   • Connection

✔ Privacy & Security lets you specify how much of your identity is shared with the rest of the online community through these subcategories:

   • Cookies

   • Images

   • Forms

   • Passwords

   • Master Passwords

   • SSL

   • Certificates

   • Validation

✔ Advanced settings fine-tune specific system and network behaviors:

- Scripts & Plugins
- Cache
- Proxies
- HTTP Networking
- Software Installation
- Mouse Wheel
- Offline & Disk Space

## *Adjusting your appearance*

"Please brush your hair!" might be the first thing that comes to mind when you think about appearance. Fortunately, it's easier to configure Netscape 7, and it remembers every change, too!

Figure 6-4 shows appearance options that allow you to specify which elements of Netscape 7 should be launched when the program is started. By default, it launches only *Navigator* (the Web browser).

Netscape 7 is the name for the entire suite of tools. Navigator is the Web browser itself.

If you're using Netscape Mail as your e-mail program, select the Messenger Mail check box to have that automatically open, too.

You can also easily launch any of these tools by clicking the appropriate icon on the bottom left of the main Netscape window, as shown in Figure 6-5. From left to right, the icons launch

✔ Navigator

✔ Mail

✔ Instant Messenger

✔ Composer

✔ Your e-mail Address Book.

Leave the ToolTips option checked. It makes Navigator pop up helpful little yellow notes if you leave the cursor over an icon for a second or two.

**Figure 6-5:**
The launch
shortcut
icons in
Netscape 7.

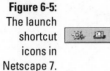

**Figure 6-5:**
The launch
shortcut
icons in
Netscape 7.

### Fonts

Click the Fonts subcategory listing under Appearance on the left pane of the dialog box to see a new set of font options, as shown in Figure 6-6. Usually, you won't have to change these options.

If you'd prefer to have both the variable width and fixed-width (typewriter) text on the browser page a bit larger, you can change the options here: Choose the next size up from the current setting for both

✔ **Proportional** (the default text on most pages)

✔ **Monospace** (code listings and other fixed-width material)

By convention, the fixed width font is always smaller than the variable width font, but you can change it to whatever is pleasing for your eyes.

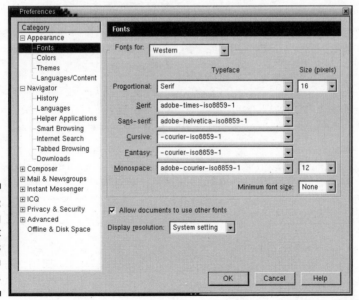

**Figure 6-6:**
Adjusting
Font
preferences
in
Netscape 7.

The other option here — Allow Documents to Use Other Fonts — is to optionally override fonts included by Web sites. Don't change this setting; many sites use technology for text presentation that enhance the layout and presentation.

### Colors

The Colors subcategory is shown in Figure 6-7. If you've surfed the Web, you're familiar with the standard color scheme of black text, blue underlined hypertext reference links, and purple underlined links for places you've previously visited. Here's where you can change this scheme and fine-tune things to your heart's content!

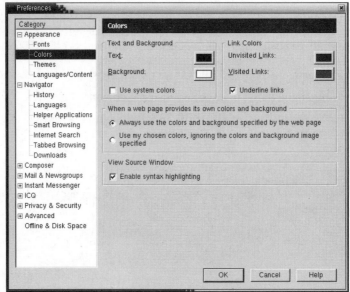

**Figure 6-7:**
Color
preferences
in
Netscape 7.

To change a color, click the little color box. This produces an attractive set of colors in a grid, as shown in Figure 6-8. Click the desired color. The selected color replaces the previous color for links, background, or whatever you wanted to alter.

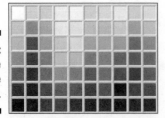

**Figure 6-8:**
The
Netscape
color picker.

You can change other colors and turn off the underlining of hypertext references if you want, but most modern Web sites already do their own alterations of the appearance to ensure the best possible design.

If you prefer a specific color scheme, or you don't like it when Web pages hide the hypertext references by disabling underlines, changing colors, and so on, then check the radio button adjacent to Use My Chosen Colors, Ignoring the Colors and Background Image Specified. Keep your fingers crossed that it always works!

## *Navigating preferences*

Preferences under the Navigator category control the internal behavior of the browser. As shown in Figure 6-9, the default Navigator preference lets you specify whether to

✔ Start new windows with the home page or a blank page

✔ Alter your home page

✔ Fine-tune what's shown in the toolbars

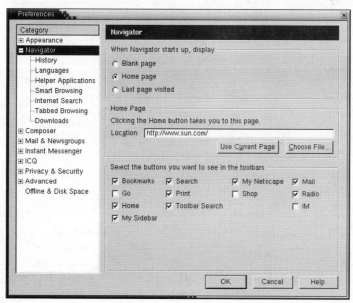

**Figure 6-9:**
Navigator
preferences.

# There's no place like your home page

It's useful to visit Sun.com sporadically, but the content doesn't change often enough to make it an exciting choice for your home page. Instead, I recommend some alternatives:

✔ **Slashdot** (www.slashdot.org) is a popular discussion and news site for computer aficionados, with an entertaining mixture of news, science, technology, and, well, just weird stuff.

✔ **Google News** (news.google.com) offers a terrific overview of the latest news as reported in a wide variety of news and information outlets. It changes all the time and offers easy access to the terrific Google search engine.

✔ **ESPN** (www.espn.com) is a great choice for the sports junkie, with its constantly updated tickers for football, basketball, baseball, NASCAR, and whatever else is happening in the sports world.

✔ **BBC News** (news.bbc.co.uk) offers a European perspective on news and the events of the day. It's updated all the time, too, but might seem a bit stark compared to a site like Yahoo! or MSN.

✔ **eBay** (www.ebay.com) if you're a collector, or just like shopping, there's no better or more compelling site online than eBay, an enormous, chaotic online auction site. Whether it's a second SPARC system or new clothes for your baby, someone's probably selling it on eBay.

You can change your home page several ways:

✔ Click in the Location box, select the current URL therein (http://www.sun.com/), and replace it with your preferred home page address.

✔ Move in the browser to the page you want, choose Edit➪Preferences to jump to this Preferences dialog box, and click the Use Current Page button.

### History

History is a useful setting. Click it to see the dialog box shown in Figure 6-10.

The History settings are important, especially if you have precious little disk space. By default, Navigator saves a copy of every Web page and every graphic on every page in an area called the *cache*. The actual cache settings are part of the Advanced Preferences category; the history setting in Figure 6-10 specifies how long the browser remembers sites.

By default, Navigator remembers nine day's worth of surfing; the program automatically deletes cached Web pages and graphics more than nine days old when you quit. Make the history long enough, and you'll eventually run out of room on your computer when everything hangs around forever.

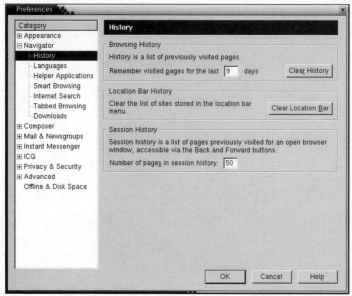

**Figure 6-10:**
Navigator
History.

Is nine the correct setting? It's difficult to say and probably depends just as much on how many sites you visit as your disk space allocation.

> ✔ If you spend hours each day visiting sites you've never visited before, you'll be building a substantial history list and cache, so you might need to reduce this to seven days, or five.

> ✔ If you read *The Wall Street Journal* when you log in, and then use only e-mail and StarOffice for the rest of the day, a nine-day history is fine.

### Languages

If you've installed several languages with your Solaris setup, you should see more than one language listed in the Languages subcategory dialog box. Otherwise, it just lists English, which is fine as-is.

### Internet Search

The Internet Search subcategory is where you can choose which search engine will, by default, process search queries entered into the Location box. My personal preference is Google, as shown in Figure 6-11.

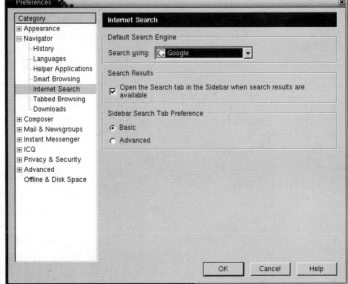

**Figure 6-11:**
Internet
Search
preferences
within
Navigator.

## Tabbed Browsing

One of the coolest features in Netscape 7 is *tabbed browsing*. Using this feature, you can have a bunch of Web pages open simultaneously, and simply click the appropriate tab to jump to the page you want to view. Figure 6-12 shows the options. If you haven't tried tabbed browsing, I recommend it!

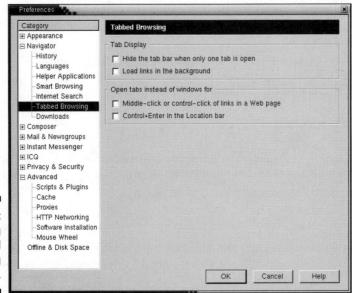

**Figure 6-12:**
Fine-tuning
Tabbed
Browsing
preferences.

### Smart Browsing

Smart Browsing is a neat idea from Netscape that has fallen on hard times. The concept is great: For each site you visit, the browser presents a What's Related button that pops up a menu of Web sites ostensibly related to the current site.

Smart Browsing is *buggy*. My experience is that the browser crashes not infrequently with this enabled.

## Advanced options

The Advanced preferences category, shown in Figure 6-13, gives you control of such enhanced capabilities as

- Fine-tuning your privacy settings
- Disabling cookies
- Allowing or disabling Java or JavaScript

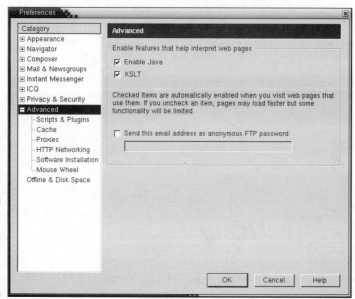

**Figure 6-13:**
Advanced
preferences
in
Netscape 7.

The default configuration is probably fine for you unless you know you need changes. For example, I enable Java and XSLT (as shown in Figure 6-13) because lots of the content on the Sun Microsystems Web site is Java-enabled. You maintain a more restrictive — and secure — browsing environment by disabling Java.

The only other Advanced preference worth considering is the Cache. This subcategory is where you can fine-tune how much disk space the browser can use for its breadcrumb trail of sites you've visited. Figure 6-14 shows this.

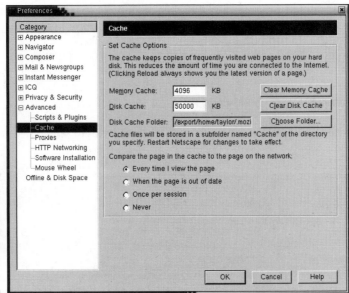

**Figure 6-14:**
Cache
preferences
in
Netscape 7.

Check the location of the disk cache folder:

✔ If you're having problems using more than your quota of disk space in Solaris, this directory is a good place to start your exploration.

✔ You can also ratchet back the amount of space allowed on the disk (the default is 50MB) if necessary by typing another value into the Disk Cache box.

# Working Effectively

In the interest of becoming an effective Web surfer, you need to know about a few buttons and links in the main browser window. Figure 6-15 shows the window.

✔ The Help menu is rightmost on the top menu bar. Click it for direct links to a number of useful Web sites within Netscape.

Figure 6-15:
Google
News in
Netscape 7.

My favorite of this list is the Security Center, where you can find tips on improving the security of your Solaris Web browser.

✔ On the Navigation bar, in addition to the usual Back, Forward, Reload, and Home buttons, there is one more to highlight: Search takes you directly to the search engine you've specified in the Internet Search preference dialog box (refer to Figure 6-11). If you type a search pattern into the Location box, instead of a URL, and then click Search, the Web browser feeds that pattern to your specified search engine and shows you the results instead. A very cool feature!

When you find a Web page that would make a great home page, choose Preferences—Navigator and click the Use Current Page button to set it as your new home page.

✔ The next row down on the Web browser is known as the bookmarks bar because it offers one-click access to your favorite bookmarks. Netscape 7 is preloaded with a bunch of useful bookmarks, including

- Radio

- My Netscape

- Shop

- WebMail

- Calendar

This feature is worth exploring. My Web browser has a customized set of bookmarks including *The New York Times, The Wall Street Journal,* and Slashdot, among others.

You can hide or display any or all toolbars a couple of ways:

✔ Select the appropriate option on the View⇨Show/Hide menu.

For example, to hide the Personal toolbar, simply select it from the View menu, and it vanishes.

As a general rule, anything preceded on the menu with a checkmark is visible, and anything missing the checkmark is hidden: every time you select an item on the Show/Hide menu it'll flip from visible to invisible, or back.

✔ Click the narrow vertical bar on the leftmost edge of the toolbar in question; it shrinks to a tiny vertical bar.

I've shrunk the Personal toolbar in Figure 6-15 and the Navigation bar in Figure 6-16.

✔ To restore toolbars to full size, simply click the tiny horizontal element.

The final element to explore in Netscape 7 is the padlock icon on the bottom-right corner of the window. For any given Web site, the padlock icon shows whether the site's secure or insecure:

✔ Secure sites have closed padlocks.

✔ Insecure sites have open padlocks.

Click the padlock icon (or choose View—Page Info and then click the Security tab), and a dialog box pops up with lots of security information for the current page, whether the page is secure or not.

Figure 6-16 shows the security information for the PayPal.com home page (`https://www.paypal.com/`).

Figure 6-16 shows that the PayPal site is secure (both because the padlock is closed and because the Security page says the page was encrypted). This is particularly important if you're entering personal data, such as

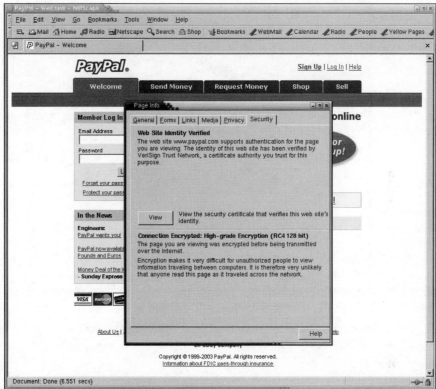

**Figure 6-16:**
Security
Info for
PayPal.com.

✔ Account and password information

✔ Credit card data

It's a good idea to make it a habit to check whether a Web site is secure before providing personal information.

In terms of shopping, you might ask yourself, "How trustworthy is an online store if it doesn't bother to encode the transmission between me and its server?" I personally avoid doing business with online stores that do not encrypt payment pages, regardless of how big and well established they are.

While I'm talking about Security, pop back to the Preferences dialog box (choose Edit—Preferences) and then move to Privacy & Security and click the subcategory SSL. You see a new dialog box, as shown in Figure 6-17.

SSL is a secure alternative to the regular Web transfer system. Information is encrypted and decrypted by your browser and the remote server. While in transit, the information is in an unreadable format; when you're checking your bank balance, no one can use the information if they intercept it.

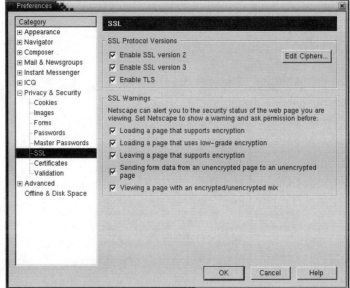

**Figure 6-17:**
Netscape 7
security
settings.

You won't have to configure either SSL2 or SSL3, but you need to enable them, as shown in Figure 6-17.

I disable all the warning dialog boxes because I check for secure sites by glancing at the padlock icon; if you don't, you can leave the warnings enabled by leaving all the boxes checked (as shown).

## Going back in time

One great feature of Web browsers from the very first introduced is that they keep track of where you've surfed prior to the current page. You can then easily back up to a previous page by clicking on the Back button or, on the more recent browsers, viewing and selecting from your surfing History. But the History window is quite a bit more useful than a way of avoiding multiple clicks on the Back button, because unlike the Back button, the History window remembers sites you've visited on previous invocations of the browser too.

Figure 6-18 shows my current history list. Choose Go⇨History to access your list.

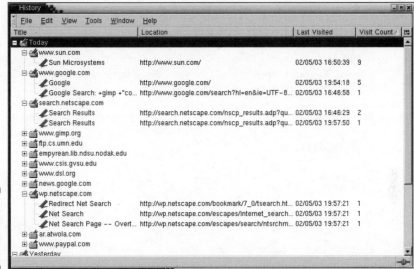

**Figure 6-18:**
Web
navigation
history.

In Figure 6-18, the entries are organized by date and sorted by frequency of visit. Unsurprisingly, Sun Microsystems is the most visited site.

✔ You can change the sort column by clicking the column name.

✔ Click it a second time to reverse the order of the sort.

To sort by page title, for example, click Title. Now it's sorted in a to z order. Click Title again, and it's reversed, in z to a order. Click a third time, and you're back to a to z order.

The History window lists all sites you've visited in the last week or two, not just since you started your current session. It's like a super Back button. How far back does it keep the list? That's what the History setting in the Preferences adjusts; by default, it's nine days.

The History feature presents a privacy challenge. To understand why, consider what your boss would see if she sauntered over to your Solaris system, opened this History window, and sorted by Visit Count. Are you secretly spending time visiting "cuteguys.com" or "singles.net" during work hours? To minimize the privacy problem, some Web surfers set their History preference to a very small value. On the other hand, if you're at work, you're supposed to be working, so maybe changing the browser isn't the best way to solve the problem!

## Managing bookmarks

If you're like most Web surfers, you either don't use bookmarks at all, or they've taken over, and your bookmark menu has dozens, or hundreds, of entries. Knowing how to manage your bookmark list is well worth a few minutes of time and makes surfing more fun.

The Personal toolbar comes with a set of bookmarks preloaded, including

- ✔ WebMail
- ✔ Calendar
- ✔ Radio

Here's how to add a few useful additional locations.

First, go to a Web site you like to visit. I'll pop over to the Dummies.com home page at `www.dummies.com/`, as shown in Figure 6-19.

**Figure 6-19:**
The Dummies Press home page.

To add the Dummies.com site to my Personal toolbar, I choose Bookmark⇨File Bookmark. The default action is to add the bookmark to my Personal Toolbar Folder. I click OK, and the new element is added to the folder, but is not displayed in my Personal toolbar. Why not? Because it's at the end of the list in the folder.

What if, in addition to moving the Dummies bookmark to make it visible, you also want to get rid of the Radio bookmark because you already have a radio and don't need one on your Solaris system?

To solve both problems, you need to open the Bookmark Editor:

1. Choose Bookmarks⇨Manage Bookmarks. The Bookmark Editor is shown in Figure 6-20. The highlighted line in the figure is the Dummies.com bookmark.

2. To change the label for this entry, right-click anywhere on the line.

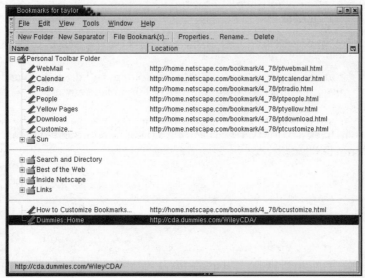

**Figure 6-20:**
The
Bookmark
Editor.

A small menu pops up with many choices. To rename it as the bookmark name choose Rename, and the Bookmark Properties dialog box appears, as shown in Figure 6-21.

Here you can

✔ Type a new title

✔ Fine-tune the location URL

✔ Add a description to help remember why you found the site so compelling

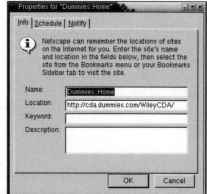

**Figure 6-21:**
The
Bookmark
Properties
dialog box.

Bookmarks can be adjusted to make your system efficient and convenient:

✔ To move a bookmark to the top of the Personal Toolbar Folder, simply click and drag it to the top.

✔ To delete a bookmark, right-click it and choose Delete from the pop-up menu.

✔ You can also create new bookmark folders and drag specific bookmarks around, which is a boon for the well-organized surfer.

When you're done fine-tuning your bookmarks, choose File⇨Close. Now you're back at your Web browser, with the new improved Personal toolbar, as shown in Figure 6-22.

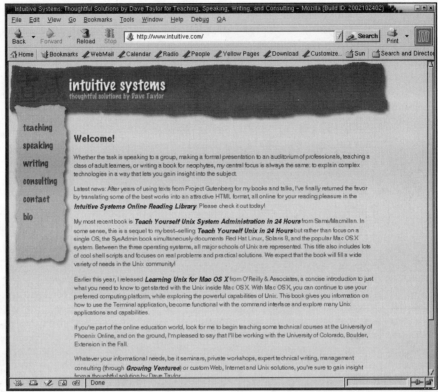

**Figure 6-22:**
The
improved
Personal
Toolbar.

# Chapter 7

# Creating Web Pages

● ● ● ● ● ● ● ● ● ● ● ● ● ● ● ● ● ● ● ● ● ● ● ● ● ● ● ● ● ● ● ● ● ● ● ● ● ● ● ● ● ● ● ● ● ● ● ●

## In This Chapter

▶ The rules of naming Web pages

▶ Entering content into your new Web page

▶ Opening up and Viewing local pages in Navigator

▶ Improving your page layout with HTML

▶ Working with the Apache Server on your Solaris system

● ● ● ● ● ● ● ● ● ● ● ● ● ● ● ● ● ● ● ● ● ● ● ● ● ● ● ● ● ● ● ● ● ● ● ● ● ● ● ● ● ● ● ● ● ● ● ●

**A**lthough it's entertaining to surf the Web, discovering what everyone else has produced, nothing is as exciting as publishing your own Web site, fiddling with the hypertext markup, and checking the server log files to see how many people read your material while you were at lunch!

Creating complex, sophisticated Web sites like the Sun.com site is obviously beyond the scope of this book (although I share some recommendations in this chapter for other Web design books), but one of the real beauties of the Web is that it's egalitarian. If you can work in either a CDE- or GNOME-based editor or launch a terminal window and edit in vi — all of which are discussed in Chapter 12 — you're ready to go.

## Naming Files

It's easy to build a simple Web page using the GNOME Text Editor application. If you're using the Common Desktop Environment, Text Edit is functionally identical and can be easily used instead.

---

# HTML essentials

Whether you're using your Solaris system as a Web server, or you have Web space on a different server (perhaps America Online or another Internet service provider), you can easily learn the basics of HTML and get started. HTML is the HyperText Markup Language: the set of notations within all Web pages that tell the Web browser how to present information.

Here's an example of HTML:

```
<P>This is a paragraph with a
    word in <B>bold</B></P>
```

As the preceding example shows, HTML is straightforward: To have the word *bold* formatted in bold, wrap the word in *tags:*

- ✔ The open bold HTML tag (B) at the start
- ✔ The close bold HTML tag at the end (it's like the open, but with a / added).

All HTML tags start with an open angle bracket and end with a close angle bracket, and most, but not all, HTML tags are pairs; they start and then end a particular presentation characteristic, like bold.

---

The first issue to consider is the name of the file. But you can't just name a file anything you'd like. There are specific rules about well-formed HTML file names on the Web:

- ✔ Spaces aren't allowed in Web filenames.
- ✔ Solaris differentiates between uppercase (capital) and lowercase letters in a filename. Welcome and welcome are actually two different files.

    Some operating systems (notably Microsoft Windows) ignore case differences.

    Use all lowercase letters for your Web page filenames. That sidesteps the problem completely.

- ✔ Use .html as the filename suffix.

    - Web browsers know what they're looking at.

    - Web servers know what kind of information they're feeding to visitors who ask for your new page.

A good first Web page name is welcome.html.

# *Entering Content*

Web pages with content are obviously more exciting than blank pages (though blank pages can be curiously relaxing at times), so you probably want some.

The process depends on the environment you're working in:

- ✔ In CDE, launch the CDE Text Edit application. Just click the Text Note icon (the little piece of paper with the pencil and red pushpin icon) on the main control bar.

- ✔ In GNOME, go to the GNOME menu on the bottom-left corner and then choose Applications➪Accessories➪Text Editor, as shown in Figure 7-1.

**Figure 7-1:**
Launching
the GNOME
Text Editor.

When the GNOME Text Editor — `gedit` — first opens, it looks like Figure 7-2.

Try entering some text into this new as-yet-unborn Web page:

```
We've come a long way since the days when Sun was
just four university students with an idea.

Twenty years down the road, much to our own surprise,
we have nearly 40,000 employees in offices around
the world. In fact, from humble beginnings as
builders of engineering workstations, we've become
a leading supplier of network servers, data storage
systems, system software, network infrastructure
applications, and much more.

But with all the changes--all the ways we have
reinvented our products and our company over
the years--one thing remains the same:

The idea that started it all.

Open network computing is still our passion,
still the driving force behind each of our
technologies, products, and services.
```

This passage is from a retrospective written by Scott McNealy, CEO of Sun Microsystems. You can find it online at `www.sun.com/2002-0225/feature/`.

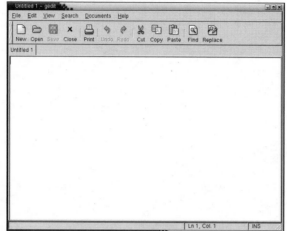

**Figure 7-2:**
GNOME
Text Editor.

After you enter the text, your text editor should look like Figure 7-3.

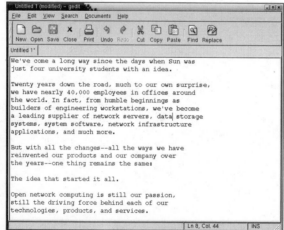

**Figure 7-3:**
Twenty
years of Sun
history, in
Text Editor.

This looks fine in Text Editor, but it's not yet a Web page. To see why, save the text to a file and then open the file in Netscape Navigator. To save the file, either

✔ Choose File➪Save

✔ Click the Save icon on the GNOME Text Editor toolbar

The Save As dialog box pops up. By default, the dialog box should open to your home directory, with the filename `Untitled 1`. Figure 7-4 shows how that looks.

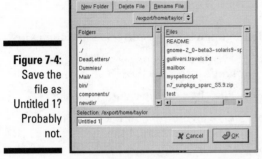

**Figure 7-4:**
Save the
file as
Untitled 1?
Probably
not.

The default location of my home directory is fine, but the filename `Untitled 1` is unacceptable: I use `welcome.html`. To change the filename, I use these steps:

1. Select `Untitled 1` in the bottom text area and replace it with `welcome.html`.

2. Click OK to save the file.

The Text Editor window should now show the name of the file in both

✔ The title bar

✔ The small tab below the New and Open buttons on the toolbar

# Viewing Local Pages

You can open a Web page in Netscape Navigator several ways, including dragging and dropping the icon onto the browser. To open the file you've created in Text Editor, follow these steps:

1. **Launch Navigator (Chapter 6 explains how) and then choose File⇨Open Page within Navigator.**

   The Open Page dialog box appears, as shown in Figure 7-5.

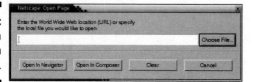

**Figure 7-5:**
Opening a
page in
Navigator.

### 2. Click the Choose File button to open another file selection dialog box.

This window is similar to the Save As dialog box shown in Figure 7-4. You should be looking at your home directory by default.

### 3. Find and select the file in the Files box on the right.

The selection box on the bottom of Figure 7-6 now has a full filename specification: /export/home/taylor/welcome.html.

**Figure 7-6:**
Selecting a
file to open.

### 4. Click OK to select the file.

You go back to the Open Page dialog box, as shown in Figure 7-5; this time, the filename is filled in properly. Figure 7-7 shows the result.

**Figure 7-7:**
Ready to
open the file
in navigator.

### 5. To open the file and see how it looks, click the Open in Navigator button.

It may surprise you that the page you created isn't laid out at all like it appears in the editor. Figure 7-8 shows what I mean. Although the file contains text, it doesn't contain any HTML markup tags, so the Web browser has no idea how to present it.

The following section explains how to add some simple HTML.

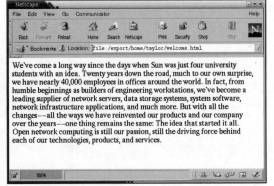

**Figure 7-8:**
The words
are right,
but the
presen-
tation
is poor.

# Improving Layout

The real pleasure of developing Web pages is learning the HyperText Markup Language and applying its many formatting and layout tags to improve the appearance of your Web page, regardless of content.

You can significantly improve this particular page with some common formatting options:

1. Add a few paragraph break tags: `<P>` and `</P>` (they're a pair so you need to start and end each paragraph).

   Wrap each paragraph of text with these two tags.

2. Add a document title, something to make it clear that Scott McNealy wrote these words.

   To accomplish this, use the H tag, which supports headers ranging between

   • Level one, the largest and most important,

      A typical level one header might look like this:

      ```
      <H1>This is my important header</H1>
      ```

   • Level six header, which is tiny and reminiscent of the proverbial small print in a contract.

The title of Scott McNealy's note containing these paragraphs of text is "Sun at 20: A look back on the future of network computing." That's what I used in this document, too. With the appropriate additions, Figure 7-9 shows the new, improved, HTML page.

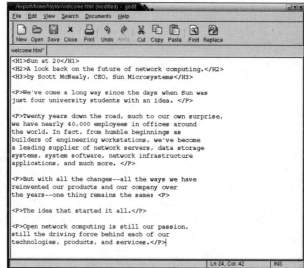

**Figure 7-9:**
The improved Web page welcome. html.

The window title now says (modified). This is a reminder that although you have entered the changes into the editor, you haven't written them to the disk and saved them.

3. Click the Save button (the little floppy disk) to write all the changes. The word (modified) should vanish from the window title.

Follow these steps to check your work:

1. Flip over to Navigator.

    • You can do this in GNOME by clicking the correct button on the bottom window bar.

    • In either GNOME or CDE, you can do it by clicking somewhere in the Web browser window itself.

2. Click the Reload button on the toolbar.

Voilà! Suddenly you've created a nice looking Web page, as shown in Figure 7-10.

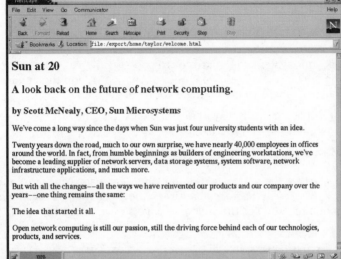

**Figure 7-10:** Finally, Scott's words look good!

## HTML by the bucketful

If you prefer to get your hands dirty building Web pages, you can find dozens and dozens of books on all things HTML. I recommend these books (all published by Wiley Publishing):

✔ *Creating Cool HTML 4 Web Pages* is a book I first wrote at the very beginning of the Web craze and have since updated and revised extensively, year after year. It's a top selling introduction to everything you need to know about HTML and how to use it.

✔ *Dynamic HTML Weekend Crash Course* is another book I wrote that goes into considerably more detail on two key modern Web technologies:

Cascading Style Sheets

JavaScript

These technologies are required knowledge for cutting-edge Web design.

✔ *HTML 4 For Dummies*, 4th Edition, by Ed Tittel and Natanya Pitts, is another good starting point, with coverage of the latest HTML tags and a helpful section on planning your site and design.

✔ *Building a Web Site For Dummies*, by David and Rhonda Crowder, is a good companion to *HTML 4 For Dummies*, with more of an emphasis on such site-design issues as

Interactive elements

Organizing your pages on the server

# Working with Apache Server

A Solaris system can be used as a fast and complete Web server, right out of the box.

For a basic configuration, follow these steps:

1. Ask your system administrator to copy the file `/etc/apache/httpd.conf-example` to `/etc/apache/httpd.conf`, and then make the few simple changes to the configuration file detailed therein.

2. After that's done, the system administrator can start up the server by typing `/usr/apache/bin/httpd`.

That's it. Your system is now running as a Web server!

To test whether the server is running, open Netscape Navigator and go to `http://127.0.0.1/`, a special address known as the *loopback address* for your computer. You see the welcome page shown in Figure 7-11.

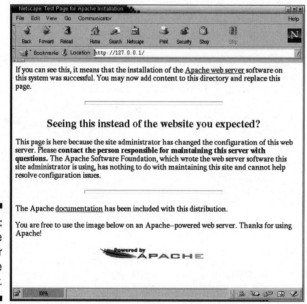

**Figure 7-11:**
Welcome
to your
Apache
Web server.

## *Publishing a Web page*

Publishing the Web page is surprisingly easy.

1. Go into Text Editor and choose File➪Save As.

   You're presented with the same dialog box shown in Figure 7-4.

2. Make sure you're in your home directory and then click the New Folder button.

   The New Folder dialog box pops up, as shown in Figure 7-12.

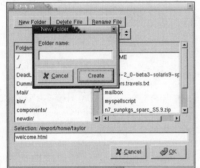

**Figure 7-12:**
Create a
new folder.

3. Type in `public_html` (yes, that's an underscore between the two words; remember, the Web doesn't like spaces) and click Create.

   You return to the Save As dialog box. This time, the Folders list should have the new `public_html` folder listed.

4. Double-click the folder to move into that subdirectory.

   Now the Save As dialog box looks like Figure 7-13.

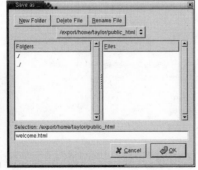

**Figure 7-13:**
Moving into
the new
`public_
html` folder.

The default name for the new file is still `welcome.html`.

5. Click OK, and the Web page is saved in the new directory.

6. Go back to the browser and open `http://127.0.0.1/~taylor/`
   `welcome.html` (where `taylor` is replaced by your account name,
   as necessary).

   You should see the same Web page shown earlier, but this time the page
   is being fed through the Web server, which means that it's accessible to
   other systems on your network and, possibly, the entire Internet.

One more touch can customize your system:

1. Ask your system administrator for your system's fully-qualified domain
   name.

   It's probably something like `aurora.intuitive.com` or `wk32.cs.`
   `colorado.edu`.

2. Change the loopback address to the correct hostname.

   Figure 7-14 shows the result for my system, with the address
   `http://aurora.intuitive.com/~taylor/welcome.html`
   displayed.

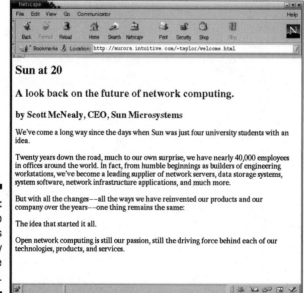

**Figure 7-14:**
The Web
page is
finally
visible
to all.

If you rename the file `index.html` within the `public_html` folder, it's the default page that's shown if a visitor requests `http://yourhost/~youraccount/` without specifying a filename.

Some systems are configured so you see a permission denied error, not your new page. If that happens, these steps should correct the problem:

1. Open a terminal window.

   Chapter 3 explains how to work at the command line.

2. Type these commands:

   ```
   chmod a+rx ~ ~/public_html
   chmod a+r  ~/public_html/*
   ```

   It should work just fine.

# Chapter 8

# Accessing Internet Services

*B*etween e-mail and the World Wide Web, it probably doesn't seem like there's much else on the Internet. But that's not the case. The Internet is also a vast repository of files, documents, and other data, free for the taking. Additionally, there are thousands of machines online where you can obtain a shell account (though mostly for a fee) and then connect directly to the system as if it were under your desk, not — perhaps — halfway around the world.

When I started working in the computer field in 1980, every few months my company's software vendor would send a "release tape," a big magnetic tape reel that we'd mount on a player and unpack onto our system. If something was broken, we'd have to either try to reverse the update or wait months for the next tape to fix the problems. The process was unimaginably slow and clunky!

Today, it's astonishingly easy to update systems and install new software. Need a new version of Netscape 7? Just connect to either the Sun Microsystems or Netscape file server and download it yourself, on demand. This tremendous improvement has helped the computer industry speed up development a hundredfold.

# Understanding FTP and Telnet Capabilities

If you've only spent time surfing the Web and passively receiving electronic mail, you might not realize that there's more to interactivity on the Internet.

For example, rather than being constrained to your computer's hard disk, you can connect to thousands of disks elsewhere on the Internet and copy files as needed. FTP, the File Transfer Protocol, allows you to do either from

 ✔ The primitive but powerful `ftp` interface
 ✔ A Web browser

    Web browers are read-only for ftp

You already know that Solaris includes a powerful command-line interface. Using the `telnet` program (or its secure big brother `ssh`), you can connect to command shells on remote computers anywhere in the world.

## FTP capabilities

The best way to imagine FTP is that it's a mechanism for attaching new hard disks to your computer, on demand.

Depending on the permissions you're granted upon connection, you can

 ✔ Read and explore content
 ✔ Upload and deposit your own files for safekeeping and storage

Most FTP connections are *read-only;* you explore the contents and copy anything you desire onto your hard disk, but you can't add your own material.

The more important limitation of the `ftp` program is that it isn't secure: Any account and password information required is sent *in the clear,* so malicious users who might be monitoring the network connection can easily "sniff" and copy your private connection details.

The secure alternative to `ftp` is `sftp`, a part of the Secure Shell (`ssh`) package. Other than the security issues, `ftp` and `sftp` are functionally identical. I strongly recommend that you use `sftp` whenever you can as a superior alternative to the `ftp` program.

## Telnet capabilities

The `telnet` program offers a simple method for connecting to command shells on remote computers, either elsewhere on your network or halfway around the world.

For reasons of system integrity and security, telnet accounts are always assigned per-person, so you have to enter your assigned account and password information. But telnet has the security limitations of the ftp application: Malicious users can potentially identify your account and password and then use them for unsavory purposes. The alternative to telnet, offering the same basic functionality, is the Secure Shell (ssh).

The ssh program (which I highly recommend) or the more widely available telnet program both offer the same functionality:

✔ After you've connected and logged in, using the command shell on the remote system is the same as working locally.

✔ If it's a Solaris system, any command-line program discussed herein will work on the remote system just as it does on your own.

If you want to find out more about how to ensure maximum security on your Solaris system, check out Chapter 17.

# Exploring the Net with FTP

Remote file access, primarily done using a protocol called FTP (File Transfer Protocol), can be accomplished two ways:

✔ **At the command line:** Many people use the command-line shell interface to access FTP archives.

This is particularly useful because it supports both

- *Downloads* (where files are brought to your system from the remote server)

- *Uploads* (where files are copied from your local system to the remote server).

✔ **Through a graphical FTP tool:** Some people don't realize that just about every Web browser is a terrific download-only FTP browser.

## Exploring FTP with a browser

A Web browser can work with an FTP-style URL, which looks something like this: ftp://ftp.sec.gov/. Open Netscape, choose File➪Open Web Location, and enter this URL. The result looks like Figure 8-1.

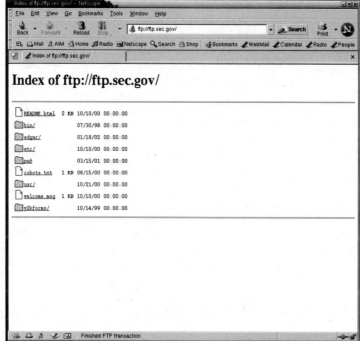

**Figure 8-1:**
The SEC
EDGAR FTP
archive, in
Netscape 7.

An FTP archive is like a remote hard disk that you can explore and download material from, as allowed by the system's file permissions.

Figure 8-1 shows that at the topmost level, this FTP server offers

- Six folders
- Three files:

> README.html
>
> robots.txt
>
> **welcome.msg**

Click the welcome.msg file, and you see a brief introductory message, like this:

```
-------------------------
  Welcome to FTP.SEC.GOV!
-------------------------

Welcome to the Securities & Exchange Commission's Public
Information Server. This file contains introductory
```

> information and will be periodically revised. This server
> features SEC public documents, information of interest to the
> investing public, rulemaking activities, and access to the
> Commission's electronic filing database, EDGAR. The public
> will be able to query the EDGAR database for any company
> currently filing electronically with the SEC. These filings
> are updated 24 hours after they are filed with the
> Commission. This server will support WWW and anonymous FTP
> and can be reached at "http://www.sec.gov" and "ftp.sec.gov"
> respectively.
> Archive note: Please read /edgar/README-2000-10-04.txt as the
> Archive structure has changed!
> Questions?  Comments. Please send e-mail to
> webmaster@sec.gov.

FTP supports both logging in to

✔ A specific account

✔ An *anonymous FTP server.*

With an anonymous server

ftp is the login

Your e-mail address as the password (usually, by convention)

Netscape defaults to an anonymous FTP connection when it displays FTP archives. It all happened invisibly with this SEC connection.

You've already accomplished a lot. You've connected to an FTP archive on a computer in Washington, D.C., requested the download of a specific file, and had that file displayed within the browser, all with just a few mouse clicks.

Click the Back button to go back to the list of folders, and then click edgar to move into the main directory of corporate filings, as shown in Figure 8-2.

This is getting more interesting! You see many folders, including historical corporate filing folders for 1997–2000, and more.

In fact, the SEC changed its FTP archive structure; in a moment, you see more recent corporate filings on this server too.

To start, click in this order:

full-index

2003

QTR1

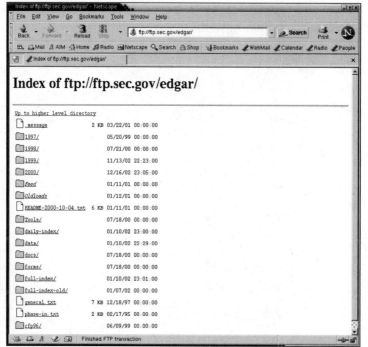

**Figure 8-2:**
The EDGAR
directory on
`ftp.sec.`
`gov.`

The full path is

```
ftp://ftp.sec.gov/edgar/full-index/2003/QTR1/
```

The results are shown in Figure 8-3. Now, click `company.idx` to see a long list of all corporate filings archived on the EDGAR system, as shown in Figure 8-4.

If you're an active investor, EDGAR is a great place to do research! From this document, you can

✔ Get the filename of the specific report on EDGAR

✔ Use Netscape to navigate to the correct file — all free, all via FTP.

## Command-line FTP

Although accessing FTP archives via Netscape is a breeze, there's one significant limitation: You can't transfer files from your local system to the server.

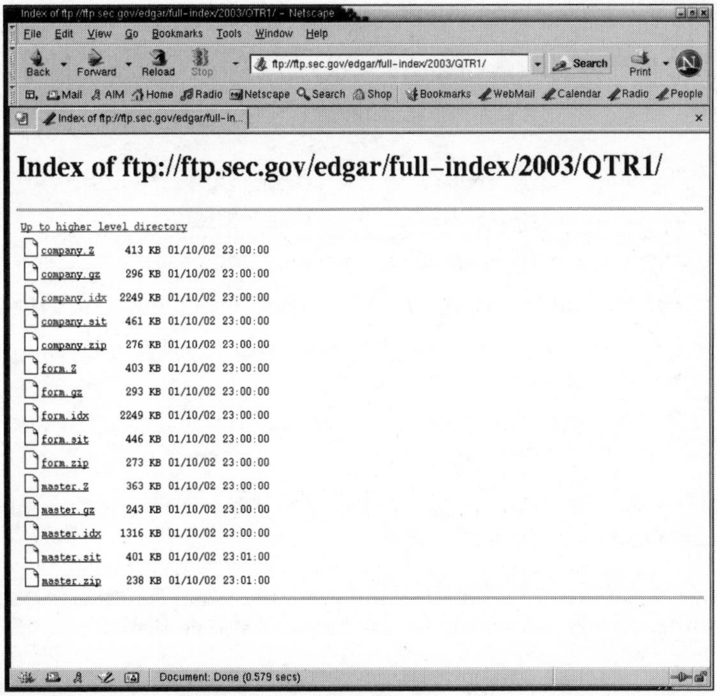

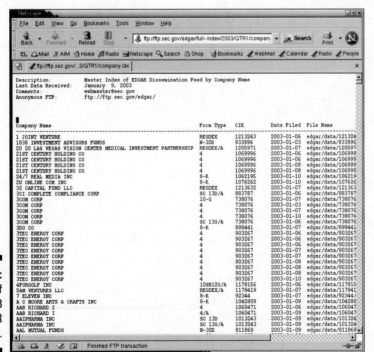

**Figure 8-3:**
First quarter
2003
corporate
filings
folder.

**Figure 8-4:**
Full listing of
Q1, 2003
EDGAR
filings.

With the command-line `ftp` program, you can do either, or both:

- ✔ Download files from the server
- ✔ Upload your files to the server

The server must have appropriate permissions to allow uploads:

- ✔ You might have an account on an FTP server that allows uploads, but requires you to use your own account and password.

  For example, many Web servers expect file uploads via FTP.

- ✔ If not, you see a permission denied error when you try to upload something.

  If that happens, seek advice from your system administrator on how to correct the permission error.

The `ftp` program requires a terminal with a command shell running. Chapter 3 explains how to launch it.

Type `ftp` at the command line, followed by the name of the FTP server you want to explore. The result looks like this if you go back to the SEC site:

```
$ ftp ftp.sec.gov
Connected to ftp.sec.gov.
220 FTP server ready.
Name (ftp.sec.gov:taylor):
```

If you had a specific account assigned on the FTP server, you could enter the account name at this prompt, but because you do not, use `ftp` as the account name:

```
Name (ftp.sec.gov:taylor): ftp
331 Guest login ok, send your complete e-mail address as password.
Password:
```

Now type in your e-mail address (or something similar, if you'd rather not give the Securities and Exchange Commission your e-mail address), and you're logged in to its FTP server:

```
230-
230------------------------------
230- Welcome to FTP.SEC.GOV!
230------------------------------
230-
230-Welcome to the Securities & Exchange Commission's Public
230-Information Server. This file contains introductory
230-information and will be periodically revised. This server
230-features SEC public documents, information of interest to
230-the investing public, rulemaking activities, and access
```

```
230-to the Commission's electronic filing database, EDGAR.
230-The public will be able to query the EDGAR database for
230-any company currently filing electronically with the SEC.
230-These filings are updated 24 hours after they are filed
230-with the Commission. This server will support WWW
230-and anonymous FTP and can be reached at
230-"http://www.sec.gov" and "ftp.sec.gov" respectively.
230-
230-Archive note: Please read /edgar/README-2000-10-04.txt as
230-structure has changed!
230-
230-Questions? Comments. Please send e-mail to
230-webmaster@sec.gov.
230-
230 Guest login ok, access restrictions apply.
Remote system type is UNIX.
Using binary mode to transfer files.
ftp>
```

This is the *welcome message* (just about every FTP server has one), which tells you what's on the system and how to get around. The last line, `ftp>`, is the prompt from the `ftp` program. To proceed, you need to type in each of the commands you want to run.

Table 8-1 has a helpful summary of the most useful `ftp` commands.

| Table 8-1 | The Most Useful `ftp` Commands | |
| --- | --- | --- |
| *Command* | *Typical Usage* | *Explanation* |
| Cd | cd edgar | Change into the named directory. Use cd .. to move back up. |
| Dir | Dir | List the contents of the current directory. |
| Get | get welcome.msg | Download the named file to the local system. |
| | | If used as get a b, then a will be downloaded and named b in the current (local) directory. |
| | | If used as get a, the file will retain its name when downloaded. |

*(continued)*

**Table 8-1 *(continued)***

| Command | Typical Usage | Explanation |
|---------|---------------|-------------|
| Help | Help | A brief but useful help message. |
| Mkdir | mkdir new | Make the named directory on the remote server, if you have the appropriate permissions. |
| Put | put welcome.html | Upload the specified file to the remote server in the current (remote) directory. |
| | | If used as put a b, then a will be uploaded and renamed b on the server. |
| | | If used as put a, then the file will be uploaded and retain its name on the server. |
| Pwd | Pwd | Shows the current directory on the remote server. |
| Quit | Quit | Quit the ftp program. |

Now that you're connected to the server, you can get a copy of the file listing from EDGAR with the command-line ftp program by typing this:

```
ftp> cd edgar/full-index/2003/QTR1
250 CWD command successful.
ftp> get company.idx
200 PORT command successful.
150 Opening BINARY mode data connection for company.idx
    (2302613 bytes).
226 Transfer complete.
local: company.idx remote: company.idx
2302613 bytes received in 10 seconds (215.12 Kbytes/s)
ftp>
```

You now have a new file in your local directory called company.idx, containing a full list of which companies have filed which documents with the SEC in the first quarter of 2003. To quit, type quit.

If you view the document and it's one very long line or otherwise in some peculiar format, you may need to download a new copy of the file. This time, type the ftp command ascii first to tell the program that it's a text file, and the appropriate end-of-line sequences should be rewritten as the material arrives.

## Connecting by Telnet

Many Solaris users work happily year after year without ever having to use the command shell to reach out and connect to a remote system. When you do need to log in to a remote system, though, you'll probably use the awkwardly named `telnet` tool. When you open up a terminal window to your own computer, you establish a Telnet-like connection. Imagine the same basic thing, but connecting to another server a few yards, miles, or even thousands of miles away.

To accomplish this, type `telnet remotehostname` at the command line. You need an account on the remote server to log in, but you can get the Telnet connection and initial login prompt without any sort of connection.

To demonstrate the concepts, the following example is a connection to a server at the University of Colorado, Boulder. The first line is the only time you interact directly with the `telnet` program rather than the remote system:

```
$ telnet spot.colorado.edu
Trying 128.138.129.2...
Connected to spot.colorado.edu.
Escape character is '^]'.

*****************************************************************
ATTENTION: This service has been disabled as part of the move
toward encrypted authentication for the Boulder campus. You
will need to switch to a secure login client, such as ssh.

For more information, step-by-step instructions, or if you
need any help, please go to
http://www.colorado.edu/its/security/encauth or call
*****************************************************************
Connection closed by foreign host.
$
```

The preceding example showed an error message then logged you out, dropping the connection and quitting the `telnet` program completely. That's okay; the example shows generally how it's done.

As another example of how `telnet` lets you connect to a remote server and work as if you were directly connected, I'll let you have a peek at my own server, which I can only connect to via `telnet` when I disable some security software.

The following example shows how, if you have an account, working with a remote system via `telnet` is a breeze:

```
$ telnet server.intuitive.com
Trying 128.121.96.234...
Connected to server.intuitive.com.
Escape character is '^]'.


login: taylor
Password:
Last login: Fri Jan 10 17:43:35 2003 from 12-253-112-102.
FreeBSD 4.4-RELEASE (VKERN) #9: Thu Jan  2 10:23:51 MST 2003


Welcome to your Virtual Server, Dave!


VPS ~ (1) : ls
HTML-Lint-0.92/        maildir@              tmp/
MT-2.51.tar           mbox                  traverse.errors
bin/                  mybin/                usr/
compat@               sbin/                 var/
dev/                  scripts/              web@
etc/                  shuttle/              webconf@
home/                 testme
VPS ~ (2) : pwd
/usr/home/dtint
VPS ~ (3) : logout
Connection closed by foreign host.
```

Once you're connected with a `telnet` session, it's just like having a terminal window open on that machine directly, except it's distant: My office is in Boulder, Colorado, whereas the intuitive.com server is located in Baltimore, Maryland. Quite a distance!

# Connecting Securely with SSH

The only problem with both `ftp` and `telnet` is that they're not secure. In fact, `ftp` is notoriously insecure, and modern Unix system administrators recommend avoiding `ftp` for any account-specific activity. Why? Because both programs send their passwords *in the clear* — unencrypted. If a bad guy, delinquent, or even malicious hacker happened to be listening on the network wire (which can be done), he'd see your account and password pair visibly travel past. In fact, a packet sniffer can be programmed to look for the string `login:` and capture the next 100 characters sent in either direction, which would include the account and password pair.

ssh (Secure Shell) is a secure replacement for both telnet and ftp.

✔ The ssh program itself is a replacement for telnet.

✔ The ssh package also includes sftp, a secure ftp program.

Outside of the invocation steps, they are pretty much functionally identical to their insecure cousins. The biggest difference is that both require you to specify the account name and server name as part of the invocation of the program.

Instead of ftp intuitive.com and then typing in taylor, you'd use:

```
$ sftp taylor@intuitive.com
Connecting to intuitive.com...
authenticity of host 'intuitive.com' can't be established.
RSA key fingerprint in md5 is:
d0:db:8a:cb:74:c8:37:e4:9e:71:fc:7a:eb:d6:40:81
Are you sure you want to continue connecting(yes/no)?
```

If you have the ssh package, and it's supported on the remote system to which you're connecting, use it. Don't use ftp or telnet. If ssh isn't an option, complain to your system administrator about the security problem, and hope it'll be fixed.

✔ If you're using anonymous FTP, it's no big deal.

✔ If you're connecting to another system over the public Internet, encryption is critical.

Because the ssh system uses public key encryption, the first step involved in any connection is to swap encryption keys. You don't have to be involved other than to acknowledge that you're visiting a site for the first time, hence the need for the public key.

Type yes at the prompt, and you'll see:

```
Warning: Permanently added 'intuitive.com,128.121.96.234'
(RSA) to the list of known hosts.
dtint@intuitive.com's password:
sftp >
```

Type in the password properly, and you're given an sftp prompt, ready to proceed. To start, type dir for a directory listing (just as you would in the ftp program):

```
sftp > dir
drwx------   17 taylor    vuser      1024 Jan  8 16:07 .
drwxr-xr-x    3 root      wheel      2048 Jan  6 21:02 ..
-rw-r--r--    1 taylor    vuser       164 May 22  2002 .login
-rw-r--r--    1 taylor    vuser       271 Apr  9  2002 .profile
-rw-r--r--    1 taylor    vuser       121 Apr  9  2002 .shrc
drwxr-xr-x    2 taylor    vuser       512 Apr  9  2002 dev
drwxr-xr-x    5 taylor    vuser      1024 Jan  5 23:27 etc
-rw-r--r--    1 taylor    vuser       898 Jan  8 16:06 .cshrc
lrwxr-xr-x    1 taylor    vuser        26 May 18  2002 web
drwxr-xr-x    2 taylor    vuser       512 Jan  7 08:24 bin
drwxr-xr-x    9 taylor    vuser       512 Dec  2  1999 usr
drwxr-xr-x    7 taylor    vuser       512 Apr  9  2002 var
drwxr-xr-x    3 taylor    vuser       512 Jan 10 19:10 tmp
drwxr-xr-x    2 taylor    vuser       512 Apr  9  2002 sbin
lrwxr-xr-x    1 root      vuser         7 Apr  9  2002 compat
drwx------    2 taylor    vuser       512 May 14  2002 .ssh
drwxr-xr-x    2 taylor    vuser       512 Sep  4 20:06 .ncftp
lrwxr-xr-x    1 taylor    vuser        24 May 18  2002 maildir
lrwxr-xr-x    1 taylor    vuser        24 May 18  2002 webconf
drwxr-xr-x    6 taylor    vuser       512 May 26  2002 home
drwxr-xr-x    6 taylor    vuser       512 May 21  2002 HTML-Lint-0.92
drwxr-xr-x    2 taylor    vuser       512 Jan  7 08:24 mybin
-rw-r--r--    1 taylor    vuser         3 May 25  2002 .counter
-rw-r--r--    1 taylor    vuser        29 May 26  2002 .aspell.english.prepl
-rw-r--r--    1 taylor    vuser        50 May 26  2002 .aspell.english.pws
-rw-------    1 taylor    vuser       773 Jul 15 04:19 mbox
drwxr-xr-x    2 taylor    vuser       512 Jan  7 08:09 scripts
-rw-------    1 taylor    vuser        79 May 26  2002 traverse.errors
drwxr-xr-x    5 taylor    vuser       512 Jan  6 01:10 .cpan
drwxr-xr-x    2 taylor    vuser       512 Oct  5 06:13 shuttle
-rw-r--r--    1 taylor    vuser         0 Oct  7 15:26 testme
-rw-------    1 taylor    vuser       929 Jan  2 16:52 .bash_history
-rw-r--r--    1 taylor    vuser   1781760 Jan  6 01:13 MT-2.51.tar
```

Table 8-2 lists the most useful SSH commands.

| Table 8-2 | Useful SSH Commands |
| --- | --- |
| *Commands* | *Functions* |
| cd path | Change remote directory to path |
| lcd path | Change local directory to path |
| get remote-path [local-path] | Download file |
| ls [path] | Display remote directory listing |
| mkdir path | Create remote directory |

| Commands | Functions |
|---|---|
| `put local-path [remote-path]` | Upload file |
| `pwd` | Display remote working directory |
| `quit` | Quit sftp |
| `rename oldpath newpath` | Rename remote file |
| `rmdir path` | Remove remote directory |
| `rm path` | Delete remote file |
| `!command` | Execute 'command' in local shell |
| `!` | Escape to local shell |

Just as `sftp` was designed to be functionally identical to `ftp`, but secure, `ssh` appears almost identical to `telnet`, except for the initial invocation:

```
$ ssh taylor@server.intuitive.com
taylor@server.intuitive.com's password:
Last login: Sat Jan 11 03:28:46 2003 from 12-253-112-102.
FreeBSD 4.4-RELEASE (VKERN) #9: Thu Jan  2 10:23:51 MST 2003

Welcome to your Virtual Server, Dave!

VPS ~ (1) : ls -F
HTML-Lint-0.92/        maildir@              tmp/
MT-2.51.tar           mbox                  traverse.errors
bin/                  mybin/                usr/
compat@               sbin/                 var/
dev/                  scripts/              web@
etc/                  shuttle/              webconf@
home/                 testme
VPS ~ (2) : logout
Connection to intuitive.com closed.
```

# Part III

# Becoming Productive with StarOffice

It's another cow box mutilation, Sheriff. Look how cleanly the case has been severed. And if my hunch is right, you won't find the motherboard within a thousand miles of here.

## In this part . . .

This part of the book introduces you to the key components of StarOffice, an excellent alternative to Microsoft Office, with a particular emphasis on StarOffice Writer, the document processing system. By the time you're done with this section, you'll have a very good idea of the power and capabilities of StarOffice and will be ready to begin your own exploration.

# Chapter 9

# Composing Documents with Writer

**In This Chapter**

▶ Creating and building new documents

▶ Increasing your efficiency with styles

▶ Saving documents

*F*or many years, the most notable absence within Solaris was the lack of Microsoft Office or a compatible suite of applications that would let Solaris users share documents, read spreadsheets, view presentations, and so on. With the introduction of StarOffice, and subsequent release of the open source OpenOffice variant on StarOffice, this problem has been solved.

Included for free with Solaris 9, StarOffice is a remarkably capable, easy to use set of programs that work well in both the Common Desktop Environment and the GNOME environment. These programs offer a high degree of inter-changeability with Windows and Mac office documents.

The showcase application of StarOffice is Writer, the document preparation and word processing environment. Clearly inspired by the interface and capabilities of Microsoft Word, Writer offers an elegantly designed and powerful environment for producing documents, whether they're just a few pages or hundreds of pages.

This chapter covers some of the most exciting parts of StarOffice, including document editing and working with styles. (Chapter 10 examines the key additional applications included with the StarOffice suite.)

# Creating New Documents

After StarOffice is installed, you can launch Writer directly from either

▶ The GNOME menu (choose Applications⇨Office⇨StarOffice)

▶ The Common Desktop Environment taskbar (click the butterfly icon).

If that doesn't work, you should be able to move into the StarOffice directory and launch the program from the terminal:

```
/export/home/staroffice6.0/program/soffice &
```

Whichever way you start Writer, you get a blank Writer screen, as shown in Figure 9-1.

▶ The main section is a virtual piece of paper upon which you can type (or cut and paste) whatever you want.

▶ Other screen features include

- A menu bar along the top

- Two toolbars

- A ruler

- A toolbar running down the left side of the window

Rather than start from scratch, I'm reading in the contents of the book *Gulliver's Travels,* which I already have on my system.

To accomplish this, choose Insert⇨File, as shown in Figure 9-2.

The file selection dialog box is different from the normal Solaris selector, but the basic concept is the same:

1. Click the Up One Level button (it has a folder with an upward pointing arrow on it) to step up the directory tree

2. Click a folder in the main view to move into a directory.

When you've found the desired file, click it to select it, as shown in Figure 9-3.

After selecting the file, click Insert. You're taken back to the original document, with the new file incorporated.

When the file is imported, Writer shows the bottom of the page, the last line of the inserted material. Jump back to the top by scrolling, or try one of the Writer shortcuts: Press Ctrl+Home to move to the first line of text. The new, more interesting document, is shown in Figure 9-4. The bottom-left corner of the window in Figure 9-4 shows that this is Page 1 of 204 total pages.

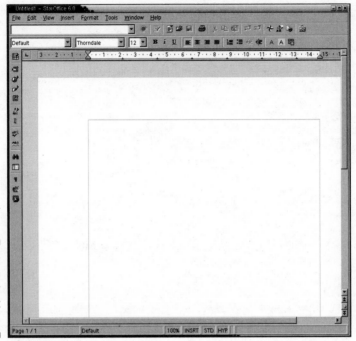

**Figure 9-1:**
StarOffice
Writer
as first
launched.

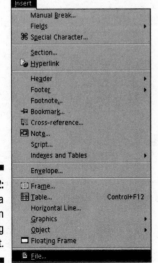

**Figure 9-2:**
Inserting a
file into an
existing
document.

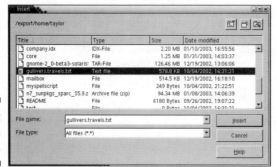

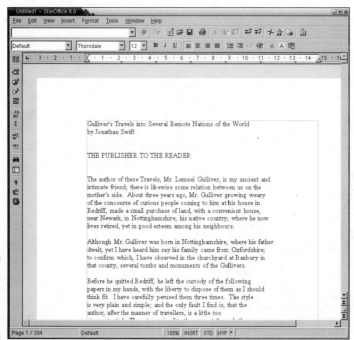

**Figure 9-4:**
*Gulliver's
Travels,*
in Writer.

# Altering the appearance of text

You can make a title appealing by making the text bold, centered, or larger:

✔ To apply bold, follow these steps:

1. Select the text with the mouse (click+drag with the left button).

2. While the text is highlighted, click the Bold button (with the B on it) on the Formatting toolbar.

The toolbar is shown in Figure 9-5, split into two lines to make it easier to read.

✔ To center the material, click the Center Text button on the same toolbar. (The button looks like four tiny lines, center-aligned.)

✔ To make the text larger, select a font size from the Font Size menu. (In Figure 9-4, the menu says 12 to indicate that the text is 12 points in size.) A variety of font sizes are shown in the pop-up menu; choose your favorite to select it.

**Figure 9-5:**
The Writer
Formatting
toolbar,
split into
two halves.

With the addition of a judiciously placed carriage return to make the centering look good, the title looks much better.

You can make many additional changes in Writer. For example, you can select THE PUBLISHER TO THE READER and then choose Format➪Paragraph.

The resulting Paragraph dialog box is complex, as shown in Figure 9-6.

**Figure 9-6:**
The many
paragraph
format
options.

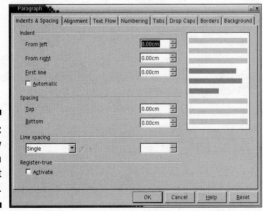

The Paragraph dialog box in Figure 9-6 has many more options than the Microsoft Word equivalent. It features eight tabs along the top:

✔ Indents & Spacing

✔ Alignment

✔ Text Flow

✔ Numbering

✔ Tabs

✔ Drop Caps

✔ Borders

✔ Background

StarOffice has an extensive, well-written online help system accessible from just about anywhere in the program. It's well worth using, whether you're a Writer neophyte or pro. Just click the Help button.

## *Tweaking colors*

Tweak the paragraph spacing, with the intent of applying a background color to make the head "THE PUBLISHER TO THE READER" stand out even more on the page.

The default top and bottom spacing (the spacing above and below the currently selected paragraph) is 0.00cm.

To change the inter-paragraph spacing, click on the tiny up arrow adjacent to the current spacing indicator to increase it to the desired amount. For example, to change the current value to 0.20cm, click the tiny up arrow twice.

1. **Click the Background tab to access an attractive color selection section of the Paragraph dialog box, as shown in Figure 9-7.**

2. **Select a color from the bottom row.**

   The large blank box on the right fills with the selected color. In this example, I selected dark violet.

3. **Click OK.**

   You see the colorful, but slightly confusing results, as shown in Figure 9-8.

   Because the original text is selected, it's shown in the inverse color to the background of the paragraph. Your display should have a weird light green for the text selected and dark violet for the rest of that line.

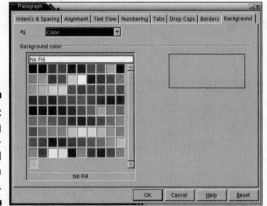

**Figure 9-7:**
Changing
the back-
ground
color of a
paragraph.

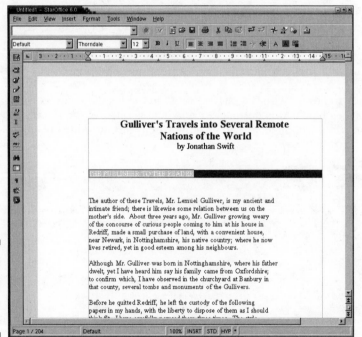

**Figure 9-8:**
Now with
the colored
paragraph
background.

Change the color of the text to white so it has more contrast with the dark violet and is therefore easier to read.

Because the text is still selected, click the Font Color button (with the small A on it), which is third from the right on the Formatting bar. (If you move your mouse over the button, the pop-up says Font Color to confirm it's the correct selection.) You see the same color palette shown earlier in the Paragraph Background selection (and also shown here in Figure 9-9). This time choose white instead of dark violet.

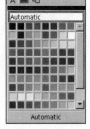

**Figure 9-9:**
The font color palette.

While the text is still selected, click the Bold button to make it bold and then click the Typeface Selection pop-up (it probably says Thorndale by default).

The resulting menu lists all known typefaces, in each typeface (a helpful way of seeing which typeface is best for your needs). Choose Arial Black.

Click somewhere on the page other than the headline you've been improving. The headline text is deselected, enabling you to see the attractive white on dark violet headline, as shown somewhat less colorfully in Figure 9-10.

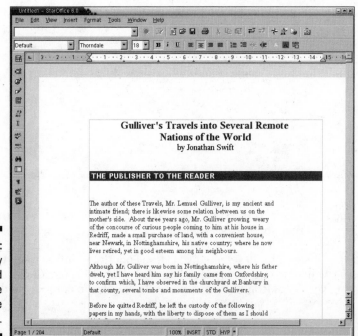

**Figure 9-10:**
A greatly improved headline in the document.

# Using Styles

If you apply formatting to every word individually in a large document, it might take a bit of time to turn a plain text file into an attractive and highly readable document. You can speed up this process with styles.

The most common task with styles is to apply a given style to a passage of text. To create styles, you have to define them. This, fortunately, is easy.

Go back to the new colorful headline and select the text on that line, then open the Stylist window with either of these steps:

- ✔ Press the F11 key
- ✔ Choose Format⇨Stylist

The Stylist window opens, as shown in Figure 9-11.

**Figure 9-11:** Working with the Writer Stylist window.

Presented in very small type, this window can be a bit baffling, but the mouseover pop-ups are a lifesaver here: Move the cursor over any of the tiny buttons to see a short description of the corresponding function.

Figure 9-11 shows about 20 predefined styles, including ten levels of headers, First Line Indent, Hanging Indent, Signature, and Marginalia.

To create a new style, follow these steps:

1. **Click the New Style from Selection button, which is the second button from the right.**

   The Create Style dialog box opens, as shown in Figure 9-12.

2. **Type in the style name — for example, "White on Purple Head" — and click OK.**

   Now the Stylist window includes the new style you've just defined.

3. **Close the Stylist window by clicking the small Close button in the top-right corner of the window.**

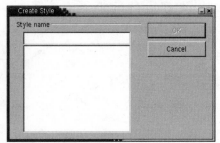

**Figure 9-12:**
Create a
new style in
Writer.

## Applying a style to text

Using styles to ensure consistency across a document is a tremendous boon to both the speed and accuracy of your document production.

You can also create special documents that are simply a collection of predefined styles by reading the Template section in the online help.

To apply a style to text, follow these steps:

1. **Select the text.**

2. **Click the Apply Style pop-up menu on the left edge of the Formatting toolbar (it probably says Default).**

   The pop-up menu shows styles defined for this document only. It's rather short currently, as shown in Figure 9-13.

3. **Select a style.**

   To apply a defined style to the selected text, click on the correct style name. For example, I select White on Purple Head. All the character and paragraph styles (typeface, size, bold, text and background color) are applied to the new material, as shown in Figure 9-14.

**Figure 9-13:**
Defined
styles for
this docu-
ment in
the Apply
Style pop-
up menu.

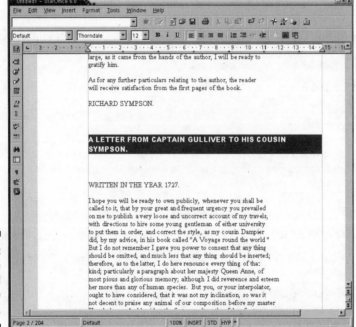

**Figure 9-14:**
A new style
applied
to the
headline.

# Saving Documents

When you've finished entering, editing, and formatting a document, save
the document to your disk. There are a couple of easy ways to save the
document:

- ✔ Click the small floppy disk button on the Function toolbar.
- ✔ Choose File➪Save.

Either way, the Save As dialog box opens, as shown in Figure 9-15.

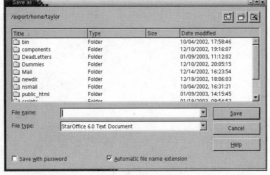

**Figure 9-15:**
Specify
where and
how to
save your
document.

As with the Open dialog box, the buttons on the top right enable you to

✔ Move up one directory level

✔ Create a new directory at the current location

✔ Jump to the default directory (usually your home directory).

You can create a new subdirectory if needed, by clicking on the New Folder button to open the Create New Folder dialog box, as shown in Figure 9-16. In this example, I'm going to create a new folder called Library for the newly formatted version of *Gulliver's Travels*.

1. Type in the name, as shown in Figure 9-16, and then click OK.

   The directory is created and now shows up on the directories list.

2. Move to the new directory and double-click on it to move into the new location.

   For example, I double-click Library to move into it. It's empty, so no files or directories are shown.

**Figure 9-16:**
Creating a
new folder.

# *Picking the optimal document format*

Click the File Type pop-up menu to see a rather bewildering array of document format options. Of these, the most useful formats are

✔ StarOffice 6.0 Text Document (the default)

✔ Microsoft Word 97/2000/XP (the most modern Microsoft Word format).

  With this format, include a `.doc` filename suffix so Microsoft Word recognizes the file.

✔ Rich Text Format, which many e-mail readers and word processing systems can read.

  With this format, include an `.rtf` filename suffix so other programs recognize the file.

If you save a Writer document as Web Page, the quality of the HTML (Hypertext Markup Language, *lingua franca* of the World Wide Web) is poor.

## Testing Cross-Platform Compatibility

I'll use the `ftp` program to transfer the document from the Solaris system to a PC running Windows XP. On that system, the file appears with the Microsoft Word icon.

Double-clicking the icon produces the result shown in Figure 9-17.

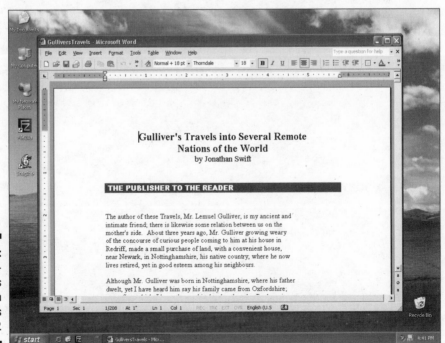

**Figure 9-17:** The document looks great in Windows XP.

# Chapter 10

# The Rest of StarOffice

*T*his chapter offers an overview of some terrific tools included in the StarOffice suite, including Calc, the spreadsheet program; Draw, the graphics editor; Impress, the presentation development tool; and the Web page builder within Writer. (Chapter 9 covers the Writer word processing program in detail.)

More than just a bunch of office-related programs thrown together, StarOffice has more integration than most Unix programs. Each program has hooks to allow invocation of the other programs, graphics and text elements can often be copied and pasted without loss of format, and the interfaces are consistent and coherent.

In addition to Writer, Calc, Draw, and Impress, the full set of programs in StarOffice includes some shortcut applications for writing specific types of documents in Writer (Agenda, Fax, Label, Letter, and Memo); the mathematical formula editor Math; V Card, a tool for making business cards; and a macro programming language called Star Basic for customizing the appearance and behavior of the StarOffice applications.

## Balancing Accounts with Calc

When I started using computers, I remember thinking that word-processing was clearly useful, but spreadsheets? Why would I ever need one of those? Time passes, and now I spend almost as much time creating and tuning complex multisheet spreadsheets as I do creating word-processing documents. Once you get the hang of working with spreadsheets, they're fun. Honest!

Here's how to use Calc to create a straightforward checkbook manager. A checkbook ledger has a small number of fields: For each transaction, you need to track the date, the check number, whether it's cleared the bank and shown up on your statement, to whom the check was written, the amount of the check, and a running balance for the account.

A few other transactions can appear in the ledger, too:

✔ An initial balance

✔ Deposits made

✔ Bank service charges

For those transactions, create a Credits column, and for the check amounts, create a Debits column, just to sound like financial mavens!

After you start Calc — probably by choosing it off the GNOME menu or CDE toolbar — the initial view is busy, as shown in Figure 10-1.

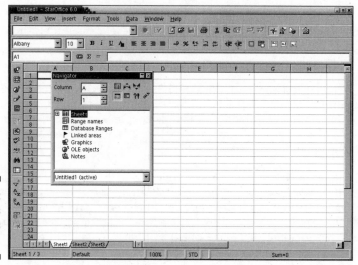

**Figure 10-1:**
Calc starts
out with lots
of options!

I prefer to dismiss the Navigator window floating atop the main spreadsheet. After doing that, you can get into the serious business of building the check-book ledger.

# *Text and numbers*

To enter data into a spreadsheet, click a box and then type the words or numbers. Press Tab to move horizontally to the next field, or Enter to move to the next spreadsheet line. Enter the following words into the columns in the first row:

- ✔ Check Number
- ✔ Date
- ✔ Description
- ✔ Cleared?
- ✔ Credit
- ✔ Debit
- ✔ Balance

Next, move the cursor to the edge of the column labels and drag the columns to maker them wider or narrower so that each has a sensible amount of space (for example, the Description column is nice and wide, whereas Cleared? is narrow). To widen the Description column, move the cursor over the line between the C and D boxes and then click+drag to the right.

You can center all the column headers by selecting them all and clicking the Center Data button on the Formatting toolbar (it's the button with four little lines, centered, in a box), and you can make them all bold by clicking the B button. Finally, to jazz up the spreadsheet, click the Background Color button on the Formatting toolbar (it's the fourth button from the right). Choose Green 8 as a background. (Green is a better color to associate with a check-book balance than red!)

The end result, with an initial balance and single check entered, looks like Figure 10-2.

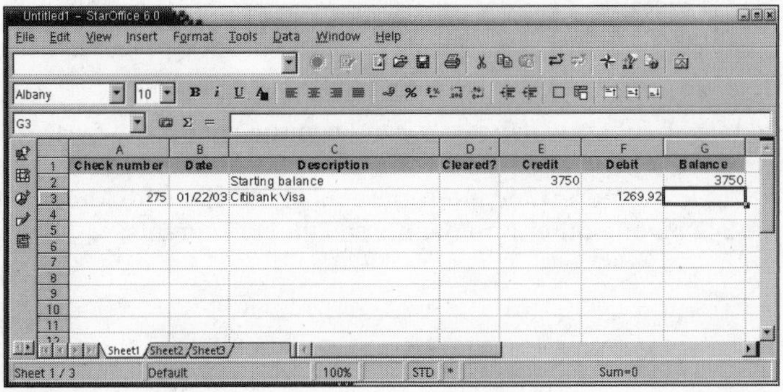

**Figure 10-2:**
You're
almost
ready to
balance
your
checkbook.

## Formulas

The Balance field isn't a value; it's a *formula*. Formulas are the heart of spreadsheets because they allow changes in a value to ripple through the entire set of calculations. Formulas are simply an equation composed of constant values, functions, and references to other cells in the spreadsheet. The balance is always the balance from the previous line plus any credits, minus any debits. Spreadsheets tend to think in terms of column x row terms. Because the current cell is G3 (row 1 is the column titles, row 2 is the starting balance), the balance in the cell above is G2, the credits value for this row is E3, and the debits value for this row is F3. Here's the actual formula you need to enter in the cell:

```
=G2+E3-F3
```

The = at the beginning tells Calc that you're entering a formula. You can also have numbers in a formula. If you want to pretend your balance is better than it is, you can use =G2+3*E3-F2 to triple any deposit!

Add a few more checkbook entries, and perhaps a deposit, and you can discover a fabulous capability of Calc. If you copy the formula cell in G3 (from the first checkbook entry) and paste it into each subsequent balance box, The spreadsheet will adjust the cell reference values appropriately. No fuss, no hassle. The result is shown in Figure 10-3.

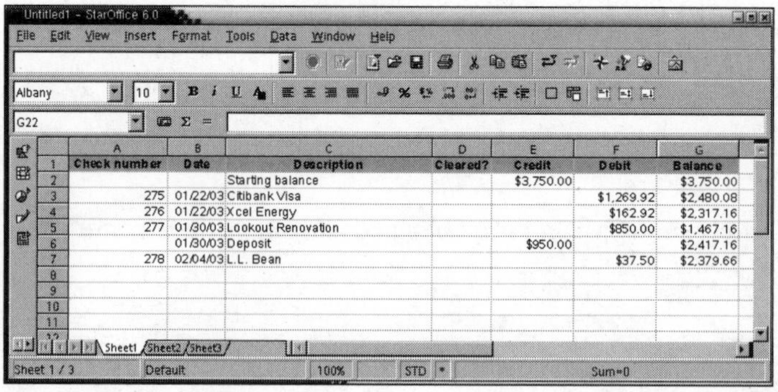

**Figure 10-3:**
This check-book ledger is nice and readable.

| | A | B | C | D | E | F | G |
|---|---|---|---|---|---|---|---|
| 1 | Check number | Date | Description | Cleared? | Credit | Debit | Balance |
| 2 | | | Starting balance | | $3,750.00 | | $3,750.00 |
| 3 | 275 | 01/22/03 | Citibank Visa | | | $1,269.92 | $2,480.08 |
| 4 | 276 | 01/22/03 | Xcel Energy | | | $162.92 | $2,317.16 |
| 5 | 277 | 01/30/03 | Lookout Renovation | | | $850.00 | $1,467.16 |
| 6 | | 01/30/03 | Deposit | | $950.00 | | $2,417.16 |
| 7 | 278 | 02/04/03 | L.L. Bean | | | $37.50 | $2,379.66 |
| 8 | | | | | | | |
| 9 | | | | | | | |
| 10 | | | | | | | |
| 11 | | | | | | | |

I could talk about spreadsheets for at least the next 150 pages. You can add more format, layout, and mathematical sophistication to your spreadsheet if you opt to learn more. Calc interoperates gracefully with Microsoft Excel and Lotus 1-2-3, among other popular spreadsheet programs.

# Creating Graphics with Draw

Whether you're a talented digital artist or just need to create a crude diagram for a presentation, StarOffice Draw offers the power and capabilities you need. Launched from the GNOME startup menu or CDE toolbar, it starts up with almost as many toolbars and buttons as Writer, as shown in Figure 10-4.

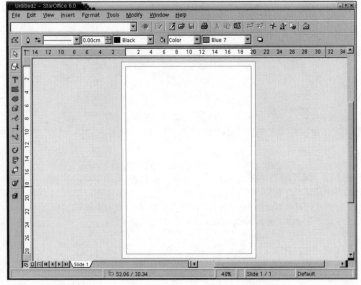

**Figure 10-4:** StarOffice Draw offers a cornucopia of drawing tools.

## Gallery

If you aren't an artist, you'll be glad to know that Draw has a gallery of clip art and other graphical objects that you can drop into an existing drawing. To access it, choose Tools⇨Gallery. A new Gallery window pops up with many categories of graphics and sound files, as shown in Figure 10-5.

To add a graphic from the gallery to an existing page in Draw, right-click the graphic and choose Insert⇨Copy from the pop-up menu. I chose the ambulance cartoon from the Problem Solving images in the gallery.

Closing the Gallery window is a bit confusing. If you click the close window icon, you close the entire Draw application. Not good. If you want to have it almost vanish but still linger a bit, click the upward-pointing triangle button in the lower-left corner of the Gallery window. That minimizes the window and leaves a small additional toolbar just below the function bar. Click that, and the gallery reappears instantly. If you want it to just go away, choose Tools⇨Gallery again, and it'll vanish.

**Figure 10-5:**
Fun problem-solving graphics in gallery.

## *Main toolbar*

Confusingly, the main toolbar in Draw is the set of functions down the left side of the window. It includes such tools as

- ✔ Text
- ✔ Rectangle
- ✔ Ellipse
- ✔ 3-D Object
- ✔ Rotate
- ✔ Draw Arrow (or Line)
- ✔ Connect Objects

To add text to my picture, I click the T button to bring up the Text tool. The Object bar (the second horizontally oriented toolbar) changes to reflect text-editing options, including

- ✔ Typeface
- ✔ Size
- ✔ Style
- ✔ Alignment
- ✔ Spacing

I'll stick with the Thorndale typeface, bump up the size to 36 points, add bold, and then click the spot in the drawing where I want text. A blob of drag handles (the tiny green boxes on the edges of a rectangle in Draw) appears; just type and ignore that momentarily. I'll type in *National Ambulance Drivers Association Picnic.* Then, while the text object is still selected, I left-click and drag an edge of the box to the desired spot in the drawing. The result is shown in Figure 10-6.

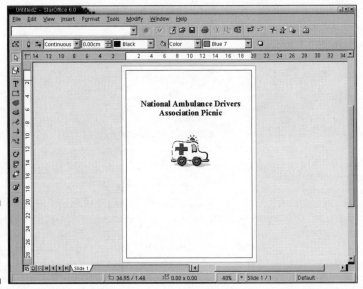

**Figure 10-6:**
Ambulance drivers need picnics too!

To wrap the new text with a rectangle with rounded corners, click the Rectangle tool on the main toolbar and hold down the mouse button. A tiny pop-up menu shows the various rectangle choices; choose the unfilled, rounded-edge rectangle. Then release the button, move the mouse to the top-left corner of the desired rectangle, and click and drag the rectangle to surround the text. The size marks are replaced by the rounded-corner rectangle.

If elements are squished together, click an element to select it. (When selected, the object gets drag handles and a bounding rectangle.) Then click and drag the object to its new place on the page.

## Cool backgrounds

To add a background fill to the entire page, use the Rectangle tool (with 90-degree corners) to define a rectangle the exact size of the page. Then click the Fill button on the Object toolbar (it's a tiny paint bucket spilling blue paint), which opens the Area dialog box. Click the Bitmaps tab and select the sky graphic, as shown in Figure 10-7.

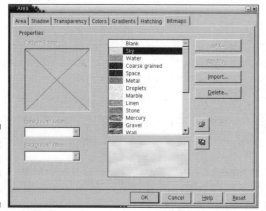

**Figure 10-7:**
Bitmap area
fill options
in Draw.

The sky graphic completely covers the text and graphic, but don't panic! With the new area still selected, click the Arrange button (two tiny gray boxes on the corners of a larger yellow box) and hold down the mouse button until the layering options appear. Select Send to Back, and watch what happens.

To finish up, let's apply a color fill to the newly created button shape, then ensure that the button label is visible over the new fill. Click the rounded-rectangle that's surrounding the text and then click the Fill button (the paint bucket). Click the Colors tab, select White, and click OK. Again, you need to push the graphic back so it's behind the text. This time, don't send it all the way to the back. Just choose Send Backward.

# Building Presentations with Impress

If you work in a business environment or are an educator, you're used to presenting complex ideas to colleagues or students. Whether it's the history of the Plantagenet family or the latest budget projections, knowing how to package your material as an attractive presentation is a great boon. That's the purpose of Impress. It's the equivalent of Microsoft PowerPoint and borrows many ideas from that ubiquitous application.

The easiest way to start StarOffice Impress is by starting Writer. Really.

In many ways, Writer is the core StarOffice application. The Impress program is really Writer in disguise.

# Starting a presentation

With Writer running, choose File⇨New⇨Presentation, which starts the AutoPilot Presentation wizard. (Sun doesn't actually call it a wizard. That's either because of a philosophical disagreement with Mr. Potter or Mr. Gates; I'll let you decide.)

1. **Decide whether you want to create a new presentation or open an existing presentation, as shown in Figure 10-8.**

   Because I want to create a new presentation, I opt for the Empty Presentation choice and click Next. The next window offers various slide designs.

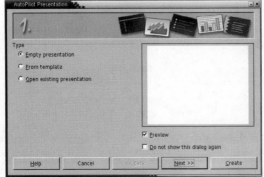

**Figure 10-8:**
The Impress AutoPilot Presentation window.

2. **Select a slide design, ensure that the output medium is correct (probably Screen), and then click Next.**

   I suggest one of the wonderful designs already defined in this library. My favorites include Celestial, Film Strip, Mondrian, and Mountain. For this presentation, Celestial will work just great.

3. **Choose the slide transition effects and the type of presentation, as shown in Figure 10-9.**

   Because the new presentation is for a group of students, I opt for Dissolve. There are some more exciting transitions here, including my favorite, Spiral Inward Clockwise.

   Depending on how fast your Solaris system is, you might also adjust the speed of the transition: Too fast, and it'll be missed, but too slow, and annoyed members of your audience will be yelling, "Just get to the next slide already!"

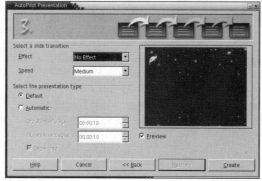

## Entering data

When you're ready to begin composing the Impress slides, click Create to build the skeleton of the new presentation.

Impress knows how to work with many types of slides, but usually the Title, Text Slides option works best. Choose it and then click OK. Now you can enter some data into this first slide.

1. **Click the text Click to Add Title and type in the title of the first slide.**

2. **Click to Add an Outline and add a few points; use Tab to move points to subpoints, and Enter to move to the next point.**

   I'll use a title of "All about Tintin" and an introductory outline, as shown in Figure 10-10. This figure also shows the slide layout and automatically applied text size and layout.

3. **To add other slides, click Insert Slide in the Presentation mini-window, or choose Insert⇨New Slide.**

4. **You can preview the newly created slide show with the many options on the Slide Show menu.**

One notable option is Slide Show, which launches a full-screen presentation of every slide, perfect for when you give the presentation.

For more on Impress, choose Help about StarOffice Impress in the main StarOffice help system.

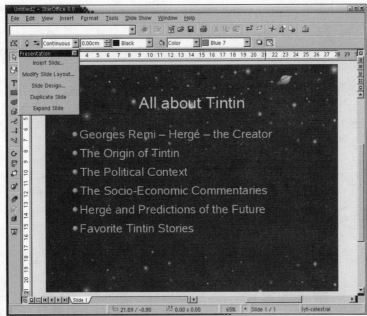

# Developing Web Pages

The Web page editor in StarOffice, sometimes called StarOffice Web for the command-line script `sweb` that launches the program, is really just Writer wearing yet another hat.

Chapter 9 covers other aspects of Writer.

StarOffice Web produces *obsolete* HTML (as does Writer). While consistent with HTML 3.2, most of how StarOffice approaches formatting specific elements (such as the extensive use of the FONT tag) has been replaced with the more powerful Cascading Style Sheets of HTML 4.0. If you're planning a complex Web page, you would do well to consider a more sophisticated tool. If you're building something simple, this is probably not a big deal.

The best way to begin editing an HTML page is to choose File➪New➪HTML Document. This pops up a blank page in Writer that appears almost identical to a blank document. The only difference is that the default text style is Text Body instead of Default.

Simply enter the text you want, formatting normally in Writer, centering, and so on.

- ✔ To create HTML-specific items, choose the text as appropriate and then apply the proper style.

- ✔ To add a horizontal rule, move the cursor to an appropriate spot and then choose Horizontal Line from the Style pop-up menu.

- ✔ To create a level one header, select the desired text and then apply the Heading 1 style.

- ✔ To insert a hyperlink, move to the desired spot and then choose Insert➪Hyperlink, which brings up the Hyperlink dialog box, shown in Figure 10-11.

  I filled in the two key fields in Figure 10-11:

  - • URL to reference

  - • Text displayed on the page

  Enter the link information and click Apply to have the link added to the Web page. (The dialog box doesn't go away. Just click the Close button to close it.)

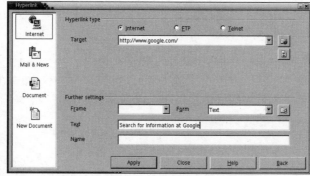

**Figure 10-11:**
The complex Hyperlink dialog box.

One annoyance is that the link is included in tiny text. Again, simply select the hyperlink and then change the typeface size. You can also center the link, as I've done on my page. The result of my efforts is shown in Figure 10-12.

To view the HTML source of the page, choose View➪HTML Source. The source HTML is shown for the developing page, as shown in Figure 10-13.

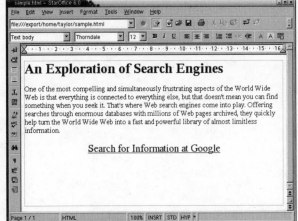

**Figure 10-12:**
A rudimentary Web page in Writer.

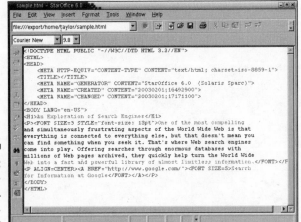

**Figure 10-13:**
The underlying HTML source.

# Part IV
# Editing and Controlling Programs

The 5th Wave                    By Rich Tennant

"We take network security very seriously here."

# In this part . . .

There's not much value to having lots of files in your Solaris account if you can't work with them, so this part introduces you to the key command line tools and GUI-based applications for viewing files, analyzing file content, editing files with vi, CDE Text Editor or the GNOME Text Editor. In addition, you'll get to explore some of the internals of Solaris to understand what processes are running and how to interact with them or — if you're feeling particularly aggressive — kill them. The last chapter in this part discusses two commands near and dear to every Solaris guru: find and grep. Both are definitely worth study, as you'll see!

# Chapter 11

# Exploring Text Files

● ● ● ● ● ● ● ● ● ● ● ● ● ● ● ● ● ● ● ● ● ● ● ● ● ● ● ● ● ● ● ● ● ● ● ● ● ● ● ●

## *In This Chapter*

▶ Viewing files within the graphical user interface (GUI)

▶ Viewing files at the command line

▶ Analyzing files with `wc` and `spell`

● ● ● ● ● ● ● ● ● ● ● ● ● ● ● ● ● ● ● ● ● ● ● ● ● ● ● ● ● ● ● ● ● ● ● ● ● ● ● ●

*O*ne of the most common tasks that you'll encounter working with a computer is viewing and editing text files. Whether they're Web pages written in HyperText Markup Language (HTML), e-mail messages written in plain text, or programs written in Perl or C, you'll probably find yourself spending an awful lot of time reading material on your screen and digitally manipulating words.

To that end, in this chapter, I focus on ways to view and analyze the contents of files by using standard Solaris tools, starting with the graphical user interface–based Text Note application. Then I jump directly to the command line and the remarkable capabilities available at your disposal there. Read on here to garner the basic tools you need to maneuver these tools before you begin editing within them. (Get the skinny on editing in Chapter 15.)

# *Viewing Files within the GUI*

The easiest way to view the contents of a file is, logically enough, to double-click it while in the graphical user interface (GUI). Unlike Windows and Macs, a couple of graphical environments are available within the Solaris environment:

✔ My preference is the GNU Network Object Management Environment (GNOME).

✔ You may personally prefer either of these environments:

- Common Desktop Environment

- The stripped, minimalist TWM (think nihilist, and you'll have the basic idea of TWM)

When you double-click a text file icon (typically visually identified as a small rectangle with dots that looks like a piece of paper with writing, from about 25 feet away), the window manager launches the program it thinks is the best match for that file type. Sometimes files have different icons and can also be identified by their suffixes. Many text files are for specific purposes and might have different icons, including

✔ .html for Web pages

✔ .c for C Programming Language source code files

✔ .sh for shell scripts

## Viewing in GNOME

Suppose that you're perusing your file system with Nautilus (the file system browser if you're running GNOME) or the Common Desktop Environment (CDE) file viewer, and you see a file that's worth a quick peek. (Chapter 2 explains the Solaris window managers.) Figure 11-1 illustrates how that file might look in GNOME. Just what is this gullivers.travels.txt file, and how can you see what's inside?

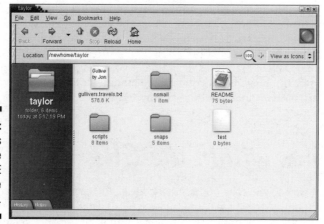

**Figure 11-1:**
Peruse files with the GNOME Nautilus file browser.

In Nautilus, view the contents of a file by simply double-clicking its icon. Nautilus displays the contents of the file directly in its own window, as shown in Figure 11-2.

In Figure 11-2, the text displayed under the file icon on the left side is slightly chopped off because of a mismatch between screen regions and typeface size. This doesn't always happen, but you'll find this sort of glitch time and again with GUIs in Unix for reasons that are a bit of a mystery to me. Just grin and get used to it!

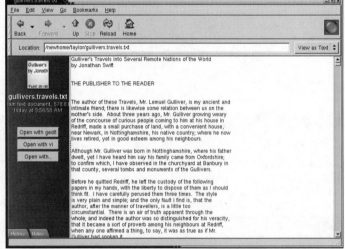

**Figure 11-2:**
A file displayed within Nautilus looks like this.

Pay attention to the list of buttons on the left side of the text under the file icon. Although you can view the contents of the file via Nautilus, you can also edit it or perhaps feed it to a formatter, compiler, mailer, meat grinder, or what have you. For a text file, your choices are

- ✔ gedit (the GNOME text editor)

- ✔ vi (the default screen-oriented editor used with terminals and xterm connections)

- ✔ Open With (an open-ended choice that lets you specify whatever program your heart might desire, such as emacs or even Netscape Navigator)

To move into an environment where you can edit this file, select one of the preceding choices. For example, click the Open with gedit button to open the file in gedit, as shown in Figure 11-3. Fortunately, your journey of discovery has had fewer perils than that of Gulliver!

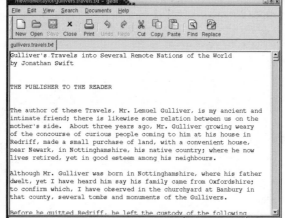

**Figure 11-3:**
View (and
edit) text
within the
gedit view.

If you choose Open With rather than Open with gedit and enter vi as the
program to use, the file opens in the vi editor, as shown in Figure 11-4.

**Figure 11-4:**
Another
way to edit
a text file in
GNOME:
Open the file
with the vi
editor.

# Browsing in CDE

The CDE file browser, shown in Figure 11-5, is undeniably less attractive than
Nautilus but offers the same basic functions. One of the options on the login
screen is to switch window managers, if you want to use CDE instead of
GNOME for a test run. (Chapter 2 covers this in more depth, if you're curious.)

Similar to Nautilus, the CDE file browser displays different icons based on file type to help you differentiate content. Common icons that you'll find here enable you to differentiate between plain text files, HTML documents, and directories.

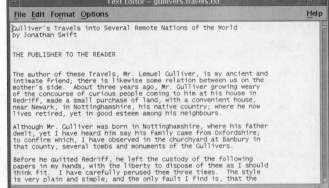

**Figure 11-5:** File browsing the CDE way.

Double-clicking the icon for `gullivers.travels.txt` reveals the contents of the file, as shown in Figure 11-6.

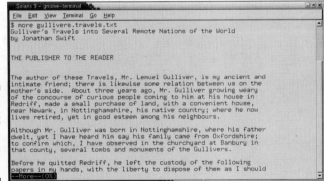

**Figure 11-6:** Use Text Editor to read files within CDE.

There is a subtle but important difference between how GNOME and CDE work:

✔ In GNOME, Nautilus displays the file directly without having to launch a separate program.

✔ CDE file browser is purely a file-browsing tool. It needs to open Text Editor to let you see the contents of the file.

Text Editor is a fairly rudimentary text editor, but it works for lightweight (think *quick*) editing jobs. If you'll be doing more complex edit work, consider a more powerful tool like StarOffice for formatting (see Chapter 9), or vi or emacs (Chapter 15) for lots of text massaging.

# Viewing Files at the Command Line

The command line is plebian, mundane, and visually uninteresting. It's also

- ✔ Fast
- ✔ Flexible
- ✔ Capable

Get to the command line by opening a terminal window with either of these steps:

- ✔ From the GNOME menu within GNOME
- ✔ On the CDE control bar, the Local Computer option on the pop-up menu above the CPU monitor

Solaris is case sensitive. Ls and ls are two different commands; only one will work as you want.

To view a directory, for example, use the handy ls (list files) command with the -F flag to have directories marked with a trailing / character. Why bother with -F? Because if you're looking at a large directory, being able to immediately see which are directories and which are files can be helpful. You'll see the following display ($ is the shell prompt; your shell prompt may be different, but the command you type is identical):

```
$ ls -F
gullivers.travels.txt      README              snaps/
nsmail/                    scripts/            test
```

As shown in Figure 11-1, there's no question that exploring the file system with a GUI-based tool is more attractive and probably easier to understand. But what if you want to see all the files with their exact size, permissions, and date of creation? How do you accomplish that in the GUI browser? It's not so easy.

At the command line, you simply add an additional command flag — -l — for long listing format:

```
$ ls -lF
total 1192
-rw-r--r--   1 taylor   other   592673 Oct  4 09:56 gullivers.travels.txt
drwx------   2 taylor   other      512 Oct  4 13:26 nsmail/
-rw-r--r--   1 taylor   other       75 Oct  4 12:52 README
drwxr-xr-x   2 taylor   other      512 Oct  4 13:26 scripts/
drwxr-xr-x   2 taylor   other      512 Oct  4 13:37 snaps/
-rw-r--r--   1 taylor   other        0 Oct  4 10:02 test
```

The preceding example gives the important information about the file:

✔ You can see how big `gullivers.travels.txt` actually is: 592,673 bytes (line 3).

✔ Only the owner (taylor) can *write* to the file (edit its contents).

✔ It was created on October 4 at 9:56 a.m. (line 3).

The sequence of characters at the beginning of each line of output is the *permission string:*

✔ The first character indicates the file type in the first space:

  • - is a regular file.

  • d is a directory.

✔ The following characters are interpreted in three-character sets:

  • Owner read, write, and/or execute

  • Group

  • Everyone else

In the preceding example, the `gullivers.travels.txt` file is read + write for owner, and read-only for group and everyone else. Chapter 4 has a detailed discussion of this important topic.

To see the contents of a file, use the `cat` command. Two of its most useful features are the ability to

✔ Number all the lines of input (`-n`)

✔ Show all the otherwise hidden and mysterious control characters (`-v`), such as ^M and ^J

A typical use of `cat` is to peek inside an executable file or graphics file.

## Of cats and dogs

The cat command is short for *concatenate,* not named after one of our feline friends. The Unix command biff *is* named after a dog, but that's another story! Don't try to use cat with lengthy files because invoking the cat command has a very important characteristic: It doesn't stop until it's done showing you the entire file.

Of course, you can try it on a very long file if you have some patience. When I used the cat command on the gullivers.travels.txt file, it only took approximately nine seconds on my high-speed connection. With a slow modem, well . . . you could easily pop into the kitchen for a quick cup of tea while you're waiting for the file display to finish scrolling.

Here's what happens when I peek into the contents of one of the XPM (X Windows Pixel Map) format screen shots for this chapter. For this example, I start by using cat and then enlist the head command to constrain the results to only the first ten lines so that I'm not drowned in output:

```
$ cd snaps
$ cat -v ch1101.xpm | head -10
/* XPM */
static char * ch1101_xpm[] = {
"811 576 76 1",
"        c #000000000000",
".        c #00002020AAAA",
"X        c #000000005555",
"o        c #000020200000",
"O        c #333340405555",
"+        c #000020205555",
"@        c #333320200000",
```

Adding the -n flag changes this output:

```
$ cat -nv ch1101.xpm | head -10
     1  /* XPM */
     2  static char * ch1101_xpm[] = {
     3  "811 576 76 1",
     4  "        c #000000000000",
     5  ".        c #00002020AAAA",
     6  "X        c #000000005555",
     7  "o        c #000020200000",
     8  "O        c #333340405555",
     9  "+        c #000020205555",
    10  "@        c #333320200000",
```

Adding the -n flag adds line numbers.

Consider what tools you want to be able to read text here at the command line.

The basic shell program for displaying a file one page at a time is more, named after its ever-present prompt at the end of each screenful. Just specify the program and the name of the file to view. In this example, enter the following line:

```
more gullivers.travels.txt
```

The results are shown in Figure 11-7.

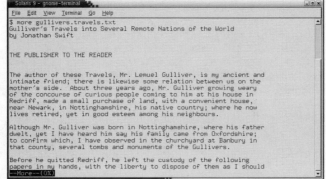

**Figure 11-7:** View a file, a screen at a time, from the more prompt.

To proceed to the next screenful of information, press the spacebar. To move down only a single line, press Enter.

The more program seems pretty simple, but it has quite a few options, including starting options and commands available at the more prompt. The most useful starting flags are listed in Table 11-1.

| Table 11-1 | Useful Starting Flags for more |
|------------|--------------------------------|
| *Flag* | *Use* |
| -s | Squeezes multiple blank lines to one. Very helpful if you're viewing files that have lots of empty lines. |
| -n | Shows only *n* lines per screenful. For example: -20. |
| +n | Starts at line *n* in the file. For example: +120. |
| +/ptrn | Starts a few lines above the first line in the file that matches *ptrn*. |

When you're at the `more` prompt, you have oodles of options. You can see them all by pressing ? (the question mark key). The list is a bit cryptic, so let me note that when it references 'k' lines of text, it means that you can type in a numeric value, then the command to have the command use the specified value rather than the default. For example, 8f will skip forward eight screenfuls of information, while f by itself skips one screen.

```
Most commands optionally preceded by integer argument k.  Defaults in brackets.
             Star (*) indicates argument becomes new default.
-----------------------------------------------------------------------------
<space>                 Display next lines of text [current screen size]
z                       Display next lines of text [current screen size]*
<return>                Display next k lines of text [1]*
d or ctrl-D             Scroll k lines [current scroll size, initially 11]*
q or Q or <interrupt>   Exit from more
s                       Skip forward k lines of text [1]
f                       Skip forward k screenfuls of text [1]
b or ctrl-B             Skip backwards k screenfuls of text [1]
'                       Go to place where previous search started
=                       Display current line number
/<regular expression>   Search for kth occurrence of regular expression [1]
n                       Search for kth occurrence of last r.e [1]
!<cmd> or :!<cmd>       Execute <cmd> in a subshell
v                       Start up vi at current line
h                       Display this message
ctrl-L                  Redraw screen
:n                      Go to kth next file [1]
:p                      Go to kth previous file [1]
:f                      Display current file name and line number
.                       Repeat previous command
-----------------------------------------------------------------------------
```

The most useful of these commands available within the `more` program are

- `space`: Shows the next screenful of information
- `q`: To quit without seeing the rest of the file
- `/ptrn`: To search for a pattern (and `n` to search for it again)
- `v`: To drop the file into `vi` and allow editing
- `:n`: To move to the next file if you specify a list of files to the program

Although it might not seem like there's much you can do with the `more` command, a number of different text file pager programs are available in Unix, although not all are available in all versions. For Solaris 9, functionally similar commands include

- `less`
- `pg`
- `page`

To use them, your best bet is to check out the man pages (type `man less` at the shell prompt, for example) or just try them on a file.

Using `more` and `page` move you forward in the file, and using `less` and `pg` can let you go back screenfuls if you decide that you want to either

 ✔ Start over

 ✔ See what's been displayed earlier

If you're in a terminal or `xterm` that has *scrolling* and a *scrollback buffer*, this capability is probably irrelevant because you can always move back through that mechanism.

# Analyzing Files with wc and spell

Although you have little apparent advantage to viewing files at the command line when compared with a slick graphical interface like GNOME, the ability to analyze and understand the contents of files through command utilities is part of what makes the command line shine as an interactive environment. You can count lines, words, and characters, discover spelling errors, and list all spelling gaffes in your documents.

Like the proverbial multitude of ways to skin a cat (which is a rather disgusting image if you think about it), you have a wide variety of ways to slice and dissect a text file by using the Unix command line and the hundreds of available commands. You can do much more here than just view a file page by page — you can calculate the most commonly used word in the file, the average length of a word, the average sentence complexity, the number of words, and even words that seem misspelled.

## Making every word count with the wc command

To find out how many words are in the file `gullivers.travels.txt`, use the `wc` (word count) command:

```
$ wc gullivers.travels.txt
   10382  106405  592673 gullivers.travels.txt
```

This output tells you that the file has 10,382 lines, 106,405 words, and 592,673 characters. If you imagine that you're on a 25-line terminal window, you'd have a rather exhausting 416 screenfuls to read the entire story (10,382 ÷ 25 = 416). (Be glad that you're not reading this file over a typical cell phone with about a 6-line display because you'd have to wade through 1,700 screens to read this short novel on your favorite Nokia or Ericsson!)

Counting words can also be important if you're a writer or student. As a writer, you often receive assignments similar to "write 500 words about . . ." or "your article can't be more than 900 words total." Now you know an easy way to ascertain this number without having to count by hand. In fact, you can specify -l, -w, and -c for lines, words, and characters, respectively. In the following, I only want to find the word count (wc -w) for this file:

```
$ wc -w gullivers.travels.txt
  106405 gullivers.travels.txt
```

## Korect yur speling with spell

Assuming that you can correctly type the name of the command, you can extract a list of misspelled words on the command line by using the spell command.

Drop the more command at the end of a pipe, and you can stop the flow of information before it begins scrolling off your screen.

```
$ spell gullivers.travels.txt  | more
11th
13th
11th
16th
17th
19th
20th
21st
24th
26th
2d
3d
abstersives
acquitted
Actium
adamantine
Agesilaus
Agrippa
Alban's
Alcoran
```

```
Amboyna
analysed
aperitives
--More--
```

Spelling-wise, well, the `spell` program isn't too bright with words that it doesn't know. The ordinals (11th, 20th, and so on) are all flagged as misspellings even though they're really not. The word *acquitted* is spelled correctly, so seeing it flagged as a misspelling is curious, too.

Regardless of whether every match is ideal, the program does generate lots of useful information. In combination with `wc`, you can quickly figure out how many spelling errors you have: The `-l` flag outputs only the number of lines in the input stream.

```
$ spell gullivers.travels.txt | wc -l
    500
```

Five hundred spelling errors! Gack!

One way to address this overly generous listing of spelling mistakes is to use a filter that automatically removes files that match a certain pattern. For example, you can chop out any word that begins with a capital letter and any word that contains a digit.

The easiest way to accomplish this is to use `egrep`, which is a cousin of the `grep` command. `egrep` works with regular expressions, a powerful, albeit arcane, set of pattern notations that look like gobbledygook but can detail just about anything. Here's how you can set it up:

1. **Start with the `(a|b)` notation to indicate that you want to match either pattern A or pattern B.**

   For the first pattern, there are two elements:

   - Specify a capital letter — `[A-Z]`.

   - Indicate that it should appear at the beginning of the line by prefacing the set with the special character `^`.

   Put them together, and your first pattern is `^[A-Z]`.

2. **The second pattern is a range of digits in a set that looks like this:**

   ```
   [0-9]
   ```

3. **An important `egrep` flag is also required: `-v`.**

   The `-v` flag reverses the logic of the match so that all lines that don't match the pattern (or patterns) are allowed.

It all combines to look like this:

```
$ spell gullivers.travels.txt | egrep -v '(^[A-Z]|[0-9])' |
         more
abstersives
acquitted
adamantine
analysed
aperitives
apophlegmatics
arbitress
asht
battalia
bedchamber
beeves
behaviour
bemired
bevil
biassed
bliffmarklub
blustrugs
bolus
burthen
c
calentures
candour
carabines
--More--
```

This clearly removes some of the false errors. How many? That's a job for wc
and its ever-helpful `-l` line-count-only flag:

```
$ spell gullivers.travels.txt | egrep -v '(^[A-Z]|[0-9])' |
         wc -l
    293
```

This output is useful, but only a tiny portion of the screen is being used
because of the one-word-per-line output format. To turn this output into a
multiple column format, use the `paste` command.

Unlike most Solaris commands that have all their flags prefaced by a dash (or
minus symbol or hyphen, depending on how you want to look at it), the
`paste` command uses the dashes as a format request:

- ✔ Use two dashes to create a two-column output.
- ✔ Use four dashes to create a four-column output.

Here's an example:

1. **Save the list of spelling errors into a temporary file so that you don't have to scan through the entire novel each time you test a command.**

   You can easily do this with the > file redirection, which saves all the spelling errors in a new file errors instead of streaming them on your screen:

   ```
   $ spell gullivers.travels.txt | egrep -v '(^[A-Z]|[0-9])'
          > errors
   $ wc -l errors
        293 errors
   ```

2. **Feed that file to the paste command and see what happens.**

   This step streams the file contents without pausing for screenfuls by using these commands:

   - cat
   - paste

   One column of data changes to four (count the number of dashes specified to the paste command to see where four came from):

   ```
   $ cat errors | paste - - - - | more
   abstersives     acquitted       adamantine      analysed
   aperitives      apophlegmatics  arbitress       asht
   battalia        bedchamber      beeves   behaviour
   bemired bevil   biassed bliffmarklub
   blustrugs       bolus   burthen c
   calentures      candour carabines       carcases
   casta   centre  cephalalgics    christian
   civilise        civilised       clamour climenole
   clyster colour  coloured        colours
   contemn coquetry        counsellors     craunch
   culverins       d       de      d'eau
   defence degul   dehul   demeanour
   demesne demesnes        desmar  despatch
   despatched      dexterous       dexterously     discoloured
   discources      dishonourable   dispair docible
   docs    donation.html   draught draymen
   drin    drurr   durst   dwuldom
   eBook   eBook's eBooks  email
   emposo  endeavour       endeavoured     endeavouring
   endeavours      endian  endians engendered
   equalled        etiam   favour  favourable
   favouring       favourite       favourites      favours
   finget  flandona        flestrin        flunec
   --More--
   ```

This isn't the most attractive output (because it isn't in neatly aligned columns), but if you can handle the messy results, it lets you review 100 of the 293 errors on a single screen.

If you want to learn Perl or awk, there are relatively straightforward ways to turn this into a neat page of aligned columns:

✔ For the skinny on Perl, check out *Perl For Dummies,* 4th Edition, by Paul Hoffman (Wiley Publishing).

✔ The best awk reference is online (it's for GNU awk, but it's functionally identical to Solaris awk):

```
www.linuxselfhelp.com/gnu/gawk/html_chapter/gawk_toc.html
```

# GUI versus the Command-Line Interface

Every time that I talk about how to do things in Solaris, I seem to get stuck on the same crazy debate: graphical interface versus command-line interface:

✔ Which is faster?

✔ Which is easier?

In this case, consider viewing text files because that's a nice, constrained category for discussion. In a nutshell, the advantages to using a GUI interface are the following:

✔ You can change the typeface used to display the text.

✔ You can fine-tune the colors and typeface size to make them as legible and readable as possible.

✔ You can position your cursor over the down arrow and then read page after page with a simple click of the mouse.

✔ You can manage graphics.

Obviously, you can't display a lovely new JPEG image of your dad's new motorcycle in a text-based environment. The main advantages of a graphical interface really don't surface until you step beyond simple text and get into either

✔ Formatted text (like this book, with bold, italics, different type faces, different sizes of type, and so on)

✔ Graphics

The advantages of a command-line interface are

✔ You can change the typeface, colors, and size to make the terminal window itself as readable as possible.

Well, that's not entirely fair because a number of people connect to Solaris systems through simple terminal interface programs or even dumb terminals (ya know, physical hardware, the kind of things you saw geeky engineers with gleaming pocket protectors staring at in horror in those 1960s sci-fi thrillers), and they definitely aren't very customizable.

✔ You can use a paging program (like `more`) to view text so each time you press the spacebar, you move forward a screenful.

✔ The command-line interface is way faster than a GUI.

One of the main arguments for a command-line interface is speed. Even with the fastest new Solaris system, the command line and its text-based interface are markedly faster than working in a graphical environment. Speed might not matter if you're scrolling a novel page by page, but if you frequently work with text files, being able to get that extra perfor-mance boost due to the increased efficiencies and power of the command line might prove to be worthwhile.

# Chapter 12

# Editing Files

· · · · · · · · · · · · · · · · · · · · · · · · · · · · · · · · · · · · · · · · · · · · · · ·

· · · · · · · · · · · · · · · · · · · · · · · · · · · · · · · · · · · · · · · · · · · · · · ·

*I*n the world of Solaris, most files are plain text without fancy typographic material, whether text, shell scripts, Web pages, or even C programs. No bold, no multiple font colors, no included graphics. Just text.

As a result, most Solaris users use vi, a powerful — albeit tricky to learn — text-only editor that lets you enter and modify text quickly.

This chapter introduces you to the basics of the text-editing tools in both CDE and GNOME and focuses primarily on how to work with the vi editor.

## Working with the CDE Text Editor

To launch Text Editor in the CDE environment, you can double-click an existing text file or start with a blank palette, an empty file. To start with a blank palette, click the arrow button immediately above the note icon on the CDE navigational bar (as shown in Figure 12-1) and then select Text Editor from the pop-up menu.

The editor starts with a blank window, as expected. Notice in Figure 12-2 that the new document has no name yet — (UNTITLED) is listed in the window's title bar — and that five menus are available.

**Figure 12-1:**
Launching
Text Editor
in CDE.

**Figure 12-2:**
Text Editor,
as first
launched.

From the left, the menus are File, Edit, Format, Options, and, far on the right, Help. The content of these menus is as follows:

- **File:** New, Open, Include, Save, Save As, Print, and Close

- **Edit:** Undo, Cut, Copy, Paste, Clear, Delete, Select All, Find/Change, and Check Spelling

- **Format:** Settings, Paragraph, and All

- **Options:** Overstrike, Wrap to Fit, Status Line, and Backup on Save

- **Help:** Overview, Tasks, Table of Contents, Reference, On Item, Using Help, and About Text Editor

To start, begin typing in some text. Because I'm working with the text from *Gulliver's Travels*, I'll begin with a brief introductory sentence.

Save yourself a lot of typing. Get a copy of the file gullivers.travels.txt from the Web at www.intuitive.com/solaris/.

If you make a mistake when typing in your text, you can either fix it with the keyboard or mouse: either backspace and fix it, or move the mouse to the problem spot and either click and erase characters to the left of the cursor with the Backspace key, or click and drag to select a problem passage, then either Backspace to delete it, or simply type the correct replacement.

## Text wrapping

By default, Text Editor expects you to press Enter each time you want to move to the next line. That's why in Figure 12-3 you can only read the last passage of the introduction I entered. By contrast, most modern text entry systems wrap the lines of text so that you can see all of your text at once.

**Figure 12-3:** Text entered, but all on one line.

Fortunately, you can change this behavior through the Options menu. Choose Options⇨Wrap to Fit. The text is instantly wrapped so that you can see everything entered so far. While you're working with the Options menu, also choose Options⇨Status Line to enable the editor to show you a useful and informative status line at the bottom of the window. The result of these two changes is shown in Figure 12-4.

**Figure 12-4:** Now you can see all the text and a status line to boot!

## *Including content from other files*

You can include the content of a file by choosing File⇔Include. This opens a standard CDE file selection dialog box, as shown in Figure 12-5. The example includes the content of the file `gullivers.travels.txt`.

If you choose Open rather than Include, the specified file replaces the current file being edited.

**Figure 12-5:** Searching for Gulliver in the Include a File dialog box.

Find the file `gullivers.travels.txt` (if you haven't downloaded it yet, there's a tip earlier in this chapter telling you where you can find it on the Web) and then click OK to open it.

The contents are almost instantaneously included into the existing edit buffer, and you're dropped down to the last line of text. Drag the scroll bar marker to the top of the file, and you'll see how the new material has been included after the existing text typed in earlier, as shown in Figure 12-6.

**Figure 12-6:** *Gulliver's Travels,* with a new introduction.

## Searching and replacing

It's easy to change all the occurrences of a pattern in text: Choose Edit⇨Find/ Change and then enter the old and new patterns in the Find/Change dialog box. Figure 12-7 changes *Gulliver* to *Kaelin* to update an old story a tiny bit.

**Figure 12-7:** Changing Gulliver to Kaelin.

Click Change All, and voilà! All changes are applied. Mr. Swift might be a wee tad appalled by this modification of his work, but I'll claim artistic license and keep going forward, okay? If you prefer to have *Gulliver's Travels* instead of *Kaelin's Travels,* simply choose Edit⇨Undo to reverse the changes.

## Saving files

Saving the file is easy. Choose File⇨Save As, to open the CDE Save As dialog box, as shown in Figure 12-8.

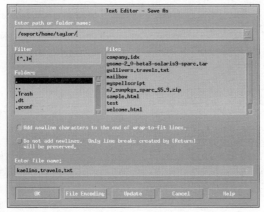

**Figure 12-8:** Saving the new document as a file.

Figure 12-8 shows that in addition to the standard filter, folder, and files windows, the Save As dialog box contains two unique options regarding how this file should be saved. You need to choose between these options:

✓ **Add Newline Characters to the End of Wrap-to-Fit Lines.** Select this option if you don't want to end up with a lot of extremely long lines.

✓ **Do Not Add Newlines. Only Line Breaks Created by [Return] Will Be Preserved.** If you're planning to open this file with a program like StarOffice Writer, you might want to deselect this option so that Writer can do its own line wrapping based on your formatting options.

Enter the filename, double-check that it's in the directory you want, and then click OK to save it. You're done!

# *Editing with the GNOME Text Editor*

The GNOME Text Editor (often called `gedit`) works much like the CDE Text Editor, as will become clear when you follow the same steps with *Gulliver's Travels* within the GNOME environment.

To launch the GNOME Text Editor, either double-click a text file icon or launch it from the GNOME menu by choosing Applications⇨Accessories⇨Text Editor, as shown in Figure 12-9.

**Figure 12-9:** Launching the GNOME Text Editor from the GNOME menu.

The GNOME Text Editor is more visually attractive than the CDE Text Editor, as shown in Figure 12-10. It's also more powerful, as suggested by the menu options. The most obvious difference is the toolbar icons, which are reminiscent of StarOffice Writer. From left to right, they are New, Open, Save, Close, Print, Undo, Redo, Cut, Copy, Paste, Find, and Replace.

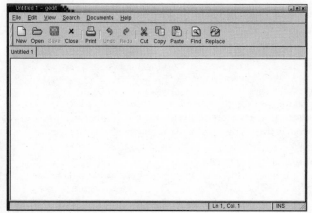

**Figure 12-10:**
The GNOME
Text Editor.

The menus are

✔ **File:** Items in the menu are:

- New
- Open
- Open Location
- Recent Files
- Save
- Save As
- Save All
- Revert
- Print Preview
- Print
- Close
- Close All
- Quit

✔ **Edit:** Items in the menu are:

- Undo
- Redo
- Cut
- Copy
- Paste
- Delete

- • Select All
- • Preferences

✔ **View:** Items in the menu are:

- • Toolbar
- • Statusbar
- • Customize Toolbar
- • Customize Statusbar

✔ **Search:** Items in the menu are:

- • Find
- • Find Next
- • Replace
- • Goto Line

✔ **Documents**

✔ **Help:** Items in the menu are:

- • Contents
- • About

One of the most useful menu options is File⇨Open Location. As its name suggests, this option enables you to easily open a Web page and examine its HTML source. You can make edits, but you can't save the Web page back to the remote server. Figure 12-11 shows the source to `www.sun.com/` as an edit window.

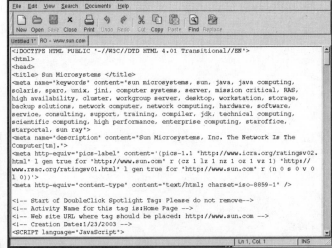

**Figure 12-11:**
The GNOME Text Editor lets you easily see HTML.

gedit offers a tabbed interface element under the toolbar:

✔ The original blank document is shown as Untitled 1

✔ The HTML source is shown as RO - www.sun.com.

If you guessed that RO is read-only, you're right!

To get back to the original blank edit window, click Close on the toolbar.

## *Including other files*

Although gedit has more capabilities than the CDE Text Editor, it doesn't have any facility to include the file's source in the existing document. To work around this, you can use cut and paste.

Click the Open button on the toolbar to open the gullivers.travels.txt file. You're presented with a typical GNOME Open File dialog box, as shown in Figure 12-12. Select the file and click OK.

**Figure 12-12:**
Opening a
file in
GNOME
Text Editor.

You now have both the original file, with the one sentence typed in, and the gullivers.travels.txt file open. Each file has its own tab.

To copy and paste *Gulliver's Travels*, follow these steps:

1. Make sure you're viewing gullivers.travels.txt (the file you want to copy)

2. Choose Edit➪Select All to select all the text

3. Click the Copy button on the toolbar to copy the text into the buffer.

4. Click the Untitled 1 tab to switch to the other window

5. Move the cursor below the text that's typed

6. Click the Paste button on the toolbar.

The result is shown in Figure 12-13.

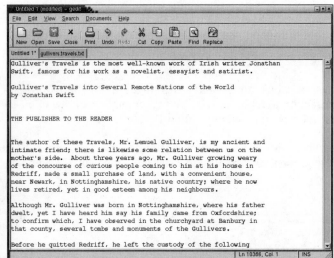

**Figure 12-13:**
Simulating
include file
contents.

## Doing a global search and replace

The basic process of globally searching for a pattern and replacing it with another is identical to the CDE Text Editor. This time, change *Gulliver* to *Terri* instead of *Kaelin*. Click the Replace button on the toolbar to open the Replace dialog box, shown in Figure 12-14.

**Figure 12-14:**
Global
search and
replace in
GNOME
Text Editor.

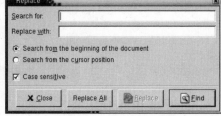

In the Search For box, enter **Gulliver**, and in the Replace With box, enter **Terri**. You also need to decide whether to search from the beginning of the document, or from the current cursor position through the end of the document. Because this is a global search and replace, select the option to search from the beginning.

Searches in the GNOME Text Editor can be case-sensitive. (For example, Gulliver will match, but gulliver and GULLIVER will not.) Usually, you want to select the Case Sensitive option — which is selected by default.

Now you're ready. Click Replace All, and you'll see a small results window that, in this case, shows the message Found and replaced 9 occurrences. A great addition!

Click OK to dismiss the information box, and click Close to dismiss the Replace dialog box. The new, perhaps improved, *Terri's Travels into Several Remote Nations of the World* is shown.

## *Saving files*

When the file is the way you want it, save it by following these steps:

1. **Click the Save button on the toolbar.**

   Although the graphic makes it look like the Save function is *grayed out* (unavailable), pay attention to the word *Save* instead: If it's black, you can use this button.

   The Save dialog box pops up, as shown in Figure 12-15.

**Figure 12-15:**
The Save
File dialog
box,
GNOME
Style.

2. **Enter the name you want and ensure that the directory location is correct.**

3. **Click OK.**

   The file is saved. You're done!

# Using the vi Text Editor

If you're a die-hard Solaris user and think that mice and graphical interfaces are for wimps and newbies, you're not alone. For those folks seeking speed over appearance, the vi editor — originally written by Bill Joy while at the University of California, Berkeley (and now a VP at Sun Microsystems) — is an excellent answer.

Working with vi is unlike anything you've seen so far in this chapter because you must do everything, from cursor motion to search and replace, from the keyboard. If this suggests that there's a bit of a learning curve, you're right. But persevere, and you'll find yourself in excellent company as you discover how to be a Solaris power user!

The vi editor runs in a *terminal window*. Chapter 3 explains how to open one.

## Understanding modes

Perhaps the most puzzling aspect of vi is that it is a modal editor. These are the two modes of operation:

- **Insert mode:** If you're in insert mode and type an *x,* the letter is added to the document at the current cursor point.

- **Command mode:** If you're in command mode, the *x* command causes the letter under the cursor to be *deleted,* not added.

Fortunately, there's a trick to starting up vi that enables a mode display function on the bottom line of the screen. This display quickly tells you whether you're in insert or command mode. Rather than specify the show-mode feature manually each time you start vi, open a terminal window and type the following:

```
echo "set showmode" >> ~/.exrc
```

Do that once, and you've created a custom preferences file for vi (yes, it should be called .virc, but that's a long story). You don't have to ever think about it again.

Chapter 3 explains the terminal and command shell in depth.

## Starting vi

You can start the vi editor from the command line several ways:

- ✔ Type vi on the command line:

  ```
  $ vi
  ```

- ✔ Specify the name of an existing file to edit or a new file to create:

  ```
  $ vi my.new.file
  ```

- ✔ You can also specify a list of filenames if you want. You can finish editing the first file, and then move to the second, and so on to modify a batch of files in sequence.

To parallel the tasks done earlier in this chapter, start vi by specifying the name you want to create:

```
$ vi ashley.travels.txt
```

The result of this command is shown in Figure 12-16.

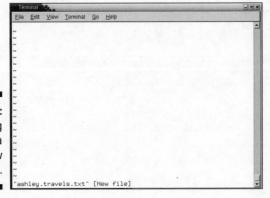

**Figure 12-16:** vi starting up with a brand new file.

The File, Edit, View, and other menus are for the terminal application, not vi. The vi program has no fancy interface elements, just whatever you type at the keyboard.

Figure 12-16 shows that vi is bare bones. There's no menu at the bottom, just a cursor at the top-left corner and a bunch of tilde symbols (~) running down the left side. The lines prefaced with tilde symbols are *placeholders,* not part of the file. They're beyond the end of the file being edited.

## Entering text

By default, the editor starts out in command mode: Type an *x,* and you'll hear a beep as the editor tells you that there's nothing to delete. You can move into insert mode several ways, depending on where you want to insert text. In fact, vi has dozens and dozens of commands, enough that I could probably write *vi For Dummies.* But I won't!

I'll stick with the basics. At the end of this chapter, I suggest some places you can go online to find out more about vi if you're interested.

- ✔ To insert just before the current cursor location (where the flashing block is sitting), press i.
- ✔ To insert just after the current cursor location, use *a* to append text.
- ✔ To insert just above the current line by creating a new blank line, use O (capital o).
- ✔ To insert into a new blank line just below the current line, use o (lowercase o).

Jump into this by pressing *i* and typing in the introductory sentence used earlier in this chapter. After you type it in, the screen looks like Figure 12-17. To make this interesting, add a few random nonsense characters at the end of what you type in.

**Figure 12-17:**
I just
entered
some text in
insert mode.

Notice that the bottom-right corner says INSERT MODE. That's the show mode feature giving a visual clue of what mode you're in.

To leave insert mode and get back to command mode, press the magic key —
Esc. Intelligently, the Esc key has no function in command mode. You can
press it any time you want to be in command mode and aren't sure what
mode you're in. It just beeps.

## Moving in the file

Because v i has no scroll bars and no mouse support, it has a set of keys that
you can use in command mode to move around.

On Solaris, you can also use the arrow keys on your keyboard unless you're
connected remotely, in which case they may or may not work.

The four key movement keys are h, j, k, and l:

  ✔ h moves one character to the left.

  ✔ j moves one line down.

  ✔ k moves one line up.

  ✔ l moves one character to the right.

Try using these four keys to move around. If these letters start to appear in
your document, you're still in insert mode and need to press the Esc key.

  ✔ You can move one word at a time with w or b, depending on whether
    you want to move forward one word or backward one word.

  ✔ You can jump to the beginning of the line with 0 (zero) and to the end of
    the line with $.

  ✔ To move page by page, when the file is sufficiently large to have pages of
    text, use

      • ^F to move forward a page

      • ^B to move back a page

      • ^D to move down half a page

      • ^U to move up half a page

  ✔ You can jump to the first line of the file with 0G (zero followed by G) and
    to the end of the file with G by itself.

Use motion keys to move to the first letter of the extraneous stuff you added
to the file. Now press the x key a few times. Each time you press it, you
should see the letter under the cursor deleted and the text slide left to fill the
now open hole. Figure 12-18 shows my results after five x commands.

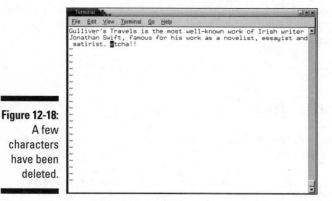

**Figure 12-18:**
A few
characters
have been
deleted.

Finish up the delete process so that there are no stray characters. Then use
the *a* append function to add a few carriage returns immediately after the
period ending the sentence. The cursor should now be on the last line, with
at least one blank line separating it from the text in the file.

## *Including other files*

To include the contents of another file, you need to jump to the vi command
line.

✔ You do this by typing :, at which point the cursor immediately jumps to
the bottom-left corner of the screen.

Type in the following command:

```
r gullivers.travels.txt
```

This is shown in Figure 12-19.

**Figure 12-19:**
Reading a
file into the
buffer.

✔ After pressing Enter, the contents of the file are injected into the buffer, exactly as you saw in the GNOME Text Editor and CDE Text Editor. This result is shown in Figure 12-20.

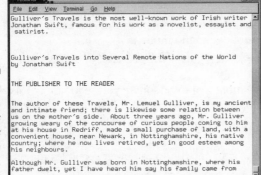

**Figure 12-20:**
With
*Gulliver's
Travels*
included in
the file.

## Doing a global search and replace

One of the ugliest parts of vi is that it's difficult to perform a global search and replace without seeing the pistons and oil stains under the hood. Just as reading in a file required a : prefix to jump to command mode, so does the search and replace.

The basic idea is that you want the editor to

✔ Search for an old pattern

✔ Replace it with a new one

In vi terms, this is

```
s/old/new/
```

However, this command by itself will only do one replacement on the current line.

✔ You need to preface it with an *address selector* that specifies the range of lines from the first to the last. The first line, unsurprisingly, is 1, and the last line is $. Now you have:

```
1,$s/old/new/
```

This is almost what you need. This will replace the first occurrence of old with new on every line. To have it replace every occurrence of old with new, add the g suffix to request that the substitution occur globally on the line. Now, finally, the command:

```
1,$s/old/new/g
```

✔ To specifically change all occurrences of Gulliver to Ashley, the complete command from command mode is

```
:1,$s/Gulliver/Ashley/g
```

Type this in, and almost instantaneously you're looking at *Ashley's Travels into Several Remote Nations of the World.*

✔ If you don't want this change applied after all, type u to undo it.

The Solaris version of vi can only undo the most recent command. It's a little quirk of vi that takes some getting used to.

✔ If you apply a global search and replace and then insert some text, the undo reverses the insertion.

✔ If you type u again, it will *undo the undo* (redo the insertion).

## *Saving files*

The final step on this journey is to save the new file. You started vi with the new filename. To save the file with that name, type one of these commands:

✔ :w writes the file and stays in vi.

✔ :wq writes the file and quits vi.

ZZ writes out the file if it has changed and then quits, without the command line (:) sequences.

If you entered more than one file, use :w to write out this file and then :n to move to the *next* file on your list.

To quit and discard the changes that you have made, add a ! to the end of the command, like this:

```
:q!
```

## Learning more about vi

Although `vi` might seem too much hassle to learn, there are a million and one capabilities in this remarkable editor, including the ability to

✔ Feed paragraphs of text to the Solaris command line and replace the text with the output of the command

✔ Read in the output of commands like `ls` and `uptime` into the file buffer

I have used `vi` for over 20 years and find it at least five times faster than any mouse- and cursor-oriented editor. If you're looking for speed and are okay with skipping the frosting and whipped cream of the graphical interface, it's worth learning.

Here are several fine online resources:

✔ A good start is `docs.sun.com`. Start with the *Solaris Advanced User's Guide* at `docs.sun.com/db/doc/806-7612`.

✔ The University of Hawaii offers *Mastering the Vi Editor* online for free download at `www.eng.hawaii.edu/Tutor/vi.html`.

✔ It's worth visiting the *Vi Lovers Home Page* at `www.thomer.com/vi/vi.html`.

# Chapter 13

# Controlling Processes

This chapter delves into the system administration side of Solaris. It explores processes and the various tools in Solaris that enable you to identify what programs are consuming the most resources on your system, how to figure out who is running those processes, and how to manage them for maximum performance on your Solaris system.

If you're used to working with a Windows system, you are probably under the impression that when you're running a program like Adobe Photoshop that's the only thing happening on the computer. That's far from the truth, though Windows does go out of its way to hide the rest of the active processes. You can tell that they're there if you leave an MP3 player running — it continues to play music even while you are busy editing photographs — and sometimes you'll get pop-ups from other programs like Norton AntiVirus letting you know an upgrade or update is available.

Solaris, coming from the Unix world, has the same ability to run multiple tasks simultaneously, but it doesn't try to hide anything from you. A number of commands can show you how many things are going on behind the scenes.

As a fundamental building block, though, Solaris works with *processes,* programs that are running or sleeping, waiting for a specific event to occur. The entire operating system and graphical interface are designed around this concept. If you have X11 and GNOME running, you might well have more than 50 processes active.

# Finding Top Processes

To figure out the busiest processes, and much more, use the prstat command. By default, it shows you the state of all processes, sorted by CPU usage, and updates the screen every ten seconds, as shown in Figure 13-1.

**Figure 13-1:**
Output of
the prstat
command.

```
Terminal                                                                         _ □ ×
File  Edit  View  Terminal  Go  Help
   PID USERNAME   SIZE    RSS STATE   PRI NICE      TIME  CPU PROCESS/NLWP
   933 taylor     13M    10M sleep     53    0   0:07:27 2.0% metacity/1
   826 root       40M    29M run       39    0  76:39:44 1.7% Xsun/1
   939 taylor     19M    13M run       49    0   0:01:18 1.3% gnome-terminal/1
   937 taylor     22M    16M sleep     56    0   0:13:50 0.5% gnome-panel/1
  3508 taylor   4568K  4280K cpu0      56    0   0:00:00 0.3% prstat/1
   928 taylor   3712K  2760K sleep     59    0   0:00:37 0.2% xscreensaver/1
  3495 taylor   4584K  4336K sleep     59    0   0:00:00 0.1% prstat/1
   755 taylor   3928K  3056K sleep     49    0   0:00:01 0.1% xterm/1
   931 taylor   9208K  5328K sleep     59    0   0:00:30 0.1% gnome-smproxy/1
  3507 taylor    936K   704K sleep     59    0   0:00:00 0.0% sleep/1
   305 root     2336K  1864K sleep     59    0   0:42:21 0.0% mibiisa/7
  3506 taylor   2608K  1504K sleep     59    0   0:00:00 0.0% bash/1
   249 root     2600K  2016K sleep     59    0   0:00:01 0.0% vold/2
   245 root     1720K  1096K sleep     59    0   0:00:00 0.0% smcboot/1
   246 root     1720K   680K sleep     59    0   0:00:00 0.0% smcboot/1
   248 root     1720K   680K sleep     59    0   0:00:00 0.0% smcboot/1
   894 taylor   4008K  2288K sleep     59    0   0:00:00 0.0% sdt_shel1/1
   208 root     2272K  1400K sleep     59    0   0:00:23 0.0% cron/1
   224 root     1416K  1096K sleep     59    0   0:00:01 0.0% powerd/3
   184 root     2184K  1456K sleep     59    0   0:00:00 0.0% lockd/2
   178 daemon   2464K  1792K sleep     59    0   0:00:00 0.0% statd/1
   201 root     3352K  1784K sleep     59    0   0:00:09 0.0% syslogd/12
Total: 81 processes, 146 lwps, load averages: 0.06, 0.36, 0.47
```

In Figure 13-1, the last line of the output shows that 81 processes are active. That's a lot of activity on a single-user workstation! In addition, some processes have more than one subprocess, called a *lightweight process* (lwp), and a total of 146 lwps are running.

In the default output of prstat, all processes are shown, sorted by CPU usage. In Figure 13-1, the GNOME window manager Metacity is the most active process, with 2.0% of the CPU time.

The Xscreensaver process is taking up CPU time (only 0.2%) even though no screensaver is currently being displayed. This is symptomatic of some poorly behaved applications that can consume computing resources even though they're invisible to the user.

If you leave prstat running, it updates the computer usage snapshot every five to ten seconds, giving you a rolling view of how your computer is being used. There are ten columns of prstat output:

✔ **PID:** The process ID (unique to each process running).

✔ **USERNAME:** The login name or real user ID of the process owner.

✔ **SIZE:** The total virtual memory size of the process.

✔ **RSS:** The *resident set size* of the process (the amount of real memory taken by the process).

✔ **STATE:** The current state of the process. Values can be

- cpu*N* (the process is running on CPU *N*)
- sleep (the process is waiting for an event to complete)
- run (the process is in the run queue waiting to be executed)
- zombie (the process has been terminated; the parent is not waiting)
- stop (the process has been stopped).

✔ **PRI:** The priority of the job: Larger numbers mean higher priority.

✔ **NICE:** The *nice value* used in priority computation. It can be used to raise or lower the priority of a given process.

✔ **TIME:** The cumulative execution time for the process.

✔ **CPU:** The percentage of CPU time used by the process.

✔ **PROCESS:** The name of the executable file running.

✔ **NLWP:** The number of lightweight processes in the process.

The information in Figure 13-1 shows that Metacity has these properties:

✔ It's being run by user taylor.

✔ It has PID 933

✔ It has a virtual memory size of 13MB

✔ It has an RSS of 10MB.

✔ It's in a sleep state (although it is using some CPU cycles),

✔ It has a relatively low priority of 53 (system jobs have a priority of 59, for example),

✔ It has no nice value

✔ It has used a cumulative seven minutes and 27 seconds of execution time.

✔ It's using 2.0% of the CPU time

✔ It has one lightweight thread (meaning that it doesn't use threads).

# *Processor Usage, by User*

prstat has an output format that's particularly useful if you're trying to identify which users are hogging the CPU resources: -t. As shown in Figure 13-2, the -t flag produces a list of processor usage summarized by user.

```
Terminal                                                          _ □ ×
File  Edit  View  Terminal  Go  Help
NPROC USERNAME   SIZE   RSS MEMORY      TIME  CPU                    ▲
   36 taylor     253M  181M    18%   0:28:21 4.2%
   34 root       131M   89M   9.0%  77:25:16 2.1%
    9 nobody      41M   27M   2.7%   0:00:00 0.0%
    1 smmsp     4280K 1432K   0.1%   0:00:13 0.0%
    1 daemon    2464K 1792K   0.2%   0:00:00 0.0%




Total: 81 processes, 146 lwps, load averages: 0.01, 0.02, 0.11    ▼
```

**Figure 13-2:**
Processor
usage, by
account.

In Figure 13-2, most of the processes are owned by either taylor or root. The
root processes are probably demons and other processes intended to run in
the background. Notice the cumulative execution time for the root processes:
a rather impressive 77 hours, 25 minutes, and 16 seconds.

Another useful flag is -s *sortkey,* which enables you to change the sorting of
the output. Possible keys are

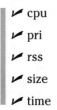

✔ cpu

✔ pri

✔ rss

✔ size

✔ time

Couple this flag with the -n flag (which lets you limit the number of lines
output) to ascertain

✔ Which applications are using the most physical memory:

```
$ prstat -s rss -n 5
   PID USERNAME   SIZE   RSS STATE  PRI NICE      TIME  CPU PROCESS/NLWP
   826 root       40M   29M sleep    49    0  76:39:49 0.0% Xsun/1
   925 taylor     25M   19M sleep    59    0   0:00:01 0.0% gnome-settings-
               /1
   937 taylor     22M   16M sleep    59    0   0:13:50 0.0% gnome-panel/1
   912 taylor     19M   14M sleep    59    0   0:00:01 0.0% gnome-session/1
   939 taylor     19M   13M sleep    49    0   0:01:21 0.0% gnome-terminal/1
Total: 79 processes, 144 lwps, load averages: 0.03, 0.04, 0.10
```

✔ Which applications are taking up the most time:

```
$ prstat -s time -n 5
   PID USERNAME  SIZE   RSS STATE   PRI NICE      TIME  CPU PROCESS/NLWP
   826 root       40M   29M sleep    49    0  76:39:49 0.0% Xsun/1
   937 taylor     22M   16M sleep    59    0   0:13:50 0.0% gnome-panel/1
   933 taylor     13M   10M sleep    59    0   0:07:29 0.0% metacity/1
   948 taylor     18M   12M sleep    49    0   0:02:58 0.0% mixer_applet2/1
   939 taylor     19M   13M sleep    49    0   0:01:21 0.0% gnome-terminal/1
Total: 79 processes, 144 lwps, load averages: 0.01, 0.04, 0.09
```

# Understanding Running Processes

Everything that's happening on your Solaris system, every program running, visible or not, is a process. Here's how individual processes are utilizing the system resources.

## What's your uptime?

To further understand how a Solaris system is being used or overused, as the case may be, use uptime, another terrifically useful command:

```
$ uptime
  9:17am  up 28 day(s), 22:25,  3 users,  load average: 0.00, 0.02, 0.08
```

In this humble one-line output, it shows you

✔ Current time

✔ How long the system has been running since its last reboot

✔ How many users are connected

✔ Load average

The load average numbers — an average count of the number of jobs in the run queue (either running or ready to run) for the last 1, 5, and 15 minutes — can be confusing for users.

Watch these values to get a sense of how busy the system is.

✔ The larger the value, the busier the system.

✔ Changes in workload can be found by comparing values:

> • If values are increasing left-to-right, then your system was busier in the past than it is currently.
>
> • If values are decreasing left-to-right, your system is busier than it has been for a while.

✔ Uptime load averages of less than one or two are the norm on a workstation and demonstrate that there's plenty of horsepower to run the necessary processes and manage the current demand on the system.

✔ If you get into two-digit load averages, things are busy.

✔ Three-digit load averages are one way that the Solaris operating system might be gasping for help, requesting another CPU or even a second computer to offload some of the busiest processes.

## *Other processor status tools*

Although `prstat` is a great program, it's a Solaris-only application. Other Unixes have commands to offer similar information, such as

```
top

monitor
```

What they all rely on is an underlying command called `ps`, which shows processor status and a lot more.

Like many Solaris commands, `ps` has a plethora of command line arguments, but these are the most useful:

✔ `-l` offers a long output format.

✔ `-L` shows information on each lightweight process.

✔ `-U` userid only lists processes for the specified login name, and you can always specify a process ID to get information about just that process.

For example, in Figure 13-1 most processes have only a single lightweight process within, whereas a process called mibiisa has 7 lwps. Now you can look inside this process to see what's what:

```
$ ps -L -l -p 305
 F S   UID   PID  PPID  LWP  C PRI NI    ADDR      SZ  WCHAN TTY   LTIME CMD
 8 S     0   305   277    1  0  40 20       ?     292    ? ?    0:00 mibiisa
 8 S     0   305   277    2  0  40 20       ?     292    ? ?   22:21 mibiisa
 8 S     0   305   277    3  0  40 20       ?     292    ? ?    3:54 mibiisa
 8 S     0   305   277    4  0  40 20       ?     292    ? ?    4:00 mibiisa
 8 S     0   305   277    5  0  40 20       ?     292    ? ?    4:08 mibiisa
 8 S     0   305   277    6  0  40 20       ?     292    ? ?    3:54 mibiisa
 8 S     0   305   277    7  0  40 20       ?     292    ? ?    4:04 mibiisa
```

## Solaris Management Console

Solaris includes a powerful, graphically oriented admin tool that encompasses many of the capabilities already shown in this chapter, and much more.

To launch the Solaris Management Console, type `smc` on the command line. After stepping through some configuration and login windows, the System Status – Processes view appears, as shown in this figure.

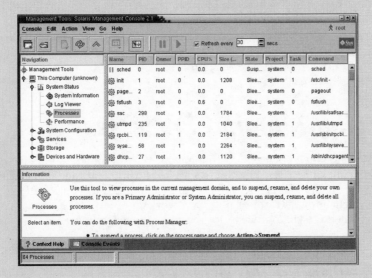

You can find out more about SMC at the Sun documentation site `docs.sun.com`. In particular, the System Administration Guide at `docs.sun.com/db/doc/806-4073` is a good place to start. Don't forget that if you've installed the AnswerBook system on your own Solaris system, the documentation is already on your computer.

Frankly, nothing here is that revealing, other than that some threads seem to get more execution time than others. If you were involved with the development of this task, you could use this information to go back into the program and try to see why lwp #2 is using almost ten times the execution time of any other lwp.

A more common usage of ps is to see all processes associated with a specific user:

```
$ ps -l -U nobody
 F S   UID   PID  PPID  C PRI NI  ADDR     SZ  WCHAN TTY    TIME CMD
 8 S 60001  4129  4128  0  40 20    ?     626    ? ?       0:00 httpd
 8 S 60001  4132  4128  0  40 20    ?     595    ? ?       0:00 httpd
 8 S 60001  4130  4128  0  40 20    ?     595    ? ?       0:00 httpd
 8 S 60001  4133  4128  0  40 20    ?     595    ? ?       0:00 httpd
 8 S 60001  4131  4128  0  40 20    ?     626    ? ?       0:00 httpd
 8 S 60001  4135  4128  0  40 20    ?     595    ? ?       0:00 httpd
 8 S 60001  4134  4128  0  40 20    ?     595    ? ?       0:00 httpd
 8 S 60001  4136  4128  0  40 20    ?     595    ? ?       0:00 httpd
```

These are the processes owned by user nobody. The processes are all owned by *parent process* (PPID) #4128, which means that process 4128 started up all the other httpd (Web server) processes.

# Managing Running Processes

How do you change what's running on your computer, either changing priority or killing a process or set of processes? It turns out that — unsurprisingly — a set of commands offers these very capabilities to you, whether you're a system administrator or not. They work differently for a regular user, but if you need to kill a process, for example, these are fine.

## Changing job priority

By default, all user processes have a nice level of zero: They are neither more nor less important than all other user jobs.

To start a process with a specific priority level, use the eponymously named nice command:

```
$ nice +5 batchjob.sh
```

This would start the named shell script with a priority that's (ready for this?) five *lesser* than a normal user job. This is a polite way of invoking long, compute-intensive processes that would otherwise monopolize the CPU. If it doesn't matter whether this batchjob.sh script finishes in three minutes or five, this is unquestionably the way to go.

Regular users cannot raise the priority of a task — that's only for root — but the full range of priorities accepted by nice are –19 to +20, where zero is the default priority. Again, higher values are lower priority processes, whereas lower values are higher priority processes.

If the process is already running, you can use `renice` to adjust its priority accordingly. If you have mpg123, an MP3 audio player, running and you ascertained that its PID is 5238, you can lower its importance to the system with:

```
$ renice +1 5238
```

You cannot raise its importance as a regular user:

```
$ renice +1 5238
renice: 5238: Cannot lower nice value.
```

Adjusting nice values appropriately is a smart way to stay in good standing with the central system administration team if you're part of a large shared Solaris environment.

## Killing unwanted processes

If you can change the priority of a running process, it should be no surprise that you can also kill a process.

- ✔ If you're a regular user, you can kill only your own processes
- ✔ If you're root, you can kill anything, even if it'll stop the entire computer dead in its tracks.

Generally, you kill processes by referencing their process IDs. To kill the MP3 player mentioned earlier, you'd use:

```
$ kill 5238
```

The `kill` program just sends a *signal* to the process; some processes ignore certain signals. A general rule is to repeat the `kill` command any time you use it to ensure that you get an error that indicates the process really was killed:

```
$ kill 5238
kill: (5238) - No such pid
```

This means that the first `kill` worked. If it hadn't worked, there would be no output, in which case it'd be time to escalate the signal to one that is more likely to work. In order, you should use the default signal, then a signal 15, and then a signal 9. Specific signals are listed with a leading dash. For example, the following command sends signal 15 (SIGINT, an interrupt signal) to process 5238:

```
$ kill -15 5238
```

## Killing processes by name

Killing processes by name is risky. If you match the wrong process, it's killed, and that's that. In Solaris, pgrep is a useful front end to pkill (the kill by name tool). It accepts all the same flags and just shows you a list of matching processes:

```
$ pgrep -l sh
    3 fsflush
  894 sdt_shell
  756 bash
  302 sshd
  920 sh
  896 bash
 4155 bash
 3463 bash
```

This lists the process ID and command name for all processes that match the pattern sh. To kill all the bash processes, for example, use:

```
$ pkill bash
```

If you kill your login shell, you'll be logged out!

# Chapter 14

# Finding Files

. . . . . . . . . . . . . . . . . . . . . . . . . . . . . . . . . . . . . . . . . . . . . .

## In This Chapter

▶ Finding files in graphical environments

▶ Searching by content with `grep`

▶ Specifying search attributes with `find`

. . . . . . . . . . . . . . . . . . . . . . . . . . . . . . . . . . . . . . . . . . . . . .

*O*ne of the most curious things about how people use computers is that although the system supports descriptive filenames, directories, and subdirectories, most users still end up with hundreds of files named `Joe-2.doc`, `sample.from.mr`, and similar, leading to crazy, impossible-to-navigate home directories.

The best way to address this is to impose some self-discipline, with logically organized folders and, at the least, well-named files. (Consider how much easier it is to understand `Eco, Umberto, 5 Feb 03` as a filename — particularly if it's in a directory called `Letters` — than a file cryptically called `ltr-eco-5.3` or similar.)

Whether or not you can accomplish this great file-naming feat, it's a sure bet that at some point you'll need a specific file without knowing where it is in your file hierarchy or perhaps without remembering the filename. That's what the various tools explored in this chapter address: finding files by

- ✔ Name
- ✔ Attributes
- ✔ Content

## Finding Files with File Manager

If you're still in the world of the Common Desktop Environment, the CDE File Manager offers some useful file search capabilities, though they are relatively hidden.

Launch the File Manager by clicking the Home Folder button (with the file cabinet on it) on the CDE taskbar, as shown in Figure 14-1. The File Manager pops up, displaying an icon for each file or folder in your home directory, as shown in Figure 14-2.

**Figure 14-1:**
The file cabinet icon launches the File Manager.

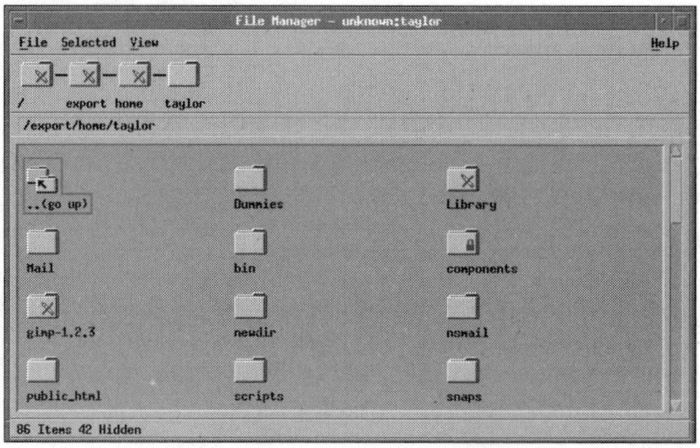

**Figure 14-2:**
The CDE File Manager.

To search for a specific file, choose File⇨Find, which opens the complex Find dialog box, shown in Figure 14-3. Here's a rundown of some options in this dialog box:

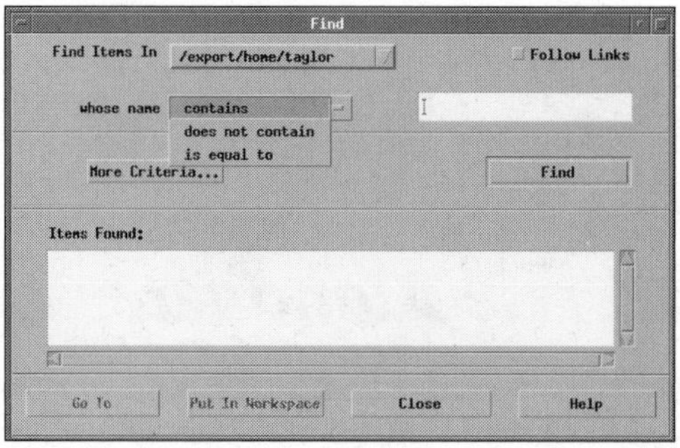

**Figure 14-3:**
The Find function in the File Manager.

✔ **Find Items In:** The default setting for Find Items In (at the top of the dialog box) is to search in the current directory. This setting is a pop-up: Click it to select another starting location for the search.

✔ **Whose Name:** This search pattern option offers the choices highlighted in the pop-up shown in Figure 14-3. You can search for files that

- Contain the pattern specified
- Don't contain the pattern specified
- Are exactly equal to the pattern specified

✔ **More Criteria:** This option offers more ways that you can search, as described in the next section.

✔ **Follow Links:** The Follow Links check box is in the top-right corner.

Links are the Solaris equivalent to Windows shortcuts or Mac aliases and are essentially shorthand ways of jumping to specific files or folders elsewhere on the Solaris system. Sometimes they point to a separate area of the file system that is huge, so the Find feature in File Manager enables you to decide whether it should ignore the links in its search.

## More find criteria in CDE File Manager

Clicking the More Criteria button opens the More Criteria dialog box, shown in Figure 14-4. This dialog box offers a variety of criteria by which you can search, as detailed here:

**Figure 14-4:**
Find, with even more criteria!

✔ **Name:** The name of the file

✔ **Content:** What's actually in the file. It can be either

- A word
- A phrase

- ✔ **Size:** The size of the file. You can search for one of these:
  - An exact file size
  - Files larger than a specified size
  - Files smaller than a specified size
- ✔ **Date Modified:** The last date modified. You can search for one of these:
  - An exact date
  - Files modified before a specified date
  - Files modified after a specified date
- ✔ **Owner:** The owner of the file (probably *you;* not too helpful)
- ✔ **Type:** The type of the file. It's one of these:
  - File
  - Directory
  - Special type of file used by the operating system only
- ✔ **Permissions:** The file permissions, such as
  - Read
  - Write
  - Execute

Of these choices, the most useful are

- ✔ Content
- ✔ Size
- ✔ Date Modified

Select them all and click OK to go back to the Find dialog box. The Find dialog box now looks like Figure 14-5.

This time the form is filled out. I'm searching for files with these attributes:

- ✔ Names contain *html*
- ✔ Contain the text *McNealy*
- ✔ Are less than 10,000 bytes in size
- ✔ Were modified in the current year

The Date Modified is tricky to figure out. The shortcut that appears in the text input box is `[[CC]YY]MMDDhhmm[.ss]`, but I bet that doesn't help you much!

**Figure 14-5:**
The Find
dialog box,
with more
options.

✔ The default information to enter is

- Month

- Day

- Hour

- Minute

Figure 14-5 shows that I've entered 01 01 00 00, or January 1 of the
current year, at 00:00, midnight.

✔ You can also specify these values:

- Seconds (although I can't imagine anyone would know file modification dates down to that level of specificity)

- Years

To find files that haven't been modified since 2001, you can use Is Before
as the modifier, and 2001010100 as the Date Modified string (got it? 2001,
January 1, 00:00).

You can search many ways by combining these attributes.

✔ To find a list of all Writer .doc files that have been modified more
recently than February 15, you can combine these attributes:

- Whose Name Contains *doc*

- Date Modified Is After 02150000.

✔ You can find all files modified since a certain date by leaving the Whose
Name box blank.

Figure 14-5 is interesting for another reason. It shows the results of my clicking Find to search my entire folder area. The two matching files are

- ✔ welcome.html in my home directory
- ✔ My public_html subdirectory

Although the Find function works well, you can't open resulting files directly. You must double-click the matched filename, or select it and click Go To. A new File Manager dialog box opens, showing the directory that contains the file. Double-click the file to see what's inside.

# Finding Files with GNOME

In GNOME, the Nautilus file system offers a separate Search for Files capability from the GNOME menu.

To launch Search for Files, follow these steps:

1. **Click the GNOME menu.**

   The Search for Files window pops up, as shown in Figure 14-6.

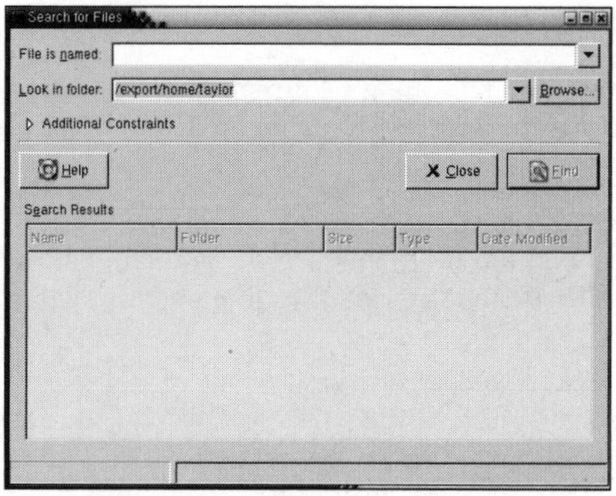

**Figure 14-6:** The GNOME Search for Files utility.

2. **To add more search constraints, click the small triangle to the left of Additional Constraints.**

   An additional search constraint section opens.

3. **Click the Available Search Constraints pop-up to see the available constraints.**

   A remarkable number of constraints are available for the search, as shown in Figure 14-7.

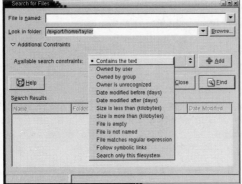

**Figure 14-7:**
Lots of
search
constraints
are
available in
the Search
for Files
dialog box.

4. **Select a constraint type from the Available Search Constraints pop-up and then click the Add button. Continue this until you've specified all desired constraints.**

I want to search for files that

- Have the pattern *html* in their name

- Have the pattern *McNealy* in the file itself

- Are less than 10,000 bytes in size

- Have been modified since the first of January

My Search for Files dialog box looks like Figure 14-8.

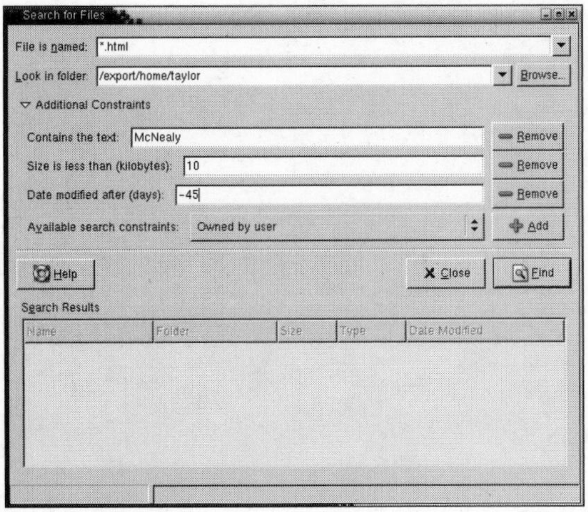

**Figure 14-8:**
Searching
for
McNealy-
related
HTML files.

There are a few differences here from the CDE file find options:

- Instead of searching for filename fragments, you need to specify a wildcard pattern: `*.html` matches all files that end with the `.html` suffix. (By comparison, `*html*` matches all files with the sequence `html` in their filename.)

- The Date Modified parameter is challenging because you specify the number of days, but in a somewhat backwards fashion. To check for files modified within the last 45 days, either specify that you want them modified `after -45` or `before 45`. It isn't logical, but it works.

5. **After you select all the desired constraints, click the Find button to see the results.**

   My search results are shown in Figure 14-9.

**Figure 14-9:**
These search results match those from the CDE File Manager.

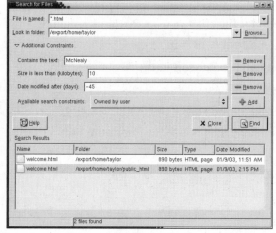

- ✔ If you double-click a match, Nautilus opens that file.

- ✔ If you right-click on a matching line, a pop-up menu opens with these options:

   - Open
   - Open Folder
   - Save Results As

I double-clicked `welcome.html` to open it, as shown in Figure 14-10. From this display window, you can open the HTML file in Netscape or any other program (including a text editor). You can find more coverage of Nautilus in Chapter 4.

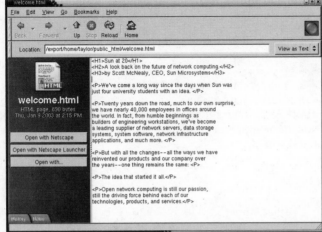

**Figure 14-10:**
The
welcome.
html file
displayed in
Nautilus.

# Searching by Content with grep

Although CDE and GNOME have graphical file search utilities, both are attractive front-ends for two Solaris command-line tools:

✔ The grep command searches a specified set of files for a *pattern*. The resulting matched lines, if any, are shown as its output.

✔ The find command can search by specific criteria, such as

  • Size

  • Owner

  • Modification date

grep gets its name from g/re/p — *global regular expression print* — a command commonly used in the ex editor when Unix was developed.

I want to use the grep command to confirm that the file welcome.html contains the pattern *McNealy*. As with every other command-line utility, you need to open a terminal window or pull up a shell. My shell is ready to go, so I enter:

```
$ grep McNealy *
welcome.html:<H3>by Scott McNealy, CEO, Sun Microsystems</H3>
```

In the preceding example, the output of grep — if there's a match — is the filename, a colon, and the matching passage. By default, grep is case sensitive; nothing happens if I type Scott McNealy's name in all lowercase, like this:

```
$ grep mcnealy *
$
```

The -i flag tells grep to ignore the case. This flag is helpful if the pattern you seek might occur in either all lowercase, mixed case, or all capital letters.

The following example shows how you can cast a wider net by either

- Shrinking the pattern down

- Looking through more files by replacing the * filename wildcard with one that also looks in all immediate subdirectories

```
$ grep -i scott * */*
gullivers.travels.txt:{3}  Britannia.--Sir W. Scott.
gullivers.travels.txt:{4}  London.--Sir W. Scott.
kaelins.travels.txt:{3}  Britannia.--Sir W. Scott.
kaelins.travels.txt:{4}  London.--Sir W. Scott.
mailbox:        "Scott Gillam" <sgillam@glenraven.com>,
welcome.html:<H3>by Scott McNealy, CEO, Sun Microsystems</H3>
newdir/gullivers.travels.txt:{3}  Britannia.--Sir W. Scott.
newdir/gullivers.travels.txt:{4}  London.--Sir W. Scott.
public_html/welcome.html:<H3>by Scott McNealy, CEO, Sun Micro
systems</H3>
```

The -l flag (lowercase *L*) offers the same basic filename pattern matching on the command line that both CDE and GNOME offer. It shows the names of the files that match, not the names and matching lines. Here's an example of the command:

```
$ grep -li scott * */*
gullivers.travels.txt
kaelins.travels.txt
mailbox
welcome.html
newdir/gullivers.travels.txt
public_html/welcome.html
```

## Using grep with mailboxes

If your e-mail is stored in various mailbox files, the grep command is an interesting way to search for addresses. In addition to simple text patterns, you can also specify some fairly complex patterns:

✔ Place a ^ at the beginning of the pattern to match lines with the pattern at the beginning of the line.

✔ Specify a $ to match the end of the line instead.

For example, "^kumquat$" will only match lines that contain the word *kumquat,* with no spaces, tabs, or other characters.

For exploring a mailbox, a natural pattern is "^From:  " (with the trailing space) to extract all the From: lines in the mailbox:

```
$ grep "^From: " mailbox
From: "Midwifery Today" <enews@midwiferytoday.com>
From: Ricardo Dunlap <ricardo@earthlink.net>
From: Lori Kats <lkats@webmail.com>
From: james@emissaryoflight.com
From: news@909shot.com
From: Dave Taylor <taylor@intuitive.com>
From: news@909shot.com
From: "Hanna Andersson" <Hanna@hannaandersson.com>
From: "Lester, Emily" <elester@kansascity.com>
From: "CallBack Centre" <akaamy@excite.com>
From: "Colette Donahue" <colette@oscar.net>
From: "Louis Good" <louisgood@carolina.com>
From: news@909shot.com
From: news@909shot.com
From: Mothering Magazine <webmaster@mothering.com>
From: "Kaelin Kelly" <kkelly@wdw.com>
From: PNR-united air lines <confirmation@uasupport.com>
From: <FrontierAirlines@flyfrontier.com>
From: news@909shot.com
From: "A Feehan" <afeehan@hotmail.com>
From: james@emissaryoflight.com
From: "Melissa Cohen Insurance Agency Inc" <mac@mho.com>
From: DonXTaylor@netscape.com
From: news@909shot.com
From: news@909shot.com
From: "Figureskater" <info@figureskaters-resource.com>
From: news@909shot.com
```

To organize your matches, you can call on two additional Solaris commands:

✔ The sort command alphabetizes lines of input.

✔ The uniq command shows only one of each unique line.

Couple these commands together, and things improve considerably:

```
$ grep "^From: " mailbox | sort | uniq
From: "A Feehan" <afeehan@hotmail.com>
From: "CallBack Centre" <akaamy@excite.com>
```

```
From: "Colette Donahue" <colette@oscar.net>
From: "Figureskater" <info@figureskaters-resource.com>
From: "Hanna Andersson" <Hanna@hannaandersson.com>
From: "Kaelin Kelly" <kkelly@wdw.com>
From: "Lester, Emily" <elester@kansascity.com>
From: "Louis Good" <louisgood@carolina.com>
From: "Melissa Cohen Insurance Agency Inc" <mac@mho.com>
From: "Midwifery Today" <enews@midwiferytoday.com>
From: <FrontierAirlines@flyfrontier.com>
From: DonXTaylor@netscape.com
From: Lori Kats <lkats@webmail.com>
From: Mothering Magazine <webmaster@mothering.com>
From: PNR-united air lines <confirmation@uasupport.com>
From: Postmaster
From: Ricardo Dunlap <ricardo@earthlink.net>
From: james@emissaryoflight.com
From: news@909shot.com
```

Because you can have multiple invocations of a command in a *pipe* (Chapter 3 explains pipes), you can now have an easy tool for finding a specific e-mail address in a mailbox file:

```
$ grep "^From: " mailbox | sort | uniq | grep -i ricardo
From: Ricardo Dunlap <ricardo@earthlink.net>
```

More tricks for using grep are detailed in the online documentation at docs.sun.com, among other places. It's a wonderful command to know, especially when coupled with the find command.

# Specifying Search Attributes with find

Though a bit more complex than grep, the find command is a great way to search through your files and directories for specific files that match certain criteria, including filename, size, owner, modification date, and much more.

✔ The standard usage for the find command is

```
find directory-or-directories flag value
```

The find command searches the specified directories for files or directories that match the specified set of flag/value criteria. For example, the following sample produces a list of all files that end with .html in (and below) the current directory:

```
$ find * -name "*.html" -print
public_html/welcome.html
welcome.html
```

Unlike almost every other Solaris command, `find` uses full-word flags, such as `-name` and `-print`. The flags and their values mingle in an English-like manner.

A common way to use `find` is to specify . as the directory to search. The program searches

- All the *visible filenames*
- All directories whose name start with . (the *invisible files* in Solaris)

For the following example, many more matches are found:

```
$ find . -name "*.html" -print
./.mozilla/taylor/kz3toqua.slt/bookmarks.html
./.mozilla/Default User/8wungi1j.slt/bookmarks.html
./welcome.html
./public_html/welcome.html
./.netscape/bookmarks.html
```

One neat result of this search is that I can see where my bookmark files are for both Netscape and Mozilla.

## Searching by size and date

To match the search criteria used earlier, you mostly need to know about the flags that `find` uses to specify file size and modification date:

✔ When specifying the value to a flag such as `-size`, you need to take into account that a specific number will only match files of that exact size.

✔ Preface the number with a - to match anything smaller than the size specified, and use + to match anything larger.

✔ Size also wants a trailing `c` on the value if you're indicating bytes; otherwise, it's interpreted as 512-byte blocks.

For dates, `find` uses the basic unit of days. Although the CDE File Manager uses month, day, hour, and minute, the GNOME Search for Files utility that uses days *ahead* or *behind* is more like the `find` command. (In fact, Search for Files uses `find` behind the scenes.)

To check a modification date, the flag is `-mtime`.

The following command checks for files with

`*.html` as their filename

A size less than 10,000 bytes

A modification time of less than 45 days

```
$ find . -name "*.html" -size -10000c -mtime -45 -print
././mozilla/taylor/kz3toqua.slt/bookmarks.html
././mozilla/Default User/8wungilj.slt/bookmarks.html
./welcome.html
./public_html/welcome.html
././netscape/bookmarks.html
```

## Searching by content

The easiest way to search by content is to wrangle grep into joining the find parade! Instead of doing it as a pipe, use the -exec flag to find, and specify the grep command as the argument:

```
$ find . -name "*.html" -size -10000c -mtime -45 -exec grep -
         i mcnealy ";"
./welcome.html:<H3>by Scott McNealy, CEO, Sun
         Microsystems</H3>
./public_html/welcome.html:<H3>by Scott McNealy, CEO, Sun
         Microsystems</H3>
```

The straightforward approach in this first example has a couple of drawbacks:

✔ It takes forever to run, because grep is invoked once for each file in your subtree, which can drag things down.

✔ The ; at the end of the line tells find where the exec expression ends.

Odd though it looks, you must include this if you use the -exec flag, so that it knows when the specified command to execute ends.

Fortunately, there's a smarter and faster way to invoke find, although it's more peculiar looking:

```
$ find . -name "*.html" -size -10000c -mtime -45 -exec grep -
         i mcnealy "{}" +
./welcome.html:<H3>by Scott McNealy, CEO, Sun
         Microsystems</H3>
./public_html/welcome.html:<H3>by Scott McNealy, CEO, Sun
         Microsystems</H3>
```

The {} sequence is replaced by the individual filenames and is optional in the default -exec expression, as shown in the first example. In this second example, replacing the ; with a + tells find to give a bunch of filenames to grep each time it's called, with the {} replaced by all the names each time.

The difference in speed is remarkable.

- ✔ The first example took almost 20 minutes to run on my system
- ✔ The second example finished in a second or two.

You can work with the `find` command many ways, but discussing them all is beyond the scope of this book. There are other directions for using `find`. Start with the `find` man page:

```
man find
```

and then referencing `docs.sun.com/`.

# Part V
# Administration and Security Issues

The 5th Wave    By Rich Tennant

Don't get your hopes up, Ted. The other end may not be plugged in.

# In this part . . .

This part of the book addresses something that might be beyond your individual responsibility: system administration and security. However, if something goes wrong on your computer, they're your files that'll be lost, corrupted or stolen, so whether you have a top-notch system administrator or not, it's wise to learn something about how to keep your system running optimally, with as many hatches battened down as possible.

The three chapters start by exploring different ways to hook a Solaris system to an existing network, including the popular Dynamic Host Control Protocol (DHCP) and the creaky Point to Point Protocol for modem access. Once that's hooked up, you'll explore the Solaris Management Console and learn the proper and safe way to stop your computer so you can unplug it. Finally, you'll learn some of the key ideas behind system security and how to ensure your system is as secure as possible.

# Chapter 15

# Connecting to the Network

● ● ● ● ● ● ● ● ● ● ● ● ● ● ● ● ● ● ● ● ● ● ● ● ● ● ● ● ● ● ● ● ● ● ● ● ● ● ● ● ●

## In This Chapter

▶ Terminology and concepts

▶ Configuring Solaris networking

▶ Fixing some DHCP glitches

▶ Quick reference for working with PPP

● ● ● ● ● ● ● ● ● ● ● ● ● ● ● ● ● ● ● ● ● ● ● ● ● ● ● ● ● ● ● ● ● ● ● ● ● ● ● ● ●

*Y*ou may have a systems administration or information technology group at your organization that manages all the "under the hood" aspects of Solaris. Even if that's the case, it's worthwhile for you to have a basic understanding of the technologies underlying the Solaris user experience.

This chapter addresses how a Solaris system connects to the network, exploring the three major protocols:

✔ Dynamic Host Configuration Protocol (DHCP)

✔ Fixed IP

✔ Point-to-Point Protocol (for dial-up connections).

# *Terminology and Concepts*

A few definitions make things easier for you in the world of networking.

✔ The Internet is a network of networks, all sharing a set of common languages, or *protocols*:

- At the lowest level of networking, Internet Protocol (IP, the denominator of the common TCP/IP protocol pair) allows machines to exchange streams of data between them.

Internet Protocol assigns each computer a unique numeric address, typically expressed as four numbers separated by dots (for example, 128.216.22.103).

- Transmission Control Protocol (TCP, the numerator of TCP/IP) ensures that the communication between two computers (which is broken into individual *packets*) goes to its destination and is assembled in the order it was sent.

  Without TCP, the middle of your e-mail messages, the last 30 lines of a Web page, and the last message from your favorite instant message buddy could be lost en route while bouncing from computer to computer.

- ✔ Other protocols on top of the TCP/IP protocol stack provide specific Internet services, including these:

  - HyperText Transport Protocol (HTTP) for Web browsers and servers

  - Simple Mail Transfer Protocol (SMTP) for e-mail interchanges

  - Domain Name Service (DNS) for mapping domain names to their unique IP addresses

A computer on a public or private network needs a few essential snippets of information:

- ✔ A unique IP address
- ✔ The address of a router or gateway to the rest of the network
- ✔ A *netmask* (which tells the computer how many other IP addresses are in the local network space)
- ✔ One or more DNS server addresses to resolve name-to-number queries

# Configuring Solaris Networking

Although you can certainly muck with system configuration files — and will do that in this chapter — the recommended method of configuring or reconfiguring a network connection is to erase the existing system configuration file and reboot.

After restarting, the system detects the missing configuration file and prompts for the necessary values, including network configuration.

It's worthwhile to take a snapshot of the essentials of your current configuration by running the network interface configuration utility ifconfig, with its -a (show all interfaces) flag specified:

```
# ifconfig -a
lo0: flags=1000849<UP,LOOPBACK,RUNNING,MULTICAST,IPv4> mtu 8232 index 1
        inet 127.0.0.1 netmask ff000000
eri0: flags=1004843<UP,BROADCAST,RUNNING,MULTICAST,DHCP,IPv4> mtu 1500 index 2
        inet 192.168.1.107 netmask ffffff00 broadcast 192.168.1.255
        ether 0:3:ba:10:dd:47
```

This shows two interfaces on this system:

- lo0 is the *loopback* interface.

  It's a convenient way for applications on the computer to communicate via the network system, but without actually having to go out to the network.

- eri0 is the *Ethernet* (network) interface.

The preceding listing shows the addresses for the network card on this Solaris system:

- The interfaces list these addresses:

  - The current IP address for the system (192.168.1.107)

  - The netmask (ffffff00)

  - The broadcast IP address (192.168.1.255).

- UP and RUNNING show that the network is currently set up correctly.

- DHCP in the list of eri0 flags shows that the system is running DHCP.

## Unconfiguration: how to repeat the out-of-box setup sequence

The easiest way to change the Solaris network configuration is to delete the existing configuration then reboot.

- Solaris checks the configuration settings during the boot process

- If Solaris finds there are no default settings, it launches the system configuration utility.

To remove the system configuration information, complete the following steps:

1. **Run** `sys-unconfig` **as root:**

   ```
   # sys-unconfig
   ```

   The output shows that this is a fairly dramatic step to take with a computer!

   ```
                              WARNING

   This program will unconfigure your system. It will cause
   It to revert to a "blank" system - it will not have a
                 name
   or know about other systems or networks.

   This program will also halt the system.

   Do you want to continue (y/n) ?
   ```

   Rather than running the current network connection protocol, I'm going to change it. Keep your fingers crossed!

2. **To continue and really delete the existing configuration, type** y **and then press Enter.**

   All the existing network services are stopped. Without any further prompts, the system is halted.

3. **Type** boot **at the** Ok? **prompt to reboot from the halt state.**

   With luck, this is the only time you ever see the Ok? prompt during boot-time.

   A series of prompts follows from this point, starting with selecting a language from those installed on the system.

4. **Enter the numeric value from the list for your preferred language.**

   Usually, English is choice 0.

   Locale choices appear now.

5. **Enter the numeric value from the list for your locale.**

   Here's what I have on my computer at this point:

   ```
   Select a Locale
      0. English (C - 7-bit ASCII)
      1. Canada-English (ISO8859-1)
      2. U.S.A. (en_US.ISO8859-1)
      3. U.S.A. (en_US.ISO8859-15)
      4. Go Back to Previous Screen
   Please make a choice (0 - 4), or press h or ? for help:
   ```

   After entering the locale, the system moves to network configurations. It begins by informing you that you're configuring the Ethernet interface:

```
Configuring network interface addresses: eri0
```

6. **When the program asks whether your system has a network card, confirm it by entering "Yes". The following instructions appear on the screen:**

```
On this screen you must specify whether or not this
        system
should use DHCP for network interface configuration.
Choose Yes if DHCP is to be used, or No if the interfaces
are to be configured manually.
NOTE: DHCP support will not be enabled, if selected,
        until
after the system reboots.
Use DHCP
--------
[X] Yes
[ ] No
```

7. **Select either DHCP-based configuration or a fixed IP address based on the configuration of your network (ask your system or network administrator if you're not sure).**

   For a DHCP-based configuration, select Yes here. (This is the default).

   For a *fixed IP address,* select No for the DHCP configuration and then enter the following values when prompted:

   - Your hostname (mine is *aurora*).

   - Your fixed IP address.

     If you're running a fixed IP network, your network administrator will have given you a unique number to enter at this point.

     My IP address is 192.168.1.107.

   - Your subnet, if you are part of one (you probably are). Answer yes to that prompt and then enter the netmask as supplied by the network administrator.

     My netmask is 255.255.255.0.

   When you complete this step, you are prompted for any additional information required by the setup program.

8. **Enable IPv6 support if you need it.**

   It's a more advanced IP addressing scheme; it can be safely enabled without adversely affecting the older IP address scheme used on most networks.

   I'll skip it. You should too, unless you have been told by your network administrator that you must have IPv6 to be able to participate fully on the network.

At this point, your settings are summarized.

- For a DHCP configuration, it's succinct:

```
       Networked: Yes
       Use DHCP: Yes
     Enable IPv6: No
```

- For a fixed IP configuration, it's lengthier:

```
              Networked: Yes
              Use DHCP: No
              Host name: aurora
              IP address: 192.168.1.107
System part of a subnet: Yes
                Netmask: 255.255.255.0
            Enable IPv6: No
          Default Route: Find one
```

- If the settings look good, you can proceed with the rest of the con-figuration options.

- If not, enter "No" and the setup program will let you alter individ-ual settings until it is correct.

9. **Accept the default values for the remaining configuration options (unless you want to experiment, in which case you can enter a new value for the specific field by typing it rather than accepting the default), except for Name Service.**

**Unless your system administration group gives you other instructions, choose** None **for Name service.**

The system automatically reboots. After a moment or two, it should boot up with your new networking options.

To check that your new network configuration details are correct, open a Web page with your browser.

- If your browser doesn't run correctly, try these steps to check whether your system is able to see the network at all:

    - Check whether ifconfig indicates UP and RUNNING.

    - Use the ping utility to ping your own system (which shows that the loopback works). Then try pinging your gateway or router (which shows that your system is still connected to the gateway).

✔ If things are still working improperly, it's time to either

- Rerun `sys-unconfig` to try some other options.

- Call your network administrator or favorite computer whiz for help!

# Fixing DHCP Glitches

The DHCP protocol is one of those fundamentally great ideas in computing: Instead of associating a specific address with each computer, have a pool of addresses and assign them on an as-needed basis for the network.

There are some advantages to this scheme:

✔ You don't need to match the number of available addresses with the number of computers.

✔ Dozens of computers can feed into a router and then one address communicates to the Internet.

My office network is configured with multiple computers sharing a single Internet IP address through a router. I pay for one IP address from my network provider, and my cable modem box also acts as a router, gateway, and DHCP server. The dozen-odd computers in my office then receive individual IP addresses within the DHCP namespace, and all invisibly share the single IP address to the outside world. Instead of taking a dozen IP addresses from the public Internet, the computers in my office only need one external IP for all systems to connect.

✔ DHCP is an open industry standard.

Just about every modern computer supports DHCP, including

- Macintosh

- Windows

- Other Unix and Linux systems

✔ You can run DHCP on your network if you're directly hooked up to the Internet via one of these services:

- High-speed network line (a *T1, T3,* and so on)

- Digital subscriber line (DSL)

- Cable modem

I have a cable modem supplying connectivity for all the computers in my office, for example.

## Hostname unknown

After you've reconfigured your system to work with a DHCP service, it's not uncommon to find that the computer has been renamed *unknown,* not the hostname you want. A surprisingly simple change to one of the configuration files fixes this.

This change isn't for the faint of heart. You'll be editing an essential part of the Solaris boot process. Be careful with the following steps. They're not difficult, but you'll want to ensure that you are very accurate with the changes to ensure nothing breaks.

The problem with hostname unknown is that Solaris expects the DHCP server to assign it a hostname. Many DHCP servers expect each computer to already have an assigned name. The result is an unknown hostname. To fix this annoying hostname unknown problem, here's what you do:

1. **Make a backup copy of the configuration file** /etc/rcS.d/S30network.sh, **just in case, like this:**

   ```
   $ cd /etc/rcS.d
   $ cp S30network.sh s30network.sh
   ```

Because filenames are case sensitive in Solaris, these are two different files. Only files in this directory that start with the letter *S* are run as the system boots up.

2. **Open the** S30network.sh **file in an editor and find the following line near the end of the file:**

   ```
   hostname="unknown"
   ```

   (Chapter 12 explains how to edit files in Solaris)

A fast way to get there with vi is to type ?unknown while in command mode. Using ? searches backwards, from the end of the file to the beginning. Because you know the patter you seek is near the bottom, it gets you there fast.

3. **Replace the line** hostname="unknown" **with the following line:**

   ```
   hostname="`shcat /etc/nodename 2>/dev/null`"
   ```

Be careful:

   • *Double quote, back quote* at the beginning of the line.

   • *Back quote, double quote* at the end of the line.

4. **Write and quit the edit session (in** vi **you can use the** :wq **command).**

5. **Double-check that the file** `/etc/nodename` **contains the name you gave the system when first configuring it, like this:**

```
# cat /etc/nodename
aurora
```

If there's no `nodename` file or it's empty, use an editor to create it. Just put your one-word hostname in it.

6. **Open the** `S30network.sh` **file in an editor and find the following line near the end of the file:**

```
hostname="unknown"
```

7. **Replace the line** `hostname="unknown"` **with the following line:**

```
hostname="`cat /etc/nodename 2>/dev/null`"
```

Again, it's

- *Double quote, back quote* at the beginning

- *Back quote, double quote* at the end of the line.

8. **Double-check both changes to ensure that the back quotes are properly inserted, by entering the following:**

```
# grep "cat /etc/nodename" S72inetsvc ../rcS.d/S30network.sh
S72inetsvc:            hostname="`cat /etc/nodename 2>/dev/null`"
../rcS.d/S30network.sh: "none") hostname="`shcat /etc/nodename
         2>/dev/null`" ;;
../rcS.d/S30network.sh: hostname="`shcat /etc/nodename 2>/dev/null`"
```

In the preceding example, the `S30network.sh` script already had the hostname set from `/etc/nodename` in the script. All three should look the same. If they don't, edit as appropriate.

9. **When you're ready, reboot.**

You should have a proper hostname!

## DNS resolution problems

When DHCP servers aren't up to snuff for a Solaris client, they might not send any DNS server information, leaving you with a system that can connect to the network, but can't do any name lookups with the domain name service.

This is easy to fix if you have the DNS server information from your ISP or system administrator (probably two or three systems identified by IP address).

1. **Go to the** /etc **directory and open a file called** resolv.conf.

   Yes, there's a missing *e* in that filename. No one knows why!

2. **If DNS isn't working, the file will be empty. Add the following lines, albeit with the DNS servers that your network administrator or Internet service provider has given you, not my AT&T IP numbers:**

   ```
   domain attbi.com
   nameserver 216.148.227.68
   nameserver 204.127.202.4
   ```

   My ISP supplied this information; your values will doubtless vary.

3. **Save the file, and run the following command to double-check that everything looks good and matches the supplied information:**

   ```
   # more /etc/resolv.conf
   domain attbi.com
   nameserver 216.148.227.68
   nameserver 204.127.202.4
   ```

   Ensure that there are no spaces before or after any periods.

   If that looks good, you can immediately do hostname lookups. Try opening a Web site in Netscape, if you want.

Great job! You're not only becoming a Solaris power user, but you're also doing pretty well in the system hacker department! Fun, eh?

# *ppp*

It's rare in the Solaris world for users to have modems as their main connection to the outside world. However, it's possible to configure a Solaris system to use the Point-to-Point Protocol (PPP) to work with a modem and automatically dial up a remote Internet service provider on demand. The configuration is tricky and beyond the scope of *Solaris 9 For Dummies* (think *Super-Detailed Solaris System Configuration Nitpicky Details For Dummies* instead).

The main program for working with PPP is the Solaris pppd command. A good place to start is to read the pppd man page with the command man pppd.

# PPP client configuration

To configure a dial-out PPP system, take the following steps:

1. **Gather preconfiguration information.**

   You want to make sure you have all the information you need from the ISP, including telephone number, modem speeds and protocols supported, account name, and password.

2. **Configure the modem and serial port.**

   You can find good documentation on this at `docs.sun.com` if you need it.

3. **Configure the serial line communication.**

   You want to ensure that the serial line talks properly to the modem at the right speed, using the right number of bits and parity, and so on.

4. **Define the conversation between the dial-out machine and the peer (or server).**

   This is one of the most essential steps; you can read about it in the chat man page.

5. **Configure information about a particular peer — PPP options for a specific server.**

6. **Call the peer. Type in the** `pppd` **command (as root) to hopefully initiate the connection.**

All of these steps are documented in great detail at the URL referenced at the end of this chapter.

# PPP server configuration

One great Solaris feature is that it can be a PPP server for remote systems just as easily as it can be a client. This means that you can easily set up your server as a mini-ISP, or even create an easy (and secure) mechanism for connecting from your home computer to the Solaris system at work.

However, as with the PPP client configuration, server configuration is tricky but, fortunately, well documented at the Sun Web site.

The necessary steps for configuring a server are

1. **Gather preconfiguration information, including**

   - Peer hostnames

   - Phone numbers

   - Modem speed

2. **Configure the modem and serial port.**

   If you've configured the system as a PPP client, this may already be done.

3. **Set up the PPP options and user environments for every dial-out machine that's allowed to connect to the server. (This is the *calling peer* information)**

4. **Configure the serial line communication.**

   Again, this might already be done if you've set up the system as a PPP client.

Accounts that are allowed to connect from a remote PPP connection have the default login shell of /usr/bin/pppd to ensure that the handshake between the two occurs properly. It's not possible with the standard Solaris configuration to have guest or anonymous PPP clients (which you wouldn't want anyway for security reasons); PPP users must have their own login and password on the dial-up system.

One final step that you (or, more likely, your system administrator) should take is to set up either Password Authentication Protocol (PAP) or Challenge Handshake Authentication Protocol (CHAP) for the PPP server. Again, that's detailed at the following docs.sun.com URL.

The best reference for all the nitpicky details of configuring PPP on a Solaris 9 system is docs.sun.com/db/doc/806-4076/6jd6amqu6?a=view. Twelve chapters in this online Sun document discuss configuring modem-based Internet access!

# Chapter 16

# Essential System Administration

- - - - - - - - - - - - - - - - - - - - - - - - - - - - - - - - - - - - - - - -

## In This Chapter

▶ Exploring the Solaris Management Console

▶ Starting and stopping your system

▶ Adding user accounts

- - - - - - - - - - - - - - - - - - - - - - - - - - - - - - - - - - - - - - - -

Although you may have an information technology group or system administrator who manages the oil changes, wheel balancing, and other messy jobs under the hood of your Solaris computer, you might still be left with some administrative tasks. Even if you never learned the root password for your system, it's helpful to have an idea of some of the tasks required for configuring and maintaining a Solaris system.

The special account ID `root` has maximum permissions. As a result, any system administration task that will read or write protected files will require you to know the root password. If you don't, many administrative tools won't even start, and certainly none will work properly.

If you need the ins and outs of root accounts and root account access, that's in Chapter 17.

# Exploring the Solaris Management Console

One of the best tools available with Solaris 9 is the Solaris Management Console (SMC). Consolidating the tasks of many command-line administrative tools, SMC makes working with your Solaris box remarkably easy, once you get the hang of it.

You have a couple of options to start SMC:

- ✓ In GNOME, choose GNOME Menu⇨CDE Menu⇨Tools⇨Solaris Management Console.
- ✓ In CDE, follow these steps:
  - Click the small rectangular button above the Tools icon (which looks like a page with some check boxes)
  - Choose Solaris Management Console from the pop-up menu.
- ✓ From the command line while logged in as root, use this command:

```
/usr/sbin/smc &
```

When SMC starts up, you may see a display that indicates the console is analyzing the system to ascertain its initial configuration, as shown in Figure 16-1.

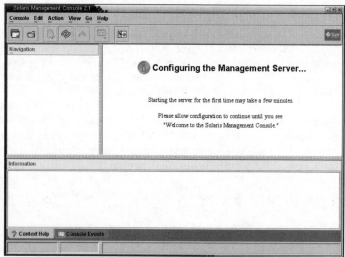

**Figure 16-1:**
The Solaris Management Console starting up.

Although it can take as long as five minutes for the program to analyze the configuration of a complex system, usually it's about a 60 to 90 second process. The main SMC view says "Welcome to the Solaris Management Console," as shown in Figure 16-2. You can now begin to explore the capabilities of SMC.

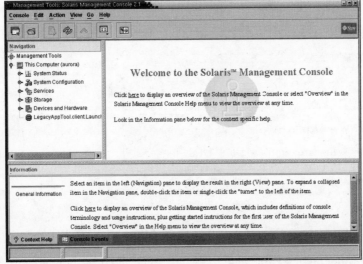

**Figure 16-2:**
Welcome to
the Solaris
Management
Console.

## Briefly exploring SMC

To see what the program knows about your system, click the tiny circular
icon adjacent to This Computer (Aurora) in the top-left window. This
Computer is expanded in Figure 16-2.

The main categories in SMC are

- System Status
- System Configuration
- Services
- Storage
- Devices and Hardware
- LegacyAppTool.client.Launcher

Select System Status to get a taste of SMC. It expands to show four options:

- System Information
- Log Viewer
- Processes
- Performance

The Performance option sounds of most interest, so click it. You then have to verify that you know the root password, as shown in Figure 16-3.

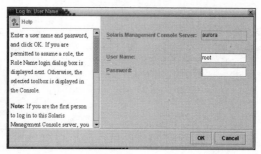

**Figure 16-3:**
Confirming
your identity
in SMC.

Enter the correct password for root and then click OK. After a moment or two, the Performance option expands to show a System choice. Open that by clicking the tiny circle icon to its left. You'll see three subcategories:

✔ Summary

✔ Projects

✔ Users

Select Summary to get a summary of the system performance levels, as shown in Figure 16-4.

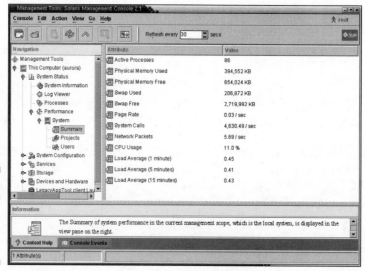

**Figure 16-4:**
Summary of
system
performance
in SMC.

The output shows several interesting statistics, though it's mostly up to you to know how to interpret them. For example, you can see that 394MB of physical memory is in use, and 654MB is available. Is that a ton of free memory, or would more physical memory improve system performance? Are 4,630 system calls per second indicative of a busy system, or a typical value for a Solaris machine that's mostly idle?

Follow these guidelines to review the utilization of your system:

✔ As long as you have unused physical memory and the Page Rate is low, you're in great shape.

✔ When you have processes demanding lots of physical memory, then

• *Swapping* (Page Rate) goes up

• Performance rapidly degrades

## Examining System Configuration

Open the System Configuration category by clicking the circle icon to the left of its name. This reveals four subcategories:

✔ Users

✔ Projects

✔ Computers and Networks

✔ Patches

Choose Users to see additional choices:

✔ User Accounts

✔ User Templates

✔ Rights

✔ Administrative Roles

✔ Groups

✔ Mailing Lists

Start by examining User Accounts. Click User Accounts to see a display similar to Figure 16-5.

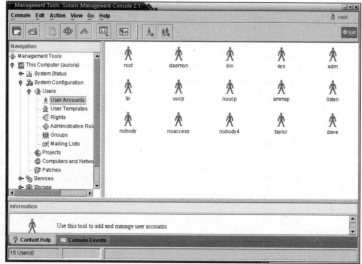

**Figure 16-5:**
User
information
in the
Solaris
Manage-
ment
Console.

Each person icon on the right side of the window represents an account on the system.

You should leave most of the functionally named accounts unchanged, such as

```
bin
sys
adm
uucp
```

The individual user accounts are worth examination. In Figure 16-6, I've clicked the account dave to see what permissions and access he has been granted.

As you can see in Figure 16-6, this SMC area shows lots of helpful information for this particular account. Tabs along the top indicate its sections:

- ✔ Password
- ✔ Password Options
- ✔ Mail
- ✔ Rights
- ✔ Roles
- ✔ General
- ✔ Group
- ✔ Projects
- ✔ Home Directory

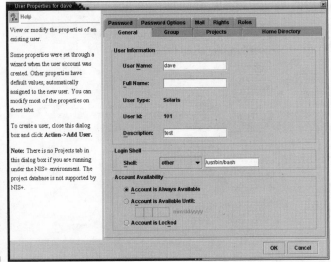

**Figure 16-6:**
User
configuration
for account
dave.

On the General tab, these are some of your options:

✔ **User Name:** You can change a user's name.

✔ **Login Shell:** You can specify which shell the user should have upon login. (Here, it's /usr/bin/bash.)

✔ **Account Availability:** You have a couple of options for controlling the time of account availability:

- Lock the account immediately.

- Configure the account to automatically lock on a specific date

  which is helpful if you have students, contractors, or other users who don't need system access forever!

Figure 16-7 shows the great Password Options tab of the User Properties window. The account dave is configured as follows:

✔ **User Must Keep For:** Each time the password is changed, the user can't change it again for 14 days.

✔ **Before Change, Alert User:** The user receives a two-day warning to change the password.

✔ **User Must Change Within:** This account requires a new password every 30 days.

✔ **Expires If Not Used For:** If the password isn't used for a period of 60 days, it automatically expires, and a new password must be entered.

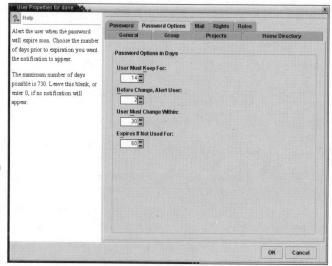

**Figure 16-7:**
Password
options for
heightened
security.

Thoughtful use of these options can significantly improve security.

Be mindful not to set timeframes too short. Users will get cranky if they're forced to change their passwords every few days.

If you're interested in exploring other aspects of the Solaris Management Console, your best bet is to start with the Sun documentation on SMC. You can find it in the *System Administration Guide: Basic Administration* located at `docs.sun.com/db/doc/806-4073`.

# Starting and Stopping Your System

A straightforward but incredibly important Solaris administrative task is shutting down or restarting your system in a manner that's operating system–friendly. Cycling power or unplugging a running Solaris system can be catastrophic, and you never want to do that!

Three commands that are mnemonically named and important to know are

```
shutdown
halt
reboot
```

# *Shutting down the system with shutdown*

The shutdown program is most typically used to change the system state from multiuser to single user for administrative purposes.

As with all the commands in this section, shutdown must be run as root.

The command has a small number of options:

```
shutdown [-y] [-g grace period] [-i init state]
```

✔ The *grace period* allows users to log out and otherwise gracefully shut down their running applications before the change in state is invoked.

✔ The *init state* allows specification of a different state if the default action of moving to single-user mode where

  • All users are shut out

  • Only the console is enabled

✔ The -y flag skips the "Are you sure?" prompt for certain state changes and is usually used within scripts rather than from an interactive shell.

Table 16-1 defines the different init states in Solaris.

| **Table 16-1** | **Init States in Solaris** |
|---|---|
| *State* | *Definition* |
| 0 | Stop the operating system. |
| 1 | Administrative or single-user state, also known as *s* or *S* state. |
| 2 | Multiuser state (default run time state). |
| 5 | Shut down so that it's safe to remove the power or otherwise physically disassemble the system. |
| 6 | Stop the system and reboot it into the default state (usually init state 2). |

As an example, drop the system into init state 5 before physically transporting it to a new cubicle:

```
# shutdown -g 30 -i 5

Shutdown started.    Mon Feb 10 16:13:07 MST 2003

Broadcast Message from root (pts/0) on aurora Mon Feb 10
        16:13:07...
The system aurora will be shut down in 30 seconds
```

Thirty seconds later, all processes are terminated, and the system halts.

## Stopping the system with halt

The halt command has one purpose in life: to stop the operating system.

Here are a few instances when you may want to use this command:

- ✔ You are suddenly notified that the power is going out in your facility.
- ✔ You realize that someone has unauthorized access, and you want to stop the system immediately.
- ✔ You just need to reconfigure or install some new hardware.

For a simple program, halt has a surprising number of command line options, as shown in Table 16-2.

| Table 16-2 | Options for halt |
|------------|------------------|
| *Option* | *Meaning* |
| -d | Force a system crash dump before rebooting. Can be useful for debugging OS performance issues. |
| -l | Suppress sending a message to the system log daemon, syslogd, about who executed halt. |
| -n | Prevent the sync before stopping. Use with caution: The disks will *not* be in sync with the operating system |
| -q | Quick halt. No graceful shutdown is attempted. |
| -y | Halt the system, even from a dial-up terminal. |

To quickly halt a system, you can use:

```
halt -qy
```

but most likely, you'll use `halt` either without any options, or with the `-d` option if you're trying to debug what's causing the operating system to get into a state where it requires a `halt`.

I recommended using `shutdown -i 5` rather than `halt` because `shutdown` is more graceful in terms of how running applications are stopped.

## Rebooting with the reboot command

The third choice for changing the state of your Solaris system is to use the `reboot` command, which, logically enough, forces an immediate reboot by default. (It's identical to `shutdown -i 6`.)

Another straightforward utility, it has four important options, as highlighted in Table 16-3.

| Table 16-3 | Options for the reboot Command |
|------------|-------------------------------|
| *Option* | *Meaning* |
| `-d` | Force a system crash dump before rebooting. |
| `-l` | Suppress sending a message to the system log daemon, `syslog`, about who executed reboot. |
| `-n` | Avoid calling `sync` and do not log the reboot to `syslogd` or to `/var/adm/wtmpx`. The kernel still attempts to sync file systems prior to reboot, except if the `-d` option is also present. If `-d` is used with `-n`, the kernel does not attempt to sync file systems. |
| `-q` | Quick. Reboot quickly and ungracefully, without shutting down running processes first. |

The most important `reboot` option is that any additional arguments are handed to the boot loader. (The boot loader is the program that controls how the operating system starts up. If you see an `Ok?` prompt on boot-up, that's the boot loader running.)

For example, if you have two disks (Solaris8 and Solaris9) and a different version of Solaris on each, you can switch from Solaris 9 to Solaris 8 by invoking:

```
reboot Solaris8
```

As with the `halt` command, Sun recommends that you use `shutdown` rather than `reboot` to ensure that all running applications are shut down gracefully.

# Adding User Accounts

A common system administration task is adding new users to a Solaris system.

- ✔ You can do most of the work with the Solaris Management Console, which has many options for account configuration
- ✔ You can use the command-line alternative `useradd`.

The `useradd` command has perhaps the most complex usage message of any Solaris command:

```
# useradd
UX: useradd: ERROR: invalid syntax.
usage:  useradd [-u uid [-o] | -g group | -G group[[,group]...] | -d dir |
            -s shell | -c comment | -m [-k skel_dir] | -f inactive |
            -e expire | -A authorization [, authorization ...] |
            -P profile [, profile ...] | -R role [, role ...]]
            -p project [, project ...] login
        useradd -D [-g group | -b base_dir | -f inactive | -e expire
            -A authorization [, authorization ...] |
            -P profile [, profile ...] | -R role [, role ...]] |
            -p project
```

Fortunately, you don't have to specify every option every time!

To understand how this works, suppose that you want to create the account `sjobs` for your friend and colleague Al Joe. The key information you'll want to know is

- ✔ Desired account name
- ✔ Full user name
- ✔ Home directory
- ✔ Login shell

If Al wants the default login shell `ksh` and his account home will be in `/export/home` along with everyone else, then the account addition command is

```
useradd -s /usr/bin/ksh -c "Al Joe" -d /export/home/ajoe ajoe
```

Unfortunately, `useradd` is a lazy command, so although this created an appropriate entry in the password file `/etc/passwd`, it hasn't built Steve's home directory or set an initial password.

# Creating a new home directory

Because you must be `root` to run `useradd`, it's straightforward to create Steve's home directory:

```
# mkdir /export/home/sjobs
# chown sjobs /export/home/sjobs
```

 If you use the `-m` flag to `useradd`, the home directory is created. However, the files from the `/etc/skel` directory are not copied into the new directory.

To do the job well, copy in some of the files from the `/etc/skel` directory, which contains standard account configuration files:

```
# ls /etc/skel
local.cshrc    local.login    local.profile
```

Copy each of these files into Steve's new home directory, with the `local` prefix stripped (so they become dot files):

```
# cd /export/home/sjobs
# cp /etc/skel/local.cshrc .cshrc
# cp /etc/skel/local.login .login
# cp /etc/skel/local.profile .profile
```

The next step is to ensure that Steve owns the files. (The wildcard pattern matches all files that begin with a dot and are followed by a lowercase letter and any subsequent sequence of letters, numbers, and punctuation.)

```
# chown sjobs .[a-z]*
```

Now double-check that all is well:

```
# ls -al
```

```
total 10
drwxr-xr-x   2 sjobs    other    512 Feb 10 17:10 .
drwxr-xr-x  12 root     root     512 Feb 10 17:08 ..
-rw-r--r--   1 sjobs    other    136 Feb 10 17:10 .cshrc
-rw-r--r--   1 sjobs    other    157 Feb 10 17:10 .login
-rw-r--r--   1 sjobs    other    174 Feb 10 17:10 .profile
```

Looks great. The one remaining problem is that Steve's account doesn't have a password set.

## Setting the account password

To set an account password as root, specify the name of the account as an argument to the passwd command and then type in the desired password twice:

```
# passwd sjobs
New Password:
Re-enter new Password:
passwd: password successfully changed for sjobs
```

You can also fine-tune the account password settings with the passwd command, something that's unique to Solaris in the Unix world. The important flags — all of which overlap the Password Options shown in Figure 16-7 — are described in Table 16-4.

| Table 16-4 | Important Password Settings with passwd |
|---|---|
| **Option** | **Meaning** |
| -f | Forces the user to change the password at the next login by expiring the password for name. |
| -l | Locks the password entry for name. |
| -n *min* | Sets the minimum field for name. The min field contains the minimum number of days between password changes for name. If min is greater than max, the user may not change the password. Always use this option with the -x option, unless max is set to 1 (aging turned off). In that case, min does not need to be set. |
| -w *warn* | Sets the warn field for name. The warn field contains the number of days before the password expires and the user is warned. |
| -x *max* | Sets the maximum field for name. The max field contains the number of days that the password is valid for name. The aging for name will be turned off immediately if max is set to -1. If it is set to 0, the user is forced to change the password at the next login session, and aging is turned off. |

To give Steve the same password settings shown in Figure 16-7, the command would be

```
# passwd -n 14 -w 2 -x 30 sjobs
passwd: password information changed for sjobs
```

You can quickly delete an account several ways:

- ✔ Use the `-d` flag to passwd.
- ✔ Use `-l` to lock the account.
- ✔ Change the password to something you know but the user doesn't know.

# Chapter 17

# Keeping Your System Secure

An important underpinning of any system security efforts is how Solaris views users and user permissions. If you're used to Windows or a Macintosh computer, you're familiar with a structure where — fundamentally — anyone who uses the computer has complete access to the system. Any user can add device drivers, delete programs, explore the file system and open any files found, and so on.

The newest Windows and Macintosh operating systems are more sophisticated, but their security models are less robust than a Solaris system. Sun Microsystems and the Unix development community have spent decades trying to find the perfect balance between high and reliable security, and non-intrusive barriers for users. And they've done a pretty darn good job!

## Accounts and Permissions

The core idea behind Solaris security is that different users have different sets of permissions on the system.

If you're user taylor and you use ls to compare your ID against the ownership and permissions of a specific file or directory, you can immediately determine whether or not you can access it. For example:

```
$ id
uid=100(taylor) gid=1(other)
$ ls -ld .
drwxr-xr-x  35 taylor    other          2048 Feb  8 11:33 ./
$ ls -ld /
drwxr-xr-x  44 root      root           1536 Feb  7 17:21 /
```

You can see that my user ID is `taylor` and I'm part of group `other`. Here's a look at the permissions as revealed in the preceding example:

- **My home directory:** You can see that the directory is also owned by `taylor`, so I have full permissions to read, write, and otherwise fiddle with that directory.

- **The top-level / directory:** The owner doesn't match my user ID, and the group doesn't match my group. Therefore, my permissions on this directory are read and execute only. I can list the contents of the / directory but cannot alter it.

One special user is exempt from this permission model: the `root` user. The administrator ID `root` bypasses all permission issues and can read, write, and execute any file or directory regardless of its permissions. Much of Unix system security revolves around trying to ensure that only authorized users can access the root account.

More fundamentally, security is often about trying to ensure that

- All accounts are secure
- Users cannot access the data or files of others without the owners granting explicit permission.

Don't think of security as a box that can be built and nailed down around your computer.

- Your system security is more akin to a specific point along the no-security-maximum-access and maximum-security-no-access continuum.
- The more secure you make the system, the harder it is to use.
- It's impossible to make any system on a public network completely secure.

This chapter deals with making a Solaris system secure enough for most users. If you need an level of increased security, you'll want a more advanced book; start by checking out the Solaris online library at `docs.sun.com/`. You can ratchet up security many ways, including using

- Firewalls
- Proxy servers
- Security monitoring systems like Tripwire

# Ensuring Account Password Security

The most obvious way to increase security is to make sure that all the user accounts are set up properly. An account without a password, or an account entry in the `/etc/passwd` file that's malformed, can lead to

✔ Unauthorized users on your system

✔ Authorized users gaining more permissions than they've been formally granted.

Solaris has two useful tools for checking the password file:

> `pwck` to check the file format
>
> `passwd` to see a summary of account configurations.

## Validating the password file

The password file check program `pwck` doesn't have much to say if the file is formatted properly:

```
# pwck
#
```

Without any output, one can presume that everything in the password file looks fine. But see what happens if a user somehow ends up with a colon in the fullname (gecos) field of his or her entry in the password file:

```
# pwck

hacker::0:1: ::hack the planet!:: ://usr/bin/bash
        Too many/few fields
```

Clearly even a visual inspection reveals that the hacker account is suspicious:

✔ There's no password.

> In the password file, colons separate fields, and the second field should have an *x* to indicate that the encrypted password is in a shadow file for additional security. By having no value in this second field, you know that this account has no password!

✔ More importantly, the fifth field contains the illegal value `::hack the planet!::` rather than the user's name. The additional colons throw Solaris for a loop.

To fix this, you need to edit the password file to delete the bad entry. The best way to do this is with the `vipw` program. This ensures that another administrator doesn't corrupt the password file while you're changing it. The password file has an entry for every account on the system, as shown here:

```
# cat /etc/passwd
root:x:0:1:Super-User:/:/usr/bin/bash
daemon:x:1:1::/:
bin:x:2:2::/usr/bin:
sys:x:3:3::/:
adm:x:4:4:Admin:/var/adm:
lp:x:71:8:Line Printer Admin:/usr/spool/lp:
uucp:x:5:5:uucp Admin:/usr/lib/uucp:
nuucp:x:9:9:uucp:/var/spool/uucppublic:/usr/lib/uucp/uucico
smmsp:x:25:25:SendMail Message Submission Program:/:
listen:x:37:4:Network Admin:/usr/net/nls:
nobody:x:60001:60001:Nobody:/:
noaccess:x:60002:60002:No Access User:/:
nobody4:x:65534:65534:SunOS 4.x Nobody:/:
taylor:x:100:1:Dave Taylor:/export/home/taylor:/usr/bin/bash
dave:x:101:1:test:/export/home/dave:/usr/bin/bash
sjobs:x:103:1:Steve Jobs:/export/home/sjobs:/usr/bin/ksh
crack::0:hacktheplanet:/:/bin/sh
hacker::0:1: ::hack the planet!:: :/:/usr/bin/bash
```

Use `vipw` to remove only the last line, and things should be okay. Double-check to make sure they are

```
# pwck
#
```

## Summarizing account data with passwd

The `passwd` program, accessed with the `-s` summarize flag, can help identify inappropriate password entries:

```
# passwd -sa
root      PS
daemon    LK
bin       LK
sys       LK
adm       LK
lp        LK
uucp      LK
nuucp     LK
smmsp     LK
listen    LK
nobody    LK
```

```
noaccess   LK
nobody4    LK
taylor     PS
dave       PS
sjobs      PS    02/11/03    14    30    2
```

Steve, with account `sjobs`, has password aging enabled (see Chapter 16), so the output for his account is

- ✔ Date of the last password change

- ✔ Minimum days between password changes

- ✔ Maximum days without a password change

- ✔ Number of days prior to expiring a password that the user should be warned.

The second column for every account listed is the status:

- ✔ PS means it's password-protected.

- ✔ LK means it's locked.

- ✔ NP stands for no password.

In the output of the `/etc/passwd` file in the preceding section, you'll see that the `passwd` command did not identify the account `crack`, which has no password. This is not good at all!

To ensure that every account is checked, do something more sophisticated on the command line:

```
# for name in `cut -d: -f1 /etc/passwd`
> do
>    passwd -s $name
> done
```

This shell loop performs a couple of steps:

- ✔ Extracts each account name in the `passwd` file. (It uses `cut`, which uses the `:` as the field delimiter and lists only the first field — the account name — in the output.)

- ✔ Test each account explicitly with the `passwd -s` command.

The output is

```
root      PS
daemon    LK
bin       LK
sys       LK
adm       LK
lp        LK
uucp      LK
nuucp     LK
smmsp     LK
listen    LK
nobody    LK
noaccess  LK
nobody4   LK
taylor    PS
dave      PS
sjobs     PS       02/11/03     14     30        2
passwd: User unknown: crack
Permission denied
```

The `User unknown` error is troubling because the account name `crack` came from the `/etc/passwd` file. This is something you need to investigate further!

## Checking for additional root accounts

Another way to find the `crack` account is to search for accounts with the user ID value of zero. The fastest way to do this is to use `grep` and `":0:"` as the pattern:

```
# grep ":0:" /etc/passwd
root:x:0:1:Super-User:/:/usr/bin/bash
crack::0:hacktheplanet:/:/bin/sh
```

There's that bad account, `crack`. Not only does it not have a password, but it's also set up as another `root` account. (Any account with user ID 0 is considered a `root` account, with all access and privileges that implies.) You need to remove this dangerous, unauthorized root account entry as soon as possible!

## Tweaking default password settings

A Solaris configuration file controls the default setup of passwords for new accounts. It's worth a quick peek:

```
# cat /etc/default/passwd
#ident   "@(#)passwd.dfl 1.3     92/07/14 SMI"
MAXWEEKS=
MINWEEKS=
PASSLENGTH=6
```

MAXWEEKS and MINWEEKS are password aging options. *Eight* and *one* are good values for these options. These options put the following restrictions on passwords:

✔ Passwords are good for only a maximum of eight weeks

✔ Passwords cannot be changed for a week after they've been updated.

# Identifying Proper File Permissions

It's important to ensure that files and directories have appropriate permissions.

To check and ensure that users have reasonable sets of permissions for their home directories, for example, list all the directories in long format by using ls:

```
# ls -l /export/home
total 38
drwxr-xr-x    2 root    root     512 Oct  4 17:01 TT_DB
drwxr-xr-x   11 root    other    512 Dec 10 19:32 adabas
drwxrwxrwx   12 dave    other    512 Feb  6 14:59 dave
drwxr-xr-x    3 root    other    512 Dec 19 14:11 gnome
drwxr-xr-x    8 root    other    512 Dec 12 13:10 imagemagick
drwx------    2 root    root    8192 Oct  2 11:45 lost+found
drwxr-xr-x    9 1010    staff   1536 Oct 24 17:56 mozilla
drwxr-xr-x    2 sjobs   other    512 Feb 10 17:10 sjobs
drwxr-xr-x    6 root    other    512 Oct  2 16:22 staroffice6.0
drwxr-xr-x   35 taylor  other   2048 Feb 11 10:38 taylor
```

You can see that permissions vary between these extremes:

✔ The *relatively closed permissions* of lost+found (which turns out to be used by the low-level file system recovery utility fsck and should be left alone)

✔ The completely open directory for account dave.

Most likely, dave would be upset if other users stored huge files in his account or deleted his mailbox, both of which could happen with a completely open permission setting.

To fix this, you may have a couple of options:

✔ As root, simply change the permissions.

✔ Send an e-mail notification to users who may have problematic settings.

You can fix the permissions yourself, this time:

```
# chmod go-w /export/home/dave
# ls -l /export/home/dave
total 0
```

Oops! If you're just listing a directory, the contents are shown by default. To force the directory itself to be shown, add the -d flag:

```
# ls -ld /export/home/dave
drwxr-xr-x  12 dave  other   512 Feb 6 14:59 /export/home/dave
```

Fixing individual directories is one solution, but the better strategy is to ensure that files and directories are created with the correct permissions in the first place.

## *Working with umask*

The umask setting controls the permissions granted to a new file or directory when created, and each user can have a different setting. Unfortunately, umask isn't a permission setting to duplicate; it's the opposite of what you want.

If you want to have permission -rwx-r-x-, then you want octal permission 750. (Chapter 4 covers file permissions.) For a umask that would produce that permission, you need to specify the opposite of 750, the value that results if you subtract the desired mask from 777:

$$
\begin{array}{r}
777 \\
- 750 \\
\hline
027
\end{array}
$$

That's the umask setting desired: 027.

To identify the current umask value, type umask:

```
# umask
022
```

Subtract this value from 777 to get the resulting permissions: 777 – 022 = 755, which can also be expressed as -rwx-r-xr-x.

To change the umask, enter a new value. It'll stick until the next time you log in, at which point it's set to the default system value and possibly reset based on the contents of a login configuration file.

Create a file and directory with each of these two `umask`s to see the difference:

```
# umask 027
# touch testfile1
# mkdir testdir1
# umask 022
# touch testfile2
# mkdir testdir2
# ls -ld test*
drwxr-x---   2 root      other      512 Feb 11 11:19 testdir1
drwxr-xr-x   2 root      other      512 Feb 11 11:19 testdir2
-rw-r-----   1 root      other        0 Feb 11 11:19 testfile1
-rw-r--r--   1 root      other        0 Feb 11 11:19 testfile2
```

The preceding example illustrate a couple of common permission cases:

✔ `testdir1` has these permissions:

   • Read and execute permission for group

   • None for any non-group users on the system

`testdir2` has read and execute permission for both group and everyone else.

✔ `testfile1` has these permissions:

   • Read and write permission for owner

   • Read-only for group

   • No access for everyone else

`umask 022` produced `testfile2`, which has read permission granted to everyone on the system.

You can change the `umask` for users directly, but it's best to e-mail them. To change the `umask` of accounts yet to be created, make the appropriate settings in the `/etc/skel` files. (See Chapter 16 for an explanation of how these files come into play when creating new accounts.)

## Finding files and programs with inappropriate permissions

Other potential security problems can be identified by checking

❘ ✔ File permissions
❘ ✔ Ownership

### Overly write-enabled files

Files that are writeable by users other than the owner can be a tip-off that something's not right. You can find these files with the wonderful find command.

To test the files within user home directories, you can use:

```
# find /export/home -type f -perm -o+w
#
```

Looks good!

### The dangerous SetUID

Executable programs or scripts may have the so-called setuid (set user ID) bit set. If it's set, anyone running that program will have the same permissions as the program's owner.

A setuid program that's owned by root is dangerous, so quickly scan all the directories in your PATH to see what's there:

```
# find `echo $PATH|sed 's/:/ /g'`  -type f -perm -4000 | head
/usr/sbin/sparcv7/whodo
/usr/sbin/allocate
/usr/sbin/sacadm
/usr/sbin/traceroute
/usr/sbin/deallocate
/usr/sbin/list_devices
/usr/sbin/sparcv9/whodo
/usr/sbin/lpmove
/usr/sbin/pmconfig
/usr/sbin/ping
#
```

The preceding output shows numerous matches, of which only the first ten are shown here.

Immediately after you do a new installation of the operating system, I recommend saving this output in a new file called something similar to /export/home/taylor/.ok-setuid. Then on subsequent runs, you can omit listing all known setuid files by using the slightly more complex command:

```
# find `echo $PATH|sed 's/:/ /g'`  -type f -perm -4000 | \
    grep -vf /export/home/taylor/.ok-setuid
#
```

The output of this command is definitely worth keeping an eye on: I'd recommend running this at least once a week on a busy system, and more often if you have lots of guest users or students.

If you're thinking this might make a good shell script, good for you! Chapter 3 shows how to turn this command into a simple script.

# Disabling Unnecessary Internet Services

One of the best ways to improve the system security is to shut off all Internet services that aren't vital to your work. If you don't plan on offering files via FTP, for example, why have it enabled?

## Starting inetd

Solaris uses the straightforward `inetd` service to manage which services are made available, all of which is defined in the `/etc/inetd.conf` file. Any line that doesn't begin with # lists an active service. (I've cleaned up the otherwise ragged paste output.)

```
# egrep -v '(^#|^1)' /etc/inetd.conf | \
    cut -f1 | paste - - - -
time
time
echo
echo
discard
discard
daytime
daytime
chargen
chargen
fs
dtspc
printer
shell
shell
login
exec
exec
comsat
talk
finger
rstatd/2-4
rusersd/2-3
walld/1
sprayd/1
name
telnet
ftp
rquotad/1
uucp
```

The `inetd.conf` file is well documented if you want to see what all of these services are doing enabled on your system. Some are obvious. If you don't want `ftp` running, you have a couple of options:

- ✔ Disable the `ftp` line by inserting a # at the beginning of the line.
- ✔ Better yet, insert #DAT# (with your initials) so that if a problem occurs, you can easily go back to see which services you disabled and which services Sun disabled.

Of these listed services, you can probably safely disable everything except these:

> `dtspc`, which is used by the CDE login subsystem
>
> `fs`, which is the X Window System font server utility.

Users on other computers don't need to know your system status or which users are logged on to your machine. If you disable nothing else, disable these three. You'll never miss them:

> `Finger`
>
> `Systat`
>
> `netstat`

## *Restarting inetd via kill*

After you've made any desired changes to the `inetd.conf` file, make the changes on your running system, too, by sending a `SIGHUP` to the running `inetd` process. This is a two-step activity.

1. Identify the process ID of `inetd`, like this:

```
# ps -ef | grep inetd
root  166     1  0   Feb 07 ?       0:00 /usr/sbin/inetd -
       s
root 7450  6943  0 12:03:45 pts/4  0:00 grep inetd
```

PID 166 is the job you seek.

2. To send a specific signal by using the `kill` program, specify the latter part of the signal name as an option (that is, to send `SIGHUP`, use `-HUP` as the option):

```
# kill -HUP 166
#
```

You don't see any confirmation that it worked. But if you do another `ps -ef`, you should not see the daemons and Internet services you've turned off in the `inetd.conf` file.

# And finally

If you've read from start to finish, this is the end of your journey (other than the useful and cool Parts of Ten you'll find just a page or two away!). You've traveled quite a road to get here, learning the ins and outs of three different operating environments simultaneously:

✔ The command line

✔ The Common Desktop Environment

✔ The new GNOME desktop environment

I've enjoyed going through this material with you and hope that you've enjoyed learning about it all.

If you have any feedback or comments, please feel free to contact me directly via e-mail at

`taylor@intuitive.com.`

Enjoy the rest of your Solaris journeys!

# Part VI
# The Part of Tens

The 5th Wave    By Rich Tennant

"We have no problem funding your Web site, Frank. Of all the chicken farmers operating Web sites, yours has the most impressive cluck-through rate."

# In this part . . .

*I* ensure that you can continue your Solaris journey in safety and comfort with my Ten Best Solaris Web Sites, The Ten Most Important Security Improvements in Solaris 9 (just in case you're still running a previous version of Solaris and need yet another reason to upgrade), and my favorite: Ten Great (free!) Additions to Solaris. All must reads!

# Chapter 18

# Ten Best Web Sites

*In This Chapter*

▶ Finding the best Solaris documentation and information online

▶ Fixing and running a big Solaris system or a small PC-based installation

▶ Pointers to everything at Everything Solaris

▶ Finding cool, Sun-endorsed software, GNU tools, GNOME, and games

*I*t goes without saying that one of the best places to explore Solaris resources, documentation, and product announcements is the official Sun Microsystems Web site at `www.sun.com/`. But there's a lot more on the Web, including three specific areas within the enormous Sun site that are well worth bookmarking in your browser.

## Excellent Online Solaris Documentation

Compared to most Unix operating systems, Solaris is well documented with both the man pages and AnswerBook system included with the distribution. However, the Sun experts have spent a lot of time exploring, analyzing, fixing, and documenting just about every facet of every Solaris version, even earlier SunOS releases. You can access all of this information online, in an easy-to-browse layout, at:

```
docs.sun.com
```

If you're running Solaris 9, click the Solaris 9 link upon entering the site to see information that applies to your version of the operating system. If you have a different version of the OS, you can find lots to explore here, too.

# Big Iron Administration Assistance

You will inevitably have to do *some* sort of administration on your Solaris system. The Sun Big System Administration site is the best resource for administration information:

```
www.sun.com/bigadmin/
```

The resources area and the discussions are worth noting. Some of the discussions on this site will blow your socks off with the authors levels of technical expertise, but others will offer a good venue for asking even rudimentary Solaris system administration questions.

# More Sysadmin at Sys Admin Magazine

*Sys Admin* has long been one of the best magazines for a Unix system administrator, and it should be no surprise that the popular Solaris servers are a common topic of discussion and feature articles. On the Web, *Sys Admin* neatly organizes its Solaris material in an area called the Solaris Corner:

```
www.samag.com/solaris/
```

The Solaris Administration "Best Practices" column is worth checking out. The author explores a variety of topics and offers thoughtful and oft-novel solutions to common sysadmin problems.

# Small but Helpful Reference Site

A modest Web site, Everything Solaris offers valuable articles and tutorials, along with some neat free applications downloads and a discussion area:

```
everythingsolaris.org/
```

The same Web designer runs similar sites for Linux and Mac OS X, so if you're interested in comparing Solaris to these other popular Unix operating systems, they too can make for interesting reading.

# Squeeze Solaris on the Intel Platform

One cool hidden capability of Solaris 9 is that it can be installed and run happily on an Intel-based personal computer. (And yes, even a slim laptop computer can run Solaris 9.) If you're interested in this option, the Solaris on Intel site is a great place to find information:

```
www.sun.drydog.com/
```

Start by reading the extensive Frequently Asked Questions material. And consider signing up for the site's highly informative — and sporadically busy — mailing list for people trying to ensure that their Solaris 9 systems live on Intel systems happily and efficiently.

# An Extensive Collection of Solaris Info

Stokely Consulting's Unix System Administrator's Resources site offers a ton of great information about Solaris and many other Unix operating systems, focused primarily — but not exclusively — on system administration.

```
www.stokely.com/unix.sysadm.resources/
```

Be sure to check out the article about setting up and configuring e-mail so that it's secure and spam is minimized; look for it on the main page. Also don't miss the listing of Unix and system administration mailing lists.

# Keep Up-To-Date on Solaris News

Solaris Central sports a wonderful design, and its main page is a log of news and coming events for the Solaris community. It's a great resource for every Solaris user, administrator or otherwise:

```
www.SolarisCentral.com/
```

Click the /sparc and /contrib links to see the many levels of information available on this site!

# Cool, Sun-Endorsed Software

Although not the largest repository of Solaris-compatible software for your Sun computer, the Sun software download area is an excellent place to get well-tested applications like the latest version of the Java runtime environment, StarOffice, or the Sun ONE Application Server.

```
www.sun.com/software/download/
```

To see what freeware is redistributed by Sun, visit

```
www.sun.com/software/solaris/freeware/
```

# Even More Cool Solaris Software

The Sunfreeware site offers a repository of Solaris software, primarily from the GNU Project (`www.gnu.org/`). Specify which Solaris version you're running to see an extensive list of software packages available:

```
www.sunfreeware.com/
```

As with the Sun documentation site, select your operating system and processor (for example, SPARC/Solaris 9) and then look through the somewhat cryptically named package list to see what's available.

If you don't have a fast Internet connection, you can order a CD-ROM of the site's top downloads for a small fee. It's well worth the savings in sanity for some Solaris users!

# Yet More Great Freeware!

Freeware4Sun offers an extensive list of downloadable software for your Solaris system. The site has a distinctive and rather funky appearance. You'll find specific areas for patches, software, GNOME, and even games! Check it out at:

```
www.freeware4sun.com/
```

Don't miss its collection of documentation and helpful FAQ.

# Chapter 19

# Ten Key Security Features

*N*o universal panacea exists for making a Solaris system completely secure, but Solaris 9 has some technologies and tools that you need to know about, whether you're administering your system or just want to ensure people don't mess with your files. You can also find more discussion of security in Chapter 17 of this book. Sun offers an excellent top-level frequently asked questions document, the Sun Solaris Security FAQ, at `www.sun.com/software/solaris/faqs/security.html`.

## Secure Shell

One of the best improvements you can make to your Solaris system is to shut off `telnet`, `rlogin`, and `ftp`, and replace these Internet services with the Secure Shell (`ssh`) package. Although the former services send the account and password information *in the clear* (that is, unencrypted), the `ssh` equivalent programs use point-to-point public key encryption, making it much harder for someone to peek into your transactions and extract account information.

## IPSec and IPK

Oddly named, IP Secure (IPSec) and Internet Key Exchange (IKE) are critical components of a Virtual Private Network, and enable encrypted IP traffic between two systems by using a robust 128-bit encryption scheme. IPSec increases security between servers so that only authorized parties can communicate.

# SunScreen Firewall

One of the most important security features of a modern Solaris system is a *firewall,* a program that screens all incoming connection requests to ensure that they're legitimate and acceptable. The excellent Solaris solution for this is Sun's SunScreen tool, which features a state-sensitive packet filter, support for IPSec/IKE, centralized management, proxy services with built-in antivirus checking, and network address translation for hiding internal IP addressing schemes.

# Secure LDAP Implementation

The Lightweight Directory Access Protocol (LDAP) offers access to a centralized directory, but not without some security risks. Sun's LDAP implementation has been enhanced for Solaris 9 and now supports both Secure Sockets Layer (SSL) and DIGEST-MD5 encryption. Secure LDAP allows you to name objects and ensure secure access to the naming service. It provides a flexible attribute-mapping mechanism and is designed for complete password management support via the directory server.

# TCP Wrappers

If you don't replace standard Unix communications utilities `telnet`, `rlogin`, and `ftp` with their Secure Shell counterparts, you can increase the security of the tools by using the access control method known as TCP Wrappers. Think of it as an authentication and authorization layer between the client and server systems. It doesn't encrypt the communication, but it helps ensure that only authorized users are accessing the identified services.

# Buffer Overflow Protection

One of the most common ways for hackers to break into a Solaris system is to exploit buffer overflows. Imagine it this way: You write a program that expects no more than a 20-letter password to be entered. But a wily hacker enters a 15,000-character entry, overflowing the space allocated for the password variable. With some apps, the overflow can end up being an executed code snippet, which clearly is very bad! Solaris 9's enhanced buffer overflow protection goes a long way toward solving this problem.

# Role-Based Access Control

Unix has always had three categories of access control: owner, group, and other. But on a modern multiuser system, a more sophisticated tool is needed; that's what role-based access control offers. By defining as many roles as needed, you can give a printer tech access only to the areas on your system that require updates for new printers being installed. Role-based access control is well worth learning about, whether you're a system administrator or just a Solaris 9 user.

# Smart Card Support

One of the most secure methods of controlling access to a Solaris system is through smart cards. By coupling traditional account passwords (known in security circles as "what you know" security) with smart cards (which operate on the basis of "what you have"), you have a solid method of limiting access, particularly from a remote location.

# Kerberos v5

Invented at MIT, Kerberos is a popular authentication scheme on a widely distributed network, particularly for single sign-on setups. The latest version of Kerberos includes improved system security and replaces the formerly separate Sun Enterprise Authentication Mechanism product. Kerberos also interoperates gracefully with MIT Kerberos and Microsoft's Active Directory, which is a boon if you have a multi-OS network.

# Solaris Resource Manager

Although it may not seem to be a security tool, the Solaris Resource Manager (SRM) is a great boon for controlling access and use of system resources. It controls resource allocation, monitoring, and control, including an improved accounting capability. For example, disabling writing to the CD-ROM device can help ensure that critical system or company files aren't copied. Preventing guest users from printing is another example of where SRM is helpful.

# Chapter 20

# Ten Great Free Add-Ons

**In This Chapter**

▶ Editors and more editors

▶ Graphical tools and desktop environments

▶ Web browsing without pictures

▶ Watching TV and, if you must, editing Word Documents

Solaris 9 includes a wealth of tools and a CDROM full of open source and other freeware from the Internet, but there's always room on a computer disk for just one more great piece of software. That's what this last chapter explores: some truly wonderful software that is sure to enhance your Solaris experience. Though it's not all guaranteed to make you more productive!

## Everything and the Kitchen Sink: Emacs

Many Solaris users swear by `emacs`, a powerful alternative to the `vi` editor. It was developed by Sun's own James Gosling, and later updated and enhanced by Richard Stallman, head of the GNU Project. If you like small, modular applications, `macs` isn't for you. But if want an editor that can do just about anything you desire, from helping you browse man pages to auto-formatting your programs, it's well worth a look. You can find it at `www.sun.com/software/solaris/freeware/`.

## Digging for GNOME

GNOME is one of the best things to happen to Solaris in a long time, from a user perspective. You can get the latest version of this powerful graphical environment, including many prebuilt GNOME applications, at `www.sun.com/gnome/`.

GNOME is covered throughout this book, but particularly in Chapter 2.

# An Attractive Alternative Desktop

A capable and arguably more visually attractive alternative to GNOME, the K Desktop Environment is a different way of looking at your desktop. It includes a suite of KDE-compatible applications, including the slick Konquerer Web browser and file system browser.

You can find KDE online at `www.kde.org/` and download it for Solaris at `www.sun.com/software/solaris/freeware/`.

# When Surfing Speed Is All That Counts

Although the latest version of Netscape Navigator (a worthy free download at `www.netscape.com/`) makes surfing the Web attractive and easy, sometimes it's useful to have a command line–based alternative. That's where lynx comes in.

Operating in a text-only mode, lynx not only is great for people with visual disabilities, but also is scriptable so you can include calls to Web sites within your shell scripts. This powerful capability makes tasks like calculating a current stock price a breeze.

Download the package at `www.sun.com/software/solaris/freeware/`.

# A Powerful and Free Database Alternative

Many database applications are available for a Solaris system — including phone books, project archives, and data catalogs — but the included choices are weak, and commercial offerings like Oracle and Syngress are expensive.

The solution is MySQL, a free and surprisingly robust database alternative, available for downloading at `www.sun.com/software/solaris/freeware/`.

# *Watch TV on Your Solaris System? Sure!*

ShowMe TV enables you to switch to working 7 days a week, 24 hours a day by having a small window on your screen showing the latest from ESPN, TechTV, Bloomberg Financial TV, or even HBO. This capability is most useful for videoconferencing and broadcasting training materials throughout a subnet or intranet. You need some hardware for video stream capture, but the software's free, and it's incredibly cool!

The ShowMe TV software and docs are available at `www.sun.com/desktop/products/software/showmetv/`.

# *StarOffice: A Great Alternative*

One of the best recent developments in the Unix community is the emergence and continued evolution of StarOffice. It's a viable alternative to the Microsoft hegemony of MS Office. Whether working with Word documents, Excel spreadsheets, or PowerPoint presentations, you can stay firmly tucked into the Solaris environment of your choice and interoperate like a guru. See `www.sun.com/staroffice/`.

StarOffice is covered in Chapters 9 and 10.

# *Interactive Multimedia Collaboration*

If you've checked out ShowMe TV and decided that it's only solving part of the distributed training and collaboration problem, a more powerful and integrated alternative is SunForum.

This amazing suite of tools is available at `www.sun.com/desktop/products/software/sunforum/`.

# *Vi on Steroids!*

For many Solaris users, `vi` is the editor of choice. But some capabilities are missing in `vi`, including

> ✔ Support for multiple edit windows
>
> ✔ An undo capability that can back up to the original file
>
> ✔ Support for the X Window System, with pull-down menus and more.

All of these have been addressed in the excellent vim package. You can find it at `www.vim.org/`.

# Games, Games, Games

If you spend a lot of time using your computer for work, it's nice to occasionally take a short break and play a game. Because of the ubiquitous nature of the X Window System underlying both GNOME and CDE, a *ton* of games are available, from Tetris clones to Chess, from Backgammon to Mahjongg, and even an air-traffic-control game.

To check out the range of offerings (though not every game is built for Solaris), start at `www.gnu.org/directory/games/`.

# Index

## • H •

## • I •

### • *T* •

• *Z* •

# Notes

# Notes

# Notes

# Notes

# FOR DUMMIES®

## A world of resources to help you grow

## HOME, GARDEN & HOBBIES

**0-7645-5295-3**

**0-7645-5130-2**

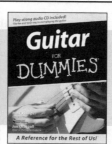

**0-7645-5106-X**

### Also available:

Auto Repair For Dummies
(0-7645-5089-6)

Chess For Dummies
(0-7645-5003-9)

Home Maintenance For
Dummies
(0-7645-5215-5)

Organizing For Dummies
(0-7645-5300-3)

Piano For Dummies
(0-7645-5105-1)

Poker For Dummies
(0-7645-5232-5)

Quilting For Dummies
(0-7645-5118-3)

Rock Guitar For Dummies
(0-7645-5356-9)

Roses For Dummies
(0-7645-5202-3)

Sewing For Dummies
(0-7645-5137-X)

## FOOD & WINE

**0-7645-5250-3**

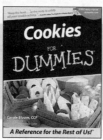

**0-7645-5390-9**

**0-7645-5114-0**

### Also available:

Bartending For Dummies
(0-7645-5051-9)

Chinese Cooking For
Dummies
(0-7645-5247-3)

Christmas Cooking For
Dummies
(0-7645-5407-7)

Diabetes Cookbook For
Dummies
(0-7645-5230-9)

Grilling For Dummies
(0-7645-5076-4)

Low-Fat Cooking For
Dummies
(0-7645-5035-7)

Slow Cookers For Dummies
(0-7645-5240-6)

## TRAVEL

**0-7645-5453-0**

**0-7645-5438-7**

**0-7645-5448-4**

### Also available:

America's National Parks For
Dummies
(0-7645-6204-5)

Caribbean For Dummies
(0-7645-5445-X)

Cruise Vacations For
Dummies 2003
(0-7645-5459-X)

Europe For Dummies
(0-7645-5456-5)

Ireland For Dummies
(0-7645-6199-5)

France For Dummies
(0-7645-6292-4)

London For Dummies
(0-7645-5416-6)

Mexico's Beach Resorts For
Dummies
(0-7645-6262-2)

Paris For Dummies
(0-7645-5494-8)

RV Vacations For Dummies
(0-7645-5443-3)

Walt Disney World & Orlando
For Dummies
(0-7645-5444-1)

**Available wherever books are sold. Go to www.dummies.com or call 1-877-762-2974 to order direct.**

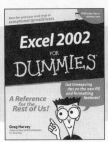

# FOR DUMMIES®

## Helping you expand your horizons and realize your potential

### INTERNET

**0-7645-0894-6**

**0-7645-1659-0**

**0-7645-1642-6**

### DIGITAL MEDIA

**0-7645-1664-7**

**0-7645-1675-2**

**0-7645-0806-7**

### GRAPHICS

**0-7645-0817-2**

**0-7645-1651-5**

**0-7645-0895-4**

# FOR DUMMIES®

## The advice and explanations you need to succeed

---

## SELF-HELP, SPIRITUALITY & RELIGION

0-7645-5302-X

0-7645-5418-2

0-7645-5264-3

## PETS

0-7645-5255-4

0-7645-5286-4

0-7645-5275-9

## EDUCATION & TEST PREPARATION

0-7645-5194-9

0-7645-5325-9

0-7645-5210-4

---

FOR

# DUMMIES®

We take the mystery out of complicated subjects

## WEB DEVELOPMENT

Creating Web Pages FOR DUMMIES

**0-7645-1643-4**

HTML 4 FOR DUMMIES

**0-7645-0723-0**

Dreamweaver MX FOR DUMMIES

**0-7645-1630-2**

### Also available:

ASP.NET For Dummies
(0-7645-0866-0)

Building a Web Site For Dummies
(0-7645-0720-6)

ColdFusion "MX" For Dummies (0-7645-1672-8)

Creating Web Pages All-in-One Desk Reference For Dummies
(0-7645-1542-X)

FrontPage 2002 For
(0-7645-0821-0)

HTML 4 For Dummi
Reference
(0-7645-0721-4)

Macromedia Studio
All-in-One Desk Ref
For Dummies
(0-7645-1799-6)

Web Design For Du
(0-7645-0823-7)

## PROGRAMMING & DATABASES

C++ FOR DUMMIES

**0-7645-0746-X**

XML FOR DUMMIES

**0-7645-1657-4**

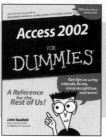

Access 2002 FOR DUMMIES

**0-7645-0818-0**

### Also available:

Beginning Programming For Dummies
(0-7645-0835-0)

Crystal Reports "X" For Dummies
(0-7645-1641-8)

Java & XML For Dummies
(0-7645-1658-2)

Java 2 For Dummies
(0-7645-0765-6)

JavaScript For Dummies
(0-7645-0633-1)

Oracle9i For Dummies
(0-7645-0880-6)

Perl For Dummies
(0-7645-0776-1)

PHP and MySQL For
Dummies
(0-7645-1650-7)

SQL For Dummies
(0-7645-0737-0)

VisualBasic .NET For
Dummies
(0-7645-0867-9)

Visual Studio .NET A
Desk Reference For
(0-7645-1626-4)

## LINUX, NETWORKING & CERTIFICATION

Red Hat Linux 7.3 FOR DUMMIES

**0-7645-1545-4**

Networking FOR DUMMIES

**0-7645-0772-9**

A+ Certification FOR DUMMIES

**0-7645-0812-1**

### Also available:

CCNP All-in-One Certification For Dummies
(0-7645-1648-5)

Cisco Networking For Dummies
(0-7645-1668-X)

CISSP For Dummies
(0-7645-1670-1)

CIW Foundations For Dummies with CD-ROM
(0-7645-1635-3)

Firewalls For Dumm
(0-7645-0884-9)

Home Networking F
Dummies
(0-7645-0857-1)

Red Hat Linux All-in
Desk Reference For
(0-7645-2442-9)

TCP/IP For Dummie
(0-7645-1760-0)

UNIX For Dummies
(0-7645-0419-3)

**Available wherever books are sold.**
**Go to www.dummies.com or call 1-877-762-2974 to order direct.**